ORDERS TO NOWHERE

ORDERS TO NOWHERE

The after action report from a career Marine's transition back to the civilian world

Lieutenant Colonel Michael Grice, USMC (Retired)

Printed by CreateSpace
Charlston, South Carolina
www.createspace.com
Cover images © Shutterstock

LCCN: 2013920522
ISBN: 1492985686
ISBN-13: 978-1492985686

3d Edition

NOTE: This revised edition of *Orders to Nowhere* includes recent changes in medical benefits, transition programs, TRICARE, and other facets of the dynamically changing environment that surrounds military to civilian transition as of December 2013. This book is a journal of the author's experiences during the transition from active duty to civilian life. The content is accurate as of the time of publication, and it is sold with the understanding that neither the publisher nor the author are engaged in professional career services. For further assistance, contact a professional transition specialist. For updates on material in this book, go to www.orderstonowhere.com.

To my family:

Thank you for your patience, love, and understanding through all of the time that I was far away in the service of our nation. I am home now. This time for *good.*

Acknowledgements:

There are literally hundreds of people who have helped make this book possible, and I could not even begin to list them all. I thank everyone who gave me advice, counsel, and the occasional chewing out along my personal and memorable journey down the road to nowhere.

Table of Contents

Table of Contents (continued)

Preface: What is this all about?

Hello there! Welcome to a travelogue and after action report from the curious adventure that was, and continues to be, the conversion from military service back to civilianhood. It chronicles my switch from the challenging and exciting way of life that I loved as a United States Marine to the other side of the metaphorical fence as I reentered the civilian world that I had abandoned nearly three decades earlier. Being a Marine is a wonderful career, full of peaks and valleys and excitement and boredom and everything else that makes a military life unique. Taking off the cloth of the nation and facing unexpected choices, such as which clothes to wear, when to get up in the morning, and what to do all day without a uniform on proved to be a shock to the system that I was not really prepared for. This is the story of my journey through transition; through the not-too frequent highs, the all-too frequent lows, and everything in between.

This book is really two stories that are inseparably intertwined. It is the after action report from my own experiences during transition as well as a self-help book to assist you, the reader, with the daunting task of leaving the military. The first few chapters chronicle the difficult decision to leave the military and the multitude of issues and ramifications that come with deciding to get out. From there on _Orders to Nowhere_ focuses on the lessons that I learned during my own transition into retirement. The lessons were quite often painful to experience and quite frustrating, but they were not unique to my situation. They apply to pretty much everyone who hangs up their uniform: Soldiers, Sailors, Airmen, Marines, Coast Guardsmen, Officers, Enlisted, Careerists, and those who serve a single enlistment. The transition experience is largely the same for everyone, and if you want to get right to the lessons learned you can skip ahead to chapter three.

All stories have an arc and mine is no different. My arc began a lifetime ago when I was a know-it-all teenager back in high school. I had always wanted to join the military, and after watching every war movie ever made and talking to recruiter after recruiter I made my decision to join the Marine Corps Reserve. At the ripe old age of 17 (and with my mother's begrudging consent and signature on the enlistment papers) I raised my right hand and swore an oath to support and defend the Constitution of the United States, and with that pledge I began my new life.

Unlike most recruits, I didn't immediately ship out for bootcamp after swearing the oath. I was still in my senior year at Broomfield High, so I spent six months or so in the Delayed Entry Program anxiously awaiting the day I would ship out for recruit training. I had already signed on the dotted line and received my first set of official Marine Corps orders that would send me off to the Marine Corps Recruit Depot in Sunny San Diego, where a scant few days after I threw my high school graduation cap into the air I would be introduced to my newest and bestest friends in the world: my Marine Corps Drill Instructors.

Time passed and the big day arrived. It was June 24th, 1985, and my recruiter picked me up and drove me to the airport. In typical Marine Corps fashion, it was dark, it was early, and it was unsettling. I was trepidatious to say the least, so with a lump in my throat I hugged my mom goodbye and headed off in pursuit of my destiny, or at least for a shot at seeing if I had what it took to become a United States Marine.

After a plane ride to San Diego and a bus ride through the imposing gate of the Marine Corps Recruit Depot, I learned that I had made what seemed at the time to be the biggest mistake of my life. My first indication that things were changing was watching the base's gate guards spit on the bus, which was filled with teenaged recruits just like me. It was not an omen of happy times ahead. I won't bore you with the details, but the next dozen weeks or so weren't much better. I did graduate that September (on Friday the 13th, no less), and with that happy graduation (much happier than the one from high school some three months before) the arc of my story rose like a rocket. I was on my way!

After ten days of leave back home I headed out to my Military Occupation Specialty (MOS) School in Fort Sill, Oklahoma, which where I learned my martial trade. I was destined to become a Field Artillery Fire Controlman (MOS Code number 0844), which means I was the guy who calculated the firing data needed by the cannon crewmen to point their guns and hit targets that were too far away for them to see. It proved to be very interesting stuff, especially considering that back then we used paper charts and slide rules to determine the data (computers were just entering the scene in the unenlightened dark days of the mid-1980s, and we didn't have them). Upon graduation from artillery school I returned home and joined my Marine Corps reserve unit, where I served as I worked my way through college.

Ultimately, I decided that I really liked this Marine Corps thing and raised my right hand again to commit myself to the arduous and rigorous opportunity presented by Officer Candidate School in my ardent fervor to become a commissioned Officer of Marines.

In a serious case of *déjà vu*, a different recruiter (with the oddly repetitive title of Officer Selection Officer, or OSO) picked me up in the early morning darkness just before dawn. I was as nervous that morning as I had been years earlier as I rode to the airport on my way to bootcamp. After a very familiar plane ride and introduction to a new set of newest and bestest Drill Instructor friends I found myself on the challenging and often miserable hamster wheel that is Officer Candidate School. Again I wondered what I had gotten myself into, and I also wondered if I could get out of it. Despite the option to *Drop on Request* (or DOR; an acronym that really spells "quit") I sucked it up and knuckled down, enduring all ten weeks along with my fellow candidates. It wasn't any fun, and in fact I found it to be much more difficult than recruit training. That's OK though. It should be hard, because as Thucydides observed: *"he, who graduates the harshest school, succeeds"* and if pain and exhaustion are metrics of the severity of the school, then I was indeed successful. I was more than a little gaunt and a lot more physically fit after the incredibly grueling experience and upon graduation I traded my Staff Sergeant's stripes for the gold bars of a second lieutenant. It was very exhilarating!

My arc continued to rise as I enjoyed a tremendously successful career and had the time of my life. Leading Marines, learning about my profession (I chose to continue in the artillery because I enjoyed my time as an enlisted artilleryman so much), and seeing the world was a fantastic and wonderful experience. There were parts that were miserable, but they were far outweighed by the sheer joy of the dynamic and exciting career that I was fortunate to pursue.

That arc continued to rise through peacetime deployments all over the country and overseas, fighting in a couple of wars, getting married, getting divorced, getting remarried, having kids, leading Marines and Sailors, and commanding numerous units and organizations. I had joined a true brotherhood of like-minded souls who were all headed in the same direction, with the same goals, aspirations, ideals, and frames of mind. Despite a few very bad days along the way, my arc rose higher and higher as I pursued the vocation that I truly loved.

All good things eventually come to an end. After nearly three decades in uniform it became my time to leave. My arc, which had been rising steadily higher and higher, plummeted like the proverbial man in the barrel trying his luck over Niagara Falls. My arc doesn't look like nice symmetric bell curve, but instead is more like the first part of a rollercoaster; moving up slowly, then more steeply, and finally reaching a precipice before careening back down to where it all started.

Suddenly I found myself in an unfamiliar and unsettling place: the "real world". Simple things that my non-military friends had been doing day in and day out for years on end were novel and intimidating to me. The warm and comfortable blanket of the Marine Corps was ripped away, and I found myself standing in the cold reality that is life on the outside. Everything was different. Take clothes, for example. Wearing the same uniform as everyone else year after year made the simple task of picking out different things to wear every day seem overwhelming. For nearly thirty years I had worn either black, brown, or olive-drab socks. That's great for green and earth-toned uniforms, but lousy for everything else. Now I had to choose from new colors and *gasp* even patterns! Argyle? Grey? Stripes? Blue? Who knew that there were so many types of socks in the world? If being stumped by a sock drawer was any indication, then I was in for a rough reentry to Civvie Street.

That unsettling discovery, along with a thousand others, led me to blog about my journey and to write this book. Coming back to the civilian world was much more difficult and disconcerting than I had ever imagined. I knew that if I was having a hard time with the transition from one side of the fence to the other then others must be mystified and confused as well.

So what does "Orders to Nowhere" mean, anyway?

Orders, in military terms, are a set of documents that tell you where you are supposed to go and what you are supposed to do when you get there. The closest parallel in the civilian world would be a job transfer from one town to another, but the big difference between the two is that civilians have the option to take it or leave it. Not so much in the military. You don't have the option of turn them down because you don't like them. That's why they call them orders.

Anyhow, that's the way it works. Every couple of years or so the Marine Corps (or the Army, the Navy, the Air Force, or the Coast Guard) issues out a set of orders to send you to your next assignment, and off you go. Pretty much everything is decided for you; where you are going, where you will be working, and even in many cases where you will live. All things considered, it is a pretty good gig because all you have to do is what you are told to do; pick up your orders at the unit administrative section and off you go.

That is until you find yourself on the off-ramp from military service, which is where I found myself before I really knew what was happening. Nearly three decades, a bunch of deployments, and a couple of wars flew by like a rocket. For the first time since big hair and parachute pants were all the rage I faced a fundamental change in life's path. I was leaving the world that I thoroughly loved (most of the time, anyway; there were times when I hated it, but that is the way it goes in the Marines) and going back to one that I left behind long before.

This book is about that change. It is an account of my personal journey from being a successful, experienced, and competitive Marine to not being one anymore. It is also a record of the many lessons that I learned along the way. Transition proved to be a remarkably and unexpectedly emotional rollercoaster ride, a personal and professional challenge, and an exhilarating though daunting experience. As each day passed I found myself learning things I didn't know, but that are second nature to pretty much everyone outside the military. I also started doing things I that I had not done in a loooooooong time, like getting to know how to use a comb and hair "product" again.

It is my fervent hope that you, the reader, will get something out of *Orders to Nowhere* that will help make the unnerving jump from the uniformed world to the civilian one a little less jarring. Nobody gets to serve forever, and for every person who wears the cloth of the nation their discharge looms on the horizon. That final day as a Soldier, Sailor, Airman, Marine, or Coast Guardsman will inevitably come, and maybe this book can help make your transition a little smoother by sharing my own trials and tribulations so that you will learn from my experience and can avoid some of the mistakes that I made along the way.

This second edition of the book has been revised and updated to provide the most up to date information about transition available as of December 10th, 2013 (which, interestingly enough, is exactly 29 years to the day after I first enlisted).

Part I: Getting Out

Chapter 1: Taking the plunge

It happens to everyone in the military. Sooner or later you take off your uniform and face the reality of a future that stands in stark contrast to the Spartan life that you have led. It doesn't matter if you serve four years or forty; everybody has to get out. Lifelong service has gone the way of horse cavalry and airships and searchlight batteries, and as a result each and every one of us who has sworn to serve our country ultimately ends up returning to civilian life as a regular citizen. A veteran to be sure, but a regular citizen nonetheless. Just like everyone else. Well, just like everyone else except for the things that you have learned while wearing the uniform, like technical skills, leadership, and how to stab the enemy with a tent stake when you run out of bullets for your rifle. Despite all of the cool things that you learn in the military, at some point everyone makes the transition from their uniformed life back to one a bit less sporty.

Transition is a nice word. It is a genteel euphemism that we in the military use to describe the transformation from uniformed defender of freedom and the American Way of Life back to the population we all came from. It makes you feel a little warm inside because it is such a nice word; great feelings about what lies ahead, but also feelings that belie just how nice parts of the transition process really aren't.

There are a lot of elegant synonyms for transition; words like *passage, conversion,* and *adjustment* come to mind. Not bad! You can read these little bits of cheerful lexicography and your blood pressure stays nice and low. "I am transitioning. How nice. It's a happy passage from my days in uniform to the rest of my life as a civilian. The conversion should be a gentle one because of all the programs and whatnot that are out there to help me along. I used to be a civilian, so the adjustment shouldn't be too bad! *La de da de da...*" These happy terms are usually accompanied by images of palm trees swaying overhead as you lounge on a nice sandy beach with a mai-tai in one hand and big fat cigar in the other.

Other synonyms are not so nice. *Upheaval. Distortion. Revolution.* "Ahhhhuuuugggghhhhh! What am I gonna do? What can I do for a living? I have no idea what to do for the rest of my life! Aaaarrrrgh!" Not so good for your blood pressure. Visions of a future sitting at a highway off-ramp with a cardboard sign offering to work for food compete with the strong desire to see how fast you can make it all the way to the bottom of a bottle of scotch go dancing around inside your head as you reach for the antacids and Alka-Seltzer.

The truth of the matter is that the transitional process is often only looked at from one perspective: the perspective of *"getting out"* and not *"what's next"*. We all tend to focus on the day of our End of Active Service (EAS) because that is when the camouflaged carriages of our careers turn into ordinary old pumpkins. Woe to those that don't get everything done before midnight on that fateful and final day, but all too often Marines (and Sailors and Airmen and Coast Guardsmen and Soldiers) don't pay close enough attention to the morning that comes after their last night in uniform. What are you going to do next? All of a sudden everything on the list is checked off (or it should be) and you have nobody telling you where to go, what to do, and what to wear as you do it. It is just you, alone with your thoughts and probably a splitting headache from the farewell party the night before.

There is nothing wrong with sitting around in your underwear for a week or so burning through bags of Cheetos and cases of beer as you ponder what lies ahead, but that isn't much of a plan for the rest of your life. As the giddy feeling of hanging it up wears off, it is usually replaced with a burgeoning feeling of dread at the uncertainty of what lies ahead, not to mention an epic case of indigestion from all of that junk food and cheap beer. Like a hangover, the after effects of your last day in uniform are often not quite what you wanted or expected, and by then it is too late to go back in time and perform those actions that needed to be done months before. Without a plan things can go horribly awry. Just ask anyone who thought that dropping out of high school would lead to a great jet-setting way of life these days. *You make your own luck* a great man once told me, and sometimes we all need to be told what we need to do even though we don't want to hear it. *You* need to take charge of your transition, and the sooner you do so the better.

As the commanding officer of a combat unit I made a point of sitting down and having a serious discussion with each and every Marine and Sailor who was leaving the command. Many were moving on to new duty stations, but many others were getting out of the service. The conversations with those approaching the end of their enlistment invariably turned to what they planned to do with their lives, and the answers usually fell into one of two possibilities.

"So, John (or Bob or Bill), what are you going to do when you get out?"

"Go back to school, sir." This is the answer I got about 80% of the time.

"Great! Good for you. Where? What will you study?"

There were a million different answers to this question, but they all boiled down to variations of:

"I am going to (fill in the name of college or school or apprenticeship at _____)."

or, the answer I received the other 20% of the time:

"I dunno."

The first answer led to a great discussion of life after military service and the joys of college because the benefits available with the Post 9/11 GI Bill are quite frankly spectacular. Those Marines and Sailors were well on the way to a successful life on Civvie Street because they had made a plan and were ready to make it happen.

As for the second answer, well, that led to a completely different dialog which focused on not ending up like the homeless guy holding the cardboard "unemployed veteran - please help!" sign at road intersections. Some were receptive; some just looked at me with the hollow stare as they inwardly prayed that the bad man (me!) would just stop talking. But I wouldn't. After torturing them for a while, I would wheedle a commitment out of them to do something, anything, but to commit to having a plan.

I think it worked. I still receive emails and Facebook hits from a lot of them. It is very gratifying to hear that a Marine or Sailor with whom I had such a conversation is now well on his way to graduating from college, and I run into many of them along the path that is life.

One memorable example involved a young corporal who got out of the Marine Corps many years ago, and long after he hung up his uniform our paths crossed at Disneyland. He was there with his young family, and was happy to report that he had listened to my advice and that it helped him make the decision to pursue an apprenticeship with a railroad line. Now he has a great life as a locomotive mechanic.

Unfortunately, I also receive appeals for help from those who didn't have a plan or who found life on the other side of the fence much different than they remembered. While it may seem like an opportunity to turn that into an "I told you so" moment, that is not at all helpful. Instead, I do what every Marine that I ever asked for advice did for me. I try to see how I can help. That's what Marines do, and you know what? It is just as gratifying because you know that someday down the road the person you help today will send you an email or drop you a note to let you know how things turned out. And odds are that they will turn out just fine as long as they commit to doing something with their lives.

So how do you decide when to leave? For a lot of military folks the decision is made for them by the Department of Defense because they either cannot reenlist or have reached the maximum service limit. For others, they may be medically separated due to wounds received in combat or to accident or illness. For the rest of us, though, we are faced with a decision that we have to make. When should we head for the off-ramp?

For me, the decision was an incredibly difficult one while at the same time one of the easiest that I have ever had to make. It was difficult because I loved the life I led in the military, and it had been my home for nearly three decades. It was easy because the decision made itself.

I woke up one day and realized it was time to go.

Every Marine, Soldier, Sailor, Airman, and Coast Guardsman has a unique story written by his or her military career. Although every one of them starts at recruit training or officer candidate school and ends with a discharge or retirement ceremony, the days, weeks, months, and years between the beginning and the end are uniquely different. In my case, I woke up that fateful morning and realized that I had done everything that I wanted to do in the service of my country: I had seen the world, led men and women in peace and war, and been tested in the crucible of combat. Along the way, however, I had missed countless birthdays, Christmases, anniversaries, and the hundreds of "firsts" that are part of my sons' childhoods. I awoke that day and decided that I had been gone enough. It was time to devote myself to serve my other life: the one with my family and without a uniform. My wanderlust was sated. It was time to plant the flag, pour cement over my tent pins, and with my family make a lasting home.

At any rate, that is why I chose to retire from the Marine Corps and move on to a new and different way of life. All I needed to do was to get out and start over. It wasn't that easy, though. Getting out was the one thing that my time in uniform did not prepare me for, so after the decision was made I found myself facing a mountain that I didn't know how to climb. As the Chinese philosopher Lao-tzu wittily observed some 2500 years ago, a journey of a thousand miles begins with a single step.

The problem is he doesn't tell you which step to take first.

Chapter 2: *Coming out of the foxhole*

Which foxhole, you ask? It is the one that you can't simply dive back into once you climb out; it's the "I'm getting out of the military" foxhole.

So you've made your decision to hit the turn signal and head for the off-ramp that takes you back to the civilian world. If you are like me, there are really a couple of stages in making the decision. First, you make the choice to get out, which is great. That is Lao-tzu's first step on the road to transition. Second, however, you have to tell people about it. All kinds of people, like your spouse, your parents, your kids, your peers at work, your boss, your subordinates; pretty much everybody.

That is much easier said than done, or easier typed than said I suppose. Lao-tzu didn't say anything about the second step. It can be a quite intimidating!

Telling my family was pretty easy because they were part of the decision to begin with. With a sigh of relief they readily embraced the thought of me being home for the holidays, so announcing my decision was quickly and smoothly done. Telling my extended family was likewise pretty easy; an email here, a phone call there. Again, this is pretty easy to do because every single person in my family supported my career and, more importantly, my decision to move on. My friends outside the military responded in much the same way. They were very supportive, just as they always have been.

Announcing your decision is not as easy when it comes to work, though. In my experience, there are generally two types of people in the military: the aggressive meat eaters who eat what they kill and docile grazers who hover over the salad bar of life. I have prided myself on being carnivorous, and I worked diligently and aggressively to be the best enlisted Marine and officer that I could possibly be. However, when I announced my decision to depart the Marine Corps, I left the carnivorous pack and joined the cud-munching herd. With such a migration came some startling revelations. There turned out to be a lot of hurdles on the path of transition.

The first hurdle to jump over is how do you tell everyone that you are, in effect, quitting? The Marine Corps reveres its veterans and considers them as Marines for life, which is great. The Marine Corps also expects excellence from every Marine in uniform, and the institution invariably gets what is expected. There is a gulf, however, between being a contributing Marine and valued veteran. It is really more of an abyss than a gulf, though, because before you get to wear a suit or a tuxedo to the Marine Corps Birthday Ball you have to go through the mystical process known as transition. And before you start your transition, you have to tell your boss that you are going to quit, and once those words leave your mouth they cannot ever be unsaid. Just like death and pregnancy, quitting the service is pretty final.

In my case I did so by email. My boss was in Afghanistan and, as my unit had very recently returned from that exciting and adventuresome place, I wasn't. That made stopping by her office a bit difficult. At any rate, once I made the decision the electronic notice of career irrelevance headed out to the other side of the world, and within hours my email inbox received her reply. I sat at my desk and just stared at the unopened email, trepidatious to open it for fear of what it might contain. After all, I had just uttered the unmentionable words "I am retiring", and with that email my flourishing career ended. Fortunately, she was a great boss and was very thoughtful in her reply. She gave me some sage mentoring advice and asked how she could help. Whew! One down, about a zillion more to go...

Once your boss knows, you can be sure that the word will get out at the speed of heat. That is when I quickly began telling lots and lots of people, or "socializing" the news as we like to call it in the military. Interestingly, my pronouncement was invariably met with one of two responses from my military friends, seniors, peers, and subordinates: either a broad smile and "hey, that's great! What are you going to do next?" or a disdainful scowl accompanied with the epithet: "Quitter!"

The first response was always followed by a pleasant conversation. The second response, well, not so much. It was usually followed by an uncomfortable silence broken only by the sound of my ego as it plummeted to the floor and shattered into a thousand pieces.

Another interesting note is that with my announcement to transition the conversations that I had with others in uniform subtly changed. I was no longer a part of the inner circle where decisions were made and deals were done, but now stood on the fringe and watched the action that I had spent many years in the midst of. It was bruising for the ego but an inexorable part of the process. After all, it was nothing personal, but in the immortal words of the *Cosa Nostra*, "just business." The positive side is that I no longer had to stay late when things got hectic at work or tell my family that I was on a short list of people who may have to leave on a moment's notice to go somewhere hot and dangerous on the other side of the world. So it all worked out.

Anyhow, once you hit the blinker and head for the off-ramp you need to be ready for the conversations that you will have. The decision you make is your own and your families, but as with all things in the military everyone else has an opinion, and not all of them are supportive.

With the announcement of my retirement my place in the upwardly mobile lineup was over. I stepped off the express train and onto the platform, and in doing so watched my peers and friends continue to ride the rails of their dynamic careers. Some went to the Pentagon, others to the various War Colleges, and no small number headed out for places exotic or dangerous depending on which spot on the globe they landed.

With a shrug and a sigh I waved goodbye and wished them well.

I was faced with a lot of introspective pondering and self-doubt. Why did I do it? Why did I step off the train? My career was moving upward and I was very well respected in my field. To paraphrase Marlon Brando from *On the Waterfront*, I coulda been a contender for promotion and the plum assignments that lay just down the line. So why would I leave?

That is a truly complicated question. It yields only enigmatic answers that everyone who decides to hang up their uniform must find for themselves. There was no single event or crisis that drove me out. There was no enticement from the outside world that drew me away. For me, as I said earlier I simply woke up one day to the realization that it was time to go.

Leaving, however, is both bittersweet and heart wrenching. The time I chose to depart the Marine Corps coincided with the end of the best job that I had during my career, that of being the Commanding Officer of a combat unit in time of war. I had been competitively selected from an incredibly talented and experienced group of my peers to lead a highly trained and specialized unit of Marines and Sailors and to take them to fight in Afghanistan. It was an incredibly demanding and challenging assignment, but it was the most rewarding thing that I had done in my decades of wearing brown and green.

Being in command is addictive. I had been fortunate to command five different organizations at various levels during my career, and each time I handed the flag to the next guy and said goodbye to "my" Marines was a significant emotional event. My last command, however, was the most momentous because I was selected to take charge by a board of senior officers and my orders came straight from the top Marine himself: the Commandant of the Marine Corps. I was one of the lucky few chosen to command; less than one in five officers at that level are selected to do so. For a career Marine a successful command tour is a harbinger of things to come, such as a promotion, orders to a top level military school like the National War College or a fellowship to a prestigious university like Harvard or Johns Hopkins University, and the greatly increased possibility of command again in the future. For officers who aren't selected to command, however, those opportunities are much less likely. Being picked opens doors for your career that for others remain forever closed.

Assuming command is also assuming a debt; a debt to the Marines and Sailors that you lead as well as to the Marine Corps writ large. After all, if you are selected by definition you are in the top of your peer group. The expectation of most senior officers and no small number of my peers is that you, the one entrusted with such a critical and rewarding position, will give back to the Marine Corps and repay the debt incurred by being given the most important job there is: leading our young men and women in the defense of our nation.

When I chose to depart active duty and handed the flag symbolizing command to my successor, however, no small number of my peers and seniors viewed my departure with disdain. In their minds I had taken the best job but not repaid the debt that it incurred; I had in essence eaten dessert and skipped clearing the table and doing the dishes. In their minds I was selfish. I was a quitter.

I agree that assuming command incurs a debt. The trust and confidence in a commander is nearly absolute; he or she is entrusted with the very lives of fellow Americans and with the defense of the nation. Command is also a crucible of sorts. A leader leaves the job as a changed officer and a different person because he or she has learned lessons only imparted by such an incredible level of trust and responsibility. Many of those lessons are positive, such as the satisfaction and pure joy you experience when your Marines do well and your unit succeeds. Many lessons are negative, though, such as when you or your unit fails. Command means being on duty every day and night from the day you take the flag to the day you pass it on complete with early morning phone calls that come because one of your Marines is in the brig, leading them into combat, and meeting the casualty evacuation helicopter at the field hospital when your wounded Marines and Sailors are brought in bloody from a firefight. Command tempers an officer as a furnace tempers steel, and it is for this reason that the doors I wrote about earlier spring open.

The debt is a personal one that every person in uniform feels to his or her peers, friends, unit, and country. Whether you are the commanding officer of a military unit or an infantryman or a truck driver, an incredibly strong bond of allegiance becomes a part of who you are. You owe a debt to everyone you serve with and to the Marine Corps, or the Army, or the Navy, Coast Guard, or the Air Force. For me, I fully realized that a debt was indeed owed, and I am a firm believer in paying my debts. In my case, I paid my debt up front.

The debt is one that I have not been alone in discharging. Like all military households, my family has paid an enormous price throughout my career. The late nights, training exercises, and deployments were all par for the course for a military family, but in particular the wars in Iraq and Afghanistan took a disproportionate toll.

I left my family behind and deployed overseas. To combat. A lot. That isn't unusual for a Marine particularly in time of war, but in my case the deployments were punishing. I deployed to the fight four times in a span of five years; again, that isn't as much as some, but certainly more than most. I had two young children in elementary school, and the things that I missed are utterly irreplaceable. Little things like my oldest son's 6th, 7th, 8th, and 10th birthdays. Little things like being gone either in a combat zone or preparing for the fight over half of my youngest son's life by the time he hit seven years of age. Countless holiday events – Thanksgiving dinners, Christmas mornings, Easter egg hunts, and Trick-or-Treating at Halloween – spent in a foreign country while my wife and kids open presents or hunt for eggs or trick or treat without their father. The worst bit was coming home from deployment when each of my kids was little, though. It is an incredible punch to the gut when you step off the bus and your kids don't know who you are because they were too young when you left to remember that you even exist, and in my case it happened with both of them. My kids paid their part of my debt.

When I wasn't deployed I was in the field training or off at some conference somewhere. My wife, who has an incredibly demanding career of her own, held it together despite my absence. Parent-teacher conferences, trips to the doctor, homework, sports, and everything else that parents do fell to her, and she soldiered on and made it work. She paid her part of my debt.

So on that fateful day when I woke up and realized it was time to go I did so with a clear conscience. The debt had been repaid by my entire family: I had spent 30 out of the preceding 60 months dodging bullets and avoiding IEDS in a couple of combat zones while my family stayed behind and kept it together despite the crushing demands that such stressful deployments bring. My family and I have indeed paid the Marine Corps for the privilege of command and the honor of being a United States Marine.

It is a heart-wrenching decision to hang up the cloth of the nation and leave the military behind. Every person in uniform wrestles with the decision and must make it on his or her own terms. My story is unique because it is about me, but it is ubiquitous because the decision is the same for everyone. Everyone has to leave at some point, and it is important to make peace with yourself and with your family before you step off the train.

Chapter 3: _So now what?_

So you have taken the plunge and let the world know that you are moving on. Now what? Unlike pretty much every other aspect of military life with transition there is nobody grabbing you by the noggin and telling you what to do. For the first time in a long time you are on your own. In order to be successful you are going to have to take charge of your future and chart a course for a successful trip back to civilian life. It is time for a little adventure learning, some sleuthing, and to seek a bit of advice from those who are currently transitioning or have already made the jump.

Let's start with the adventure learning part. For my entire career people have told me what to do, and in doing what they said I learned a great deal. As I got older and higher in rank the telling softened from short pithy phrases like "WHAT THE F*%#$^! DO YOU THINK YOU ARE DOING??" to more genteel greetings with "Sir" on both ends of the sentence, like a "Sir" sandwich.

"Sir, would you like me to bring the HMMWV around, sir?"

"Sir, would you like some broccoli with your mystery meat, sir?"

"Sir, everyone is at the table...can we start the meeting now, sir?"

For what it's worth, Marines come by the "sir" sandwich honestly. When I was a teenaged and perpetually petrified recruit my senior drill instructor sweetly informed me that "the first and last words out of my filthy sewer would be SIR!" just like Gunnery Sergeant Hartman in _Full Metal Jacket_.

I far prefer the latter to the former, but once I started transitioning I generally got neither. I did receive the polite "Can I help you?" with an occasional "sir" thrown in for effect, but nothing reminiscent of my carnivorous days in the meat eating pack. It became the pedantic pabulum familiar to the herd. So it goes. _Welcome to the wonderful world of transition._

Back to adventure learning. I quickly ascertained that being a rank-conscious martinet would make my transition both painful and annoying, so I opted for the more low-key approach which suited me and my personality just fine. I put away the standard expectations that come with senior rank and position and wandered around the base, seeking out administrative sections where I could ask the experts what I needed to do to retire from the military. The experience was interesting.

"Excuse me Marine, but could you tell me what I need to do to initiate my retirement paperwork?"

After receiving the blankest stare I have seen since I asked my ten year old where the empty candy wrappers in his pockets came from, I asked to see his boss.

A motivated and thoroughly squared away sergeant came to the counter. He didn't know either, but he knew who did. I then talked to *his* boss (by now I had made it to the warrant officer ranks, who are the true experts in their fields of expertise) and he pointed me to just the guy I needed to talk to: a retired Marine who was in charge of outprocessing Marines who retiring. Who would have thunk it?

So, armed with the *who*, I set out to find the *where*. Where does he work and when could I meet him? Employing my best Sherlock Holmes impersonation, I employed my digital Watson (aka my tired, slow, yet generally functional work computer) for some help. After a few emails zorched through the ether to the aforementioned retired Marine in charge of retirements, I had what I needed: an appointment.

Off I went to a decrepit old concrete building where a lot of civilians and a few Marines were attentively working on whatever it was that they were working on. I met the aforementioned transition guy, and he turned out to be absolutely great. He asked for my social security number (the Holy Grail for identity thieves, but the single most important number to a military type because every aspect of his or her life is pinned to it) and entered it into his computer.

Lo and behold, he pulled up all the information I needed to start the process! Happy day!

Happy, that is, until he told me I couldn't retire yet. As Homer Simpson says: "D'oh!"

I have been around the block a more than a few times during my career, so I was smugly secure in my assumption that all I really needed to do was tell my admin shop that I was retiring. After all, that was one of the things that administrators were for, weren't they? Didn't they administrate, and wasn't processing a retirement simply an administrative process?

As I learned that day, the answer to those questions is both yes and no. Yes it is administrative, but no, it is not simple. It never is.

As I sat at the desk of the retirement counselor, I was positive that I had figured out what I needed to know in order to get the retirement ball rolling. That happy assumption was dashed upon the jagged rocks of reality when the retirement counselor cheerfully told me that I couldn't retire yet.

After my head got done exploding and my guts unclenched I asked him why. Because, he said, you are not yet eligible to retire. The pressure between my temples shot up and the room started to spin...

Backing up a bit, the basis of my smugness was that I did what I always have done during my career: I prepared for the meeting with the retirement counselor by doing my homework. I logged into Marine on Line (MOL, the Marine Corps personnel administrative website) and surfed to the retirement section and surfed around to learn about how to retire. There is a wealth of information in the site, including a nifty letter from the Commandant of the Marine Corps commending retirees for their service. In particular I read the MARCORPSEPSMAN, which is Marine-speak for the *Marine Corps Separations and Retirement Manual* (there is a rule in the military: never say in six words that which you can say in one barely pronounceable super-contraction), which had all the information that I thought I needed. Boy was I wrong!

The assumption that I could announce my retirement date was based on calculations that are explained in the manual. There are several key dates that pertain to a military career: the *Pay Entry Base Date* (PEBD), the *Armed Forces Active Duty Base Date* (AFADBD), and the *End of Active Service* (EAS). These dates, not my math, established when I could get out. And it turned out that my calculations were wrong.

The PEBD is the day that you raise your right hand and swear to support and defend this great nation of ours. For some people, that is the day they ship out for recruit training, but for most people there is a gap between signing the contract and swearing in and heading out for the legendary yellow footprints.

What are yellow footprints, you ask? They are actual silhouettes of shoes painted on the ground at the Marine Corps Recruit Depots that serve as a recruit's initiation on how to stand with their heels together and their heels together and their feet at a 45 degree angle. Said recruits get to practice standing the Marine Corps way while being informed by their new and bestest friends who wear big hats and yell a lot what a baaaaad idea it was to sign the enlistment papers. I digress.

The time gap between signing the papers and shipping out to bootcamp is filled with what is known as the *Delayed Entry Program*, or DEP. The recruit or officer candidate signs the contract and swears into the service, which establishes his or her PEBD. After a period of time, the recruiter shows up at the door and gives the unsuspecting young person a ride to the airport, whereupon the hard part begins; reporting to recruit training or officer candidate school. The day that the recruiter picks you up is your AFADBD because that is the day that your active duty service begins. Your retirement eligibility is calculated based on your AFADBD; you are eligible for retirement 20 years and one day after your AFADBD. The AFADBD only counts time on active duty though, so your DEP time doesn't count, and neither does any time that you spend off of active duty (for example, you get out and decide to come back into the clutches of the service or are in the reserves or National Guard).

For enlisted Marines and junior officers their time in service is determined by the length of their enlistment contract. Generally along the lines of four to eight years or so (it is a little different for officers), beginning with your PEBD. The last day of your contract is the day you get out, which as we learned earlier is known as your EAS. So, now we have three different dates that determine when you can transition: PEBD, AFADBD, and EAS. PEBD is when you sign up, AFADBD is when you ship out, and EAS is when you get out. Pretty simple so far.

Simple, of course, except in my case. I have both active duty and reserve service, which takes something that which should be simple and makes it much more complicated. I initially enlisted into the reserves on an eight year contract. What that meant was that I had a PEBD that was established the day I signed the contract and swore in, which has remained unchanged throughout my entire career. I established my AFADBD on the day I shipped to bootcamp, and my active duty time continued until I was released from active duty and entered reserve status, whereupon my AFADBD was suspended because I was no longer on active duty because it only applies to active duty types.

I had a great time in the Marine reserves as I pursued my undergraduate degree. So much so that I made the commitment to be an active duty officer, contingent of course on my surviving the rigors of Officer Candidate School. With that decision, several of the dates I wrote about earlier changed. My PEBD stayed the same (because I had served continuously in the reserves since in first enlisted) but I established a new AFADBD and a new EAS. My new AFADBD was the day I shipped to OCS, and my new EAS was 42 months later (again, officer's contracts are slightly different than the standard two to eight year gigs for enlisted folks). After a year on active duty, my status changed from being a reserve officer with a 42 month contract to a regular officer through a process known as "augmentation". As a regular officer my EAS changed from the last day on my contract to

"Indefinite", which means that I served until I quit, got thrown out, or retired, which I was trying desperately to do when I sat down with the retirement counselor.

Easy enough, I thought. I should be able to retire twenty years after my AFADBD. But what about the time I served in the Marine Corps reserves? Does any of that service count?

Why, yes it does, which brings us back to the shocking revelation from the retirement counselor. Any time that I had served on active duty during my reserve enlistment counted towards retirement, and even though I had studied the arcane and byzantine rules and regulations that apply to retirement and had done the math to show that I had indeed served enough time to retire, it wasn't good enough.

The problem was that I needed proof that I had served those days of active duty in the Marine Corps Reserve. Lots of proof.

It turns out that even though there are lots of records in computer databases, it turns out that there are also a lot of records that *aren't* in computer databases. Since I had enlisted back when Ronald Reagan was in his first term of office and typewriters were all the rage, there were no electronic records to prove that I had served those active duty periods while in the reserves. Even though there was an electronic record in MOL that depicted my reserve service (known as the *Career Retirement Credit Report*, or CRCR for more acronymical dominance) there was no digital copy on file of the source documentation needed to provide a record of my service.

I needed to actually prove, with original documents, that I had been in the reserves. More importantly, I needed documentation of each and every day that I served on active duty because each active duty day (for training, deployments, and such) would count towards my AFADBD, in effect moving it backwards in time.

Holy mackerel! I needed documents pushing three decades in age! Whatever to do?

Fortunately for me (and to the chagrin of my family) I am a bit of a pack rat. In a box somewhere in my garage there laid a folder, and in that folder laid every paystub (known as the *Leave and Earnings Statement* or LES for you acronym lovers) that I had ever been issued. So, donning my best felt hat and with a whip in one hand and a flashlight in the other, I did my best Indiana Jones impersonation and went spelunking into the depths of my garage, searching for the box that held my salvation. After an indeterminate time spent grunting and sweating and cursing and searching I found the box. And the folder.

Happy day! I blew the dust off of the long neglected sheaf of papers and sorted through the mass of archaic dot-matrix documents. I plopped down at the kitchen table to sift through the three inch thick pile of faded paper, and a within a few hours had disinterred the source documents for every day of active duty served during my reserve time.

Unfortunately, it was then when things got complicated. My friendly local retirement counselor informed me that he was happy I had found the documents, but that there was nothing he could do with them. For that, I needed to go higher. A lot higher. All the way up to the Headquarters of the United States Marine Corps, where there was bound to be someone, somewhere, who could help me.

Since I was (and still am) happily living in the San Diego area, the requirement to bring my pile of papers to an office in Northern Virginia was quite problematic. Faced with a 3000 mile road trip, I abashedly swallowed my pride and looked around for some help. Unfortunately, I had no idea where to find the help I needed.

*   *   *   *   *

Lessons Learned:

The purpose of this book is to help with military transition. From here on out chapters will end with a recap of the key lessons learned during the journey of transition. Here are the salient points from this chapter:

- ☐ Do your research. Find out what rules and regulations apply to your situation (service, active/reserve time, etc.) *before* you talk to someone in the admin shop. That will help you have a much more intelligent conversation than I had, and will smooth out the rough spots.

- ☐ Get your administrative ducks in a row. Make a folder of all pertinent information such as leave and earning statements, enlistment contracts, commissioning documents, etc. This is particularly important for reservists and those with or broken service time, as there may be no other record of your service.

- ☐ Do what I didn't do: talk to people and get advice! I didn't, and it set me back a month or so as I pulled my head out of the sand and organized my files.

- ☐ Find a copy of your service's retirement and separations manual. I learned a ton by reading through the MARCORSEPSMAN. It will provide you a great foundation from which you can ask the right questions of the right people.

Chapter 4: _Advice is useful._ _Who knew?_

Transitioning from a career in the military is a bit more complicated than one might think, as I continued to painfully learn through my various and clumsy misadventures. Rather stupidly I had managed to make it more difficult on myself through my own ignorance and the boneheaded assumption that I knew everything that I needed to know, which proved to be shockingly incorrect.

So there I was, sitting with my retirement counselor when he informed me that my best-laid plans for departing active duty were fundamentally flawed. I had made all of the calculations to determine the date of my retirement based on my enlisted and commissioned officer service from both active duty and in the reserves, but all of my mathematical gyrations were in vain because I had to show my math along with the source documents that backed it up. D'oh!

I left his office dazed and confused.

In the best fashion of reality-deniers everywhere I went back to work and lamented about my fate. Dame fortune smiled upon me, however, when a senior officer heard me bemoaning my misfortune. After he told me to quit whining, he offhandedly directed me to contact a friend of his who had recently retired (!) and was now in charge of the retirement branch (irony or apropos?) back in Quantico.

The clouds parted, the birds sang, and my half empty glass was suddenly and miraculously half full. With that happy bit of information I realized that things were not as dire as I had thought. Giddily I asked my savior if he had any advice to go with the news about his friend.

"Just drop him a line," said the sage. "Tell him I told you to call and he'll take care of you."

He was right. I sent off an email and within an hour I had a response. Although my quandary seemed epic in proportions to me, he was a little too high in the food chain to deal with my "minor" problem. He did have just the people to help, though, and with another email I was almost there. After reiterating my dilemma yet again to yet another retired Marine who happened to be in charge of just the _officer_ retirements, I was linked up with a most polite and supremely helpful woman who as _the_ person in charge of verifying retirement dates.

I could have given her a big hug and a sloppy kiss, but fortunately for the both of us internet technology isn't quite that advanced as of yet.

After a brief email exchange, I called her on the telephone so she could set me straight on what I needed to do to. She directed me to find every source document that showed my reserve service. Since I had already braved the Dante-esqe cavern of my garage and had found them, the hard part of finding them was done.

"Scan 'em and send 'em in." she said. "I'll let you know in a week where you stand."

Several hours of furious scanning later, I sent off email after email with my records attached as .pdf files. As with all things related to transition, it was a chore. The scans were relatively large files, and the internal email system attachments cannot exceed a megabyte or so. As a result I spammed her inbox like a teenage hacker but once they were all transmitted I just had to be patient for her to review them.

And so I waited.

A week is a long time to wait. The stakes were, for me anyway, pretty high. The crux of the issue was the magical date on which I could retire, which I had calculated to fall before the end of the year was actually, according to the retirement counselor, sometime the following year. Although only a few months may seem to be no big deal, it would prove to be a significant emotional event for me if it proved to be the case. If so, I would have to find another assignment in the interim, and it would be an assignment where nobody would really want me around (because I was retiring) and my usefulness would be pretty limited because I wouldn't be there very long. I would have been as relevant as a typewriter in a computer lab and just about as annoying. Besides, I had already told everyone from my kids to my boss that I was retiring soon, and boy would I look like a complete idiot if I had to take it back.

So that week passed at a glacial pace, with every day seeming longer than the day before. After watching the grey hairs on my head sprout like a slivery chia pet, a week passed, and sure enough she dropped me a line to let me know how my math stood up in comparison to hers. My calculations were off by about a week or so, which in the grand scheme of things was not enough to really matter. The day was literally saved! My retirement date was officially set on the same date that I had calculated and advertised. Hooray! I wouldn't have to go back to my boss with my hat in hand, and I wouldn't be begging my family for forgiveness. I wanted to give my new found friend in Quantico a big hug and a kiss, but computing technology hadn't progressed enough in a week to make it possible.

Again, that was probably for the best.

*   *   *   *   *

Lessons learned:

- ☐ The best resource is all around you. It is the people you work with, and more specifically, the people you work *for*. Senior people know a whole lot about a whole lot and can give you some great advice, but only if you are smart enough to ask for it. In addition, they are invariably connected to other people who can help you out. Again, all you need to do is ask!

- ☐ Regulations and research are a great place to start when you are looking to transition, but they aren't enough. I had assumed that everything was hunky-dory with my service record, but I was wrong. As Ronald Reagan once said: "Trust, but verify...", and his statement is the cornerstone of administration in the military. Nobody was going to doubt me, but neither would they accept my word without performing their due diligence to make sure that every "i" was dotted and every "t" crossed.

- ☐ Find out who the people are that you will be working with, both locally and at higher headquarters. An email or two and a few phone calls solved a problem that had completely flummoxed me, but those emails and phone calls were to the right people. Find the right people and your transition will go much more smoothly.

- ☐ Make sure to say thank you to everyone who lends you a hand!

Chapter 5: *Cracking the code*

Although I didn't know it at the time, the act of officially setting a retirement date set a lot of things in motion about which I had no idea. My name was placed on a few lists here and there, and soon enough I began to receive emails and phone calls asking me to set up appointments and attend transition courses. It seemed a bit random at first, but all became clear when I met again with the transition specialist. Now that I had established a solid date, he said, I could move forward with the multitude of tasks that lay ahead of me. Tasks, unfortunately, that I really didn't know too much about.

As I sat in the uncomfortable Government Issue fiberglass chair beside his Government Issue faux wood desk, my friend the retirement counselor took notice of my blank stare. I was not sure where to even begin. Fortunately, he handed me what appeared to be an unremarkable handful of papers held together by a Government Issue staple.

I looked at the first page and saw that much of my future independent sleuthing about to find points of contact would be unnecessary. "Retirement Contact Numbers" it stated at the top of the sheet, and below the title were over a dozen phone numbers for the various people and organizations that I would be required to coordinate with as I transitioned. Happily I discerned the names and email addresses of some of the people who had been contacting me, seemingly out of the blue. Aha, I thought: a method to the madness. Good stuff!

I turned the page, and read words that set my heart racing.

"RETIREMENT CHECKLIST FOR RETIREES" it practically screamed from the page. Despite the repetitive syntax (although there may be a *non-retirement Checklist for non-retirees* I suppose), it was exactly what I needed.

To a Marine, and I suspect all servicemen and women, checklists hold a disproportionate level of elevated importance. Pretty much everything we do can in some way be distilled down to a list with little boxes next to every item, boxes that beg to be checked as you perform each action contained on the list. Checklists rule pretty much every aspect our martial lives, and I was gleeful to receive a checklist that would guide me through the transition process.

As an eager and young recruit I learned everything about the military by the numbers in checklist fashion, from how to lace my boots *("One - Grasp the laces in both hands! Two - Insert the aglet in the lowermost eyelets, and cross the laces right over left until you run out of eyelets!)* to the intricacies of the M-16 *("There are eight steps in the cycle of operation of the M-16A1 service rifle! They are firing, unlocking, extracting, ejecting, cocking, feeding, chambering, locking....and don't you forget it!!).* Our undershirts were folded according to the unyielding inspection requirement that they neatly fit into 6" by 6" squares and our socks were rolled into precise little spheres that, despite their olive drab color were oddly reminiscent of meatballs in a dodgy strip mall Italian restaurant. Exactly like the checklist said.

The predilection for neatly arranged lists has followed me throughout my career. I used them for everything and so did everyone else. They are used for keeping track of things, arranging a daily schedule, and pretty much everything you can imagine. They could be used for good or evil, depending on who was holding the pen that marked them. Just as corporate managers dread the arrival of a clipboard toting efficiency expert, military types cringe at the sight of a clipboard toting sergeant or lieutenant bent on holding an inspection. Necessary evils perhaps, but they share the same method of accounting and delivery; a bit of paper with a grade at the top, based on how well each item was scored on the checklist. And, of course, *everything* gets inspected in the military, so there is almost a perpetual state of anxiety that induces ulcers and makes one long for the simplicity of a firefight with Al Qaeda or the Taliban. Lists run the military.

Checklists have been thoroughly and completely etched into my psyche. I use them for everything, or at least for everything that I need to get done. In combat we used them to ensure that we had everything we needed (Grenades? *Check!* Ammo? *Check!* Water? *Check!*), and at home I write a list of household tasks with little boxes next to them and earnestly attempt to check them off as quickly as possible. My meeting at the retirement office was neatly written next to a tiny hand-drawn box in my notebook, and as soon as my meeting was done I would gleefully put a tiny "x" inside the little square and move on to the next entry.

But I digress. The arrival of this particular checklist produced the anti-cringing emotion of pure joy. It was the Rosetta stone that translated all of the gibberish of retirement into an organized and comprehensive compendium containing every box I needed to check in order to complete the transition process. Hugging the packet to my chest, I rose from the standard issue uncomfortable government issued chair and sailed out of the retirement office, marking the little box on my own checklist and happily setting out to check every box on my newly acquired agenda.

I left the retirement counselor's office with a smile on my face. He had given me exactly what I needed to chart my course for transition: a comprehensive checklist of tasks to perform along with a roster of contacts that would help me get those things done. Happily I grabbed a cup of coffee and sat down and took a good look at the list.

It was several pages long, and I won't bore you with the mundane and excruciating details, well, at least not *all* of them. I read through the whole packet and pondered what to do. Should I just start at the top of the list and charge through until I reached the end, or was there a more logical way to complete the rather lengthy assignment? I read through it again. The first two lines made me chuckle:

RETIREMENT CHECKLIST
I. CHECKLIST

More repetition! It only makes sense that the "Retirement Checklist for Retirees" would have a Checklist as the first item in the Retirement Checklist section. Maybe I could just read every other line and still get all the information I needed?

Nope. The checklist's first bullet, which was next line on the paper, quickly got my attention:

✓ *12-24 months before separation…*

Ack! I was only about nine months from the big day. According to the list I was already over a *year* behind, and I just got started.

Yikes!

I took a deep breath and read yet again through the entire document. It was arranged in reverse chronological order in a countdown of sorts to the date of official transition (my EAS). Beginning at two years out, the list quickly went to twelve then six and then three months before retirement. Since I had already missed out on over a year of preparatory work I decided to ditch performing the checklist as written and instead to figure a different way to get everything accomplished.

What I learned was that there are basically three facets of the retirement process, so I reorganized the checklist into those three areas and then arranged the various subtasks in order of importance and time sensitivity. The things that I needed to do right away hit the top of the list and those that could wait migrated towards the bottom. By regrouping the dozens of things to be done it made them more manageable, and hopefully I would be able to accomplish them more efficiently. The basic areas I came up with after studying the checklist were

1) Transition training

2) Administration

3) Medical evaluations

Transition training consisted primarily of a series of seminars and classes that prepare the "separating or retiring service member" (me!) for return to civilian life. As a retiring Marine (meaning I have more grey hair and wrinkles than those who were separating after only few years of service) I was required to attend one course and was eligible to attend two more. The required class, called the Transition Assistance Program (TAP) Employment Workshop, is required for each and every person on their way out of the military (with a few exceptions I will cover later). It covers a lot of really important topics ranging from veteran's benefits to tax rules, and you can't get out (at least not legally) without attending it. The other two courses were designed for more senior ("distinguished") people like me. The courses were designed to help with resume writing, interviewing, and other important job skills.

As for administration, this area addresses the nuts and bolts of leaving an incredibly bureaucratic profession. There are forms to fill out, papers to sign, and about a billion things to read and initial. The administrative boxes to check ranged from deciding where you would establish your home after the service (back to the town you enlisted from? Where you live now? Tahiti? They all have their upsides and downsides, but you can only choose one) to what uniform you will wear to your retirement ceremony. The administrative requirements ran for several pages and would take a long time to accomplish, but fortunately many of the items could be knocked out simultaneously as I met with various administration specialists (who are the military counterparts to the corporate Human Resources department).

The medical bit is just as important as the administrative requirements, and the list was likewise just as lengthy. For all separating and retiring service members the physical evaluation and disability rating process has potentially the greatest impact of any part of transition. Many people departing military service will have developed some physical problems that will follow them for the rest of their lives, and if they are properly evaluated and documented then they are eligible for medical care long after they take off their uniform. After all, carrying 75 to 100 pounds of equipment on your back while patrolling in 120 degree heat for weeks on end takes a toll on the knees just as operating a tank, flying a helicopter, or shooting artillery will likely make you a bit hard of hearing. It is crucial that these problems are evaluated while in uniform, however, because if they aren't a bureaucratic nightmare awaits should you try to get them evaluated as an *ex*-service member.

So, after revising the checklist into these three areas I set out to check each box on the list as quickly and efficiently as I could. With less than nine months to go until my retirement date, I immediately attacked those items that I was delinquent on and started emailing and calling the points of contact on the first page of the checklist to schedule everything else. It was going to be a bumpy ride, but at least I knew when it would end.

*   *   *   *   *

<u>Lessons learned:</u>

☐ First and foremost, time is incredibly important. The recommendation is to start transitioning two years before you take off your uniform because it takes that long to do everything properly and at a leisurely pace. I started transitioning with less than half of that time, and as a result I found myself working a lot harder than I need in order to get everything done. For many people, though, time is not a luxury that they control. If you are getting out after on enlistment, you may not be able to officially get started on transition until your command tells you to. That said, you can certainly plan ahead and accomplish many transition related tasks while still in your operational unit.

☐ All of the answers you need are out there. You just need to know where to go to find them, and in typical military fashion I can guarantee that there is checklist out there somewhere that will greatly aid you in your transition.

☐ I should have asked for the checklist up front instead of just blankly staring at the counselor until he took pity on me and handed it over. One of your first stops once you decide to retire is the administration shop that will be processing your retirement as they have a wealth of information and advice that they will cheerfully provide. All you need to do is ask.

☐ As soon as you make the decision to get out or retire you need to get organized! Once you have a copy of the appropriate checklist (retirement or separation), you should start checking things off as far out as you can. Even if you have not decided or do not know your actual transition date, there are many things that can be accomplished easily that will save you time later. For example, reviewing your personnel and medical records for accuracy and researching where you would like to live when you get out can be done at any time.

☐ Find out what administrative section will be processing your separation or retirement and schedule a meeting with them. They can provide you with contacts and guidance that you can put to good use immediately, and without the time wasted by adventure learning and trying to do it all yourself as I had done initially.

Chapter 6: Back to school with Transition Seminars

As we discovered in the last chapter there are three major undertakings to accomplish before the transition back to civilian life is complete: first, transition training, second, administration, and third, medical evaluations. Although all three of these paths are actually followed largely in parallel it is far too confusing to discuss all three at once. In order to avoid consternation (because there is already plenty of that in the transition process) we'll tackle them one at a time.

In terms of timing, the transition training bit comes first and here's why: the administration requirements for transition as well as the necessary medical evaluations are set on a timeline that is based on your EAS. Transition training, however, is not. Instead, the opportunity to educate yourself and learn about the transition process is available pretty much whenever you would like to take advantage of it whereas the other areas are closely tied to when you are actually departing the service. You have much more flexibility in the with transition classes than you do with the other aspects of getting out.

Transitioning from the military to the civilian world is a process that hearkens back to the birth of the nation. It began with George Washington bidding a fond farewell to his militia and regular soldiers at the end of the Revolutionary War and has continued on through the following centuries of war and peace. For decade after decade after decade veterans have hung up their uniforms and integrated back into society. Some have done so without missing a beat, but those individuals are rare indeed. For the rest of us, the road is a little bumpy and has some unexpected turns. Fortunately, somebody up there was looking out for those of us who are easily confused. Like me.

Much to my chagrin I discovered (and much too late to do anything about it, I might add) that there was no need to wait until the end of my career to learn about transition. I was eligible to attend classes and seminars on transition and retirement pretty much whenever I desired. That was quite a revelation! Had I only known that I could learn about the other side long before I actually decided to retire it would have made the whole process a lot easier, but to be honest the thought had never crossed my mind. I was too busy travelling around the world and serving in places notorious for the bad food, scorching deserts, and angry locals. Even so, there are a surprising number of opportunities that are set in place to learn about the transition process. We will cover many of the courses in much greater detail later in the chapter, but here is a survey of the classes that were relevant to my situation and available to a transitioning Marine in Southern California. My experience is far from unique because there are identical or similar courses are offered by all four services at posts and stations around the world:

-*TAP* (everything is an acronym, and this one stands for the *Transition Assistance Program*) which is also known for some reason as TAMP (which stands for the *Transition Assistance Management Program*). I really don't know if there is a difference between the two, but it falls in line with the military's love affair with acronyms – adding an "M" between "A" and "P" is certainly some form of improvement, and I am certain that somebody got a medal out of it. At any rate, the TAP (or TAMP, or whatever it is called in your branch of service) program is mandated by law and required by every branch of service as a prerequisite to separation from active duty (with a few exceptions which are covered in "Lessons Learned" section of this chapter). The core curriculum is designed for those leaving the service after serving a hitch or two, and it covers the legal, medical, and administrative requirements for transition as well as a lot of information of how to write a resume, what to wear to an interview (which is a HUGE deal for those of us who have not updated our duds since skinny leather ties and white shoes were the coolest thing on the dance floor) and how to get a job.

The core curriculum is about three days in length, and the individual services can add to it if they desire. The Marine Corps, for example, lengthened the program to five days and renamed it the *Transition Readiness Seminar*, or TRS. The additional two days are spent conducting assessments and evaluations of participants, financial planning, and resiliency training. In addition, the program recognizes that not all veterans are going to pursue the same path when they get out. TRS offers four "pathways" for the participants to follow: 1) College or University education, 2) Career or Technical training, 3) Employment, or 4) Entrepreneurship. The participant then receives classes and materials focused on the path that they choose to follow.

The course is of enormous importance because you cannot get out unless you attend it because your final check out sheet (a document of epic importance that we will get to know intimately later on) will not have the required notation that allows you to stop getting your hair cut and quit wearing a uniform. It lasts about a week, during which time attendance is mandatory and is the appointed place of duty for the participant. This is important, because unlike high school or college, you can get thrown into the brig for skipping class. Needless to say there is rarely a need for a truant officer to go round up class-skipping delinquents.

-*OUT, or Officers Under Twenty class.* This particular class is for officers who are separating from the service but do not meet the requirements for retirement. These officers are lieutenants and captains who have completed their obligated service of four to six years and who are going back to the civilian world. It is very similar to the TAP class, with the difference being that it focuses at the college graduate as opposed to the high school graduate level. They don't spend too much time on how to dress or what to wear, though, because these young officers are still generally in their twenties and their wardrobes haven't aged to the point of embarrassment. Yet.

-*Pre-Retirement TAP course.* This course is TAP for those who are going to retire after at least twenty years of active service. It is designed for the more "distinguished" amongst us (me included) that are greying at the temples and are at a different place in their lives than a twentysomething that will use his or her benefits to pursue a bachelor degree or attend a trade school. It covers the same required topics on benefits and whatnot as the other TAP courses, but has additional lectures and classes on things like becoming an entrepreneur, networking, and how to buy new clothes.

The required transition courses differ between the services. They all include the core TAP curriculum (which is usually a three day training seminar), but they may lengthen the program to include additional material as the Marine Corps did with TRS.

-*25+ Pre-Retirement Seminar.* More of a symposium than a seminar, this one is not required but is strongly encouraged and recommended for those who, again, have been in for a looooong time. It does not go into the benefits and administration of retirement, but instead focuses on life on the other side of the fence. In addition to helping with your job search and assistance with developing a new career there are several guest lecturers who cover topics ranging from financial management for retirement as well as financial management as a career, how to go into business for yourself with a franchise or on your own, and how to dress for success.

-*Ruehlin Seminar.* This course is a week-long seminar that caters to senior officers and enlisted who are retiring after a full career, with the definition of *senior* being length of service and advanced rank. There is often a difference as it is possible to retire after 20 or 25 years but not obtain senior rank; for example, many officers begin their careers as enlisted members and the time spent as a young and motivated warrior counts towards retirement. As such, they may have over two decades of service but are retiring as relatively junior officers, not the O-5s and O-6s that are the target population for the course. Also, some enlisted members may have the same length of time in uniform but for whatever reason doesn't achieve the higher enlisted ranks of E-8 or E-9. The course has a small student body of around fifteen attendees and is focused specifically on the process of starting a new career and all of the job hunting skills necessary to do so.

So there you have it: five different courses, seminars, or classes that anyone eligible can attend to help with transition. Amazing! Each one is a little different in its focus and intent, but each provides a slew of information that is invaluable to one on the path back to civilian life. In my particular case, I attended the Pre-Retirement TAP course as well as the 25+ Pre-Retirement and Ruehlin Seminars. Suffice it to say the wisdom I gained under the tutelage of the experienced and dedicated instructors was remarkable and very welcome. Without it I would have been not just a bumbling fool stumbling along until I found myself unemployed, but I would have missed out on education and training that my contemporaries in the private sector pay tens of thousands of dollars for.

There is a psychological aspect to attending transition seminars as well. They mark the first real and tangible steps you take down the road of transition. For most people making the jump it is the first real "transition" activity that they will perform, and with it comes acceptance that one is really leaving the military. For me, it is when becoming a member of the herd really hit home.

Where before I considered myself carnivorous to a fault, I left the pack and fell in with the herd. It is not a pejorative title in the least, but a descriptive observation of the new strata I found myself in. When you are on active duty, you are moving at a million miles an hour in about a hundred different directions. Compartmentalized thinking and multitasking are the norm; you almost never have the luxury of just tackling one problem at a time. As such, we all tend to be in a hurry, are a bit brusque in our speech, and never have time to sit back and watch the leaves blow in the wind.

Once you drop your papers and announce that you are departing the service your ride on the waves of chaos abates. You hand the flag over to the next person, turn in your blackberry, and lose your sweet parking spot – but you get your life back! All of a sudden you can take your kids to school and plan for holidays with the certainty that you won't be hanging tinsel on a tree built out of an ammunition crate made festive with olive drab paint and ornaments fashioned from hand grenades. Just as significant as those marvelous changes is your inculcation into a covey of people just like you; recently careworn, stressed out, and career-driven, but now shifting their lives to more sedate and hopeful civilian side of the fence.

No longer part of the rapacious pack, we are all members of the congenial herd. Regardless of our background – pilot, grunt, artilleryman, mechanic, whatever – we are taking the same train to the same destination. We are collectively leaving our chosen profession to pursue life on Civvie Street. Just as the Unsinkable Molly Brown observed as she watched the Titanic sink beneath the waves, we were all in the same boat, with first class and steerage passengers all lumped together. The wild ride is coming to an end, but that's ok. There are plenty of other rides out there, and for a change we get to choose which one we want to try.

I became a full-fledged salad grazer when I began attending transition seminars. I was headed to class and not to combat. Not at all unlike the first few of days in high school, I started to see some familiar faces in the seats to my left and right as the courses progressed. The big difference from my high school days is that they all had greying hair and some wrinkles as opposed to the big hair and Day-Glo neon green Wayfarer sunglasses that were cool when I left the hallowed halls of my youthful education. In a surprising departure from our martial love affair with snappy uniforms covered in sparkly trinkets the courses are conducted in civilian clothes, so there were none of the trappings that are part and parcel of martial life; no rank insignia or rack of ribbons to show our standing in the pecking order. Becoming civilians again began with the simple act of dressing like civilians, and doing so helped make us just like we used to be: equals. We were all of similar age and were similarly dressed in the standard collared shirt and khaki slacks which compose the non-uniform that military professionals all wear when they can't wear a uniform. Much as we leave the world as naked as we entered it, my cohorts and I were decamping from the service in the mufti we abandoned to don the cloth of the nation.

Just like the clothes we wore way back when before we first put on a uniform.

＊　　＊　　＊　　＊　　＊

Lessons learned:

☐ Start early! I was pretty far down the path to transition before I began attending classes. I found myself sitting with no small number of more prescient Marines and Sailors who were years away from transitioning but were smart enough to start learning about it early. All that is required to attend the classes is permission from your command (in civilian parlance, it means that your boss has to say it is OK to miss work for a few days) and a commitment to attend the course in its entirety because seating is often limited.

☐ Find out which courses are most suited to your situation. If you are getting out after four years, then obviously the Pre-Retirement courses are not for you. You may be in a situation, however, where you may not be eligible for a "senior" retirement seminar due to not having over 25 years in uniform, but there may be an empty slot you can take advantage of. Contact your local transition program coordinator to see what is available. Take every opportunity you can to educate yourself.

☐ Not everyone is required to attend the three day core TAP curriculum. As stated in Defense Department form DD 2958, the following people are exempt:

a. Service members retiring after 20 years or more of Active Federal Service (AFS) in the Military Services. (This was new to me; even though retirees are no longer required to attend the core TAP curriculum I still recommend that you do because it because it is free and you are guaranteed to learn a lot.)

b. Service members, after serving their first 180 continuous days or more on active duty, pursuant to 10 U.S.C., if they meet at least one of the following criteria: I. Provide documented confirmation of civilian employment. II. Provide documented acceptance into an accredited career technical training, undergraduate or graduate degree program. III. Have previously attended the DOL Employment Workshop.

c. Service members with specialized skills who, due to unavoidable circumstances, are needed to support a unit on orders to be deployed within 60 days. The first commander in the Service member's chain of command with authority pursuant to chapter 47 of 10 U.S.C. (also known as the *Uniform*

Code of Military Justice or UCMJ) must certify on the Individual Transition Plan checklist any such request for exemption from the DOL Employment Workshop. A make-up plan must accompany the postponement certification.

d. Recovering Service Members (RSMs) imminently transitioning from active duty, who are enrolled in the Education and Employment Initiative (E2I) or a similar transition program designed to secure employment, higher education, or career technical training post-separation.

Back to Class part 1: The Transition Assistance (Management) Program

The first transition class that I attended was the Transition Assistance Program, or *TAP* (alternatively labeled *"TAMP"* as we learned earlier). TAP/TAMP, universally referred to by military types as "tapandtamp", is the mandated and required training workshop that nearly everyone in the military must attend prior to hanging it all up. The program started in 1989 as a joint initiative between the Veterans Administration (VA), the Department of Defense (DOD), and the Department of Labor (DOL). It was designed to provide separating service members with employment and job training assistance as well counseling on VA benefits and services. It came about because prior to 1989 there was no coordinated or consistent curriculum to aid those on their way out the door; every base and service had its own version of what to do, ranging from formalized classes and aggressive job placement to nothing more than a hearty handshake and a slap on the back as you walked out the gate. Needless to say, the creation of the program back in 1989 was a great idea, and it has been helping military types become educated veterans ever since.

TAP's core curriculum is set by regulation but each service (and in many cases each base) may modify and add to the curriculum. Again, the experiences that I share in this chapter were from my attendance in various courses during my transition, and they may be different in your service or at your base. At the core, though, they are all pretty similar.

Anyhow, after meeting with my retirement counselor I began coordinating with the base transition office. I picked up the phone and called the number listed on the first page of my transition checklist, and was very pleasantly surprised to find yet another retired Marine on the other end of the phone who was thrilled that I had rung him up. He quickly put my mind at ease with his affable manner and earnest desire to help me out. After chatting for a few minutes, he asked about my circumstances *("what rank are you? Oh, that's great, sir! Retiring? How many years in? When is your last day?")* and by the end of our conversation I had reservations at both the Pre-Retirement TAP and the 25+ Pre-Retirement seminars. It was truly a joy to talk to this guy, who I had figured for a long retired military guy who just loved being around Marines.

As it turned out, I was right. Not long after our conversation I stopped by his office, which was a tiny room in a tired-looking government building's third deck (or floor for non-nautical types) and met him in person. A surprisingly spritely octogenarian, he fairly leaped from behind his desk in order to shake hands and introduce himself. With a broad grin, he confirmed my enrollment in the transition courses. As I looked around his cramped office, I saw pictures of a much younger man in what now would be considered vintage Marine Corps uniforms. He was too modest to talk about himself very much, so after a brief chat we parted company and I went on my way. Only later did I learn that he had enlisted in the Marine Corps during the Second World War and crossed the beach at Iwo Jima with a rifle in his hand, which to all Marines places him into a nearly divine status. As if that weren't enough, he went on to fight in Korea and Vietnam, ultimately retiring at the top of the enlisted ranks as a Sergeant Major. And now he spent his days helping people like me, who were likely unborn when *he* retired, transition from the service. Thank God for men such as him!

Digression aside, the schedule of events during the seminar is very similar whether you take it in Okinawa or Germany, Virginia or California. More of a workshop than a seminar, it is a series of lectures, classes, and briefings presented by knowledgeable representatives on a wide variety of topics ranging from medical evaluations to income tax considerations. The following is a list of presentations that I found to be very useful as I attended the Pre-Retirement TAP seminar at Camp Pendleton, California:

- *Welcome/Introduction:* this was just like the beginning of any other workshop that you might attend. The facilitators hand out a schedule of events and promise not to keep you late, which in the military is the standard fabrication that precedes almost any required class. I was pleasantly surprised to later discover, however, that these guys could actually keep to a schedule, and not only did we get out on time each day, we actually got a *whole hour* for lunch. They had this down to a science, and each brief was efficiently and professionally done in the time allotted. In addition, they provided a broad overview of the base transition services center and the broad spectrum of services that the organization could do for the attendees.

- *TRICARE brief.* This is a very important brief for retirees because it details the options for medical care after transition. In a nutshell, healthcare is free for active duty personnel and there are several different programs for families. Once you take off your uniform, however, the free medical gravy train comes off the rails and you then have to decide which medical insurance plan is best for you and your family. We will examine TRICARE in much more detail later.

- *Dental brief.* This was pretty quick and to the point. Just as with medical care, dental work is free for the service member and there are pretty good plans for families. As you transition, though, the free part goes away and the family options are less good, so you will have to choose which one you would like to take advantage of.

- *Survivor Benefit Plan (SBP).* If you are separating from the service without a retirement then SBP does not apply to you. However, as a retiree you will receive a pension, and SBP is an insurance plan that ensures that spouse and children will continue to receive a portion of the pension benefit after you pass on. The type of pension you receive depends on when you entered the service, and in my case my pension is based on my length of service and average monthly salary over my last 36 months of active duty. The length of service determines the percentage of the 36 month average salary you will receive for the rest of your life. Getting a pension is a pretty big deal, particularly now as there are very few companies that such a great retirement benefit. 401Ks are nice, but they require a lot of management and are subject to the whims of the stock market or other investment vehicles. For a retired military person the pension check shows up once a month (and although the government occasionally shuts down, retirement checks are usually safe). The pension check only arrives as long as the retiree is alive; once he or she kicks the bucket the pension terminates. In order to protect the family, however, the SBP allows for up to 55% of the pension benefit to transfer to the spouse (and in some cases, the children) after the passing of the retiree. Even if you are able to skip TAP because you are a 20+ year retiree, you are still required to be counseled on SBP and make the selection to either enroll or not (and your spouse has to approve non-enrollment!) Like TRICARE, there is a lot to it, and we will look more deeply into insurance considerations later on.

  - Federal Veteran's Affairs. There were several components to the VA brief, all of which were relevant and important. First there was an overview of benefits, such as loan guarantees, burial plots, and a surprisingly long list of others. The most significant brief covered the medical evaluation process which results in the determination whether or not you have incurred a service connected medical disability. Being considered disabled opens the door to other benefits, many of which are pretty amazing. While images of disability meaning life in a wheelchair rolled around my brain, I was pleasantly surprised to learn that was not the case; things like hearing loss and bad knees fell within the parameters of disabling conditions. As with insurance, we will discuss the VA in much greater detail later on because it is a remarkably complicated bureaucracy, and if you are not careful you can make mistakes that will deny you benefits later in life. Another critically important VA brief covered the GI Bill, which these days is utterly fantastic. In a nutshell, the VA will pay for school at the state school rate and also pay you a housing allowance while you attend classes, but you have to jump through a few hoops to take advantage of it. Fortunately, there are VA people and administrators whose job it is to help, and I found them to be helpful indeed. Much more on the GI Bill will be covered later on.

  - State Veteran's Affairs. Like the federal VA program, each state has benefits for veterans. California's are largely based on the level of disability, but not all of them are. Benefits range from free license plates if you are 100% disabled to free access to state parks just for being a veteran to a tuition-free college education for your kids in the California University System if you have a service connected disability. Great stuff! The benefits vary by state, so be sure to check and see what your state offers.

  - Joint Education Center (JEC). The presenter from the JEC (woohoo! another acronym!) also addressed the GI Bill, but also went into much greater detail on the various education programs available for veterans. For example, many of the schools and jobs that service members have attended and held during their careers may be eligible to transfer as college credits, and the JEC can assist with the evaluation process. It also provides counseling and help with applying for trade schools, college, or apprenticeships.

  -Disbursing and Travel. This brief covered how your pay will be settled as you get out as well as how you will be paid as a

retiree. Whether you are getting out after one tour or after 30 years, you will be receiving a final settlement check that closes out all of your benefits and debts. The disbursing folks explain what that means, and more importantly when you are likely to receive your final paycheck from the military. For retirees, they go into greater detail about how things will change once you get out. As an active service member you receive a paycheck twice a month, on the 1st and 15th of the month. As a retiree it changes to once a month with checks arriving on the 1st, so budgeting is a little more important. **It is also VERY IMPORTANT to note that state income taxes are NOT automatically withheld from you pension check, so don't get yourself into a jam with the state taxman by not setting up an automatic payroll deduction for state taxes.** They also disclose what you will be paid for and what you won't, which is significantly different from being on active duty. While actively serving your paycheck includes a tax-free housing allowance (as long as you live off base), an allowance for meals, various bonuses and special duty payments (such as reenlistment bonuses or extra pay for pilots and parachutists), and a uniform replacement allowance for enlisted members. When you retire all of those extra payments go away and you are left with only your pension. I personally don't jump out of airplanes or fly them, so I don't miss that money because I never received it. I miss the housing and food allowances, though.

- *Household Effects/Transportation.* This brief is important for those who will be retiring someplace other than their last duty station. Pretty much everyone wants to retire to Aruba or some other tropical paradise, but the realities of life generally bring that dream to a tragic end. People end up in one of three places: where they are, where they are from, or someplace completely new. Transportation to the first choice is easy because there are no benefits. You just go home, but you still have to file a travel claim for some unfathomable reason. The second choice is pretty simple as well. If you want to go back to your Home of Record (where you enlisted from), the government will pay to ship your household goods as well as pay for you and your family to travel to your homestead. In the third case, it is a little more complicated. The travel experts figure out how much it would cost to move you to your Home of Record and then apply that amount to the cost of moving you, your family, and your stuff. So, if you still want to move to Aruba and you enlisted from Iowa, you will have to make up the difference on your own.

- *Financial Readiness.* This brief covers the financial ramifications of retirement as well as strategies for the future. Since those of us in the pre-retirement class are all eligible for a pension, most of us have not really paid much attention to the variety of other opportunities out there beyond an Individual Retirement Account and maybe the Thrift Savings Plan (the military's nonmatching 401K type plan). The presenter showed us various investment strategies and a peek into what types of compensation exists on the outside world.

- *Marine Corps Community Services (MCCS).* This brief covered the opportunities that exist with MCCS, which is a broad umbrella organization that includes things ranging from portions of the Marine Corps Exchange (our base shopping mall) to recreational services such as sports equipment rental. Access to some programs change when you retire or get out of the service, which they covered in the presentation. There are also a lot of job opportunities with MCCS, which were addressed in detail as well.

- *The Psychological Factors of Retirement.* This covered the "softer" side of transition, the side that doesn't have a rigid checklist to follow or series of classes to attend. This class really addressed what happens after your last day in uniform when you will unexpectedly but invariably experience feelings of loneliness, uselessness, confusion, and in many cases, happiness and joy. We military types are not the most introspective and emotional folks out there, so this class was a real eye opener.

- *Relocation and Retired Activities.* There are a lot of resources out there that you can utilize as you transition and once you become a valued veteran, and the Relocation and Retired Activities office is the place go to access them. It is really a resource designed for those who are staying in the area because it is a link to the local community.

- *Medical records brief and review.* **This is one of the most important parts of the symposium!** After an hour long brief that covered the nuts and bolts of how you are medically evaluated by the Veterans Administration, you are afforded the opportunity to have your medical record examined by a true expert on such things (in my case, it was a great and thoroughly professional guy from the Disabled American Veterans, or DAV). It is very important that you bring your entire medical record on this day, because the class and the evaluation of your record will provide you with valuable medical insights. This is a pre-inspection of your records, and it identifies issues in time to allow you to follow up with your military medical provider about any physical maladies or problems that require attention before you retire or get out. It is a big deal because access to medical care is easy while you still wear a uniform, but not so much when you take it off for the last time. In addition, you will leave the screening with a list of recurrent medical problems that will later determine your medical disability rating, and with that disability rating the possibility of monetary compensation and VA healthcare. Much more about the medical side of transition is in succeeding chapters. **Don't miss this day at TAP/TAMP/TRS, and DON'T FORGET YOUR MEDICAL RECORD!!**

- *Job Hunting and Prospecting.* This is a class that could have been a seminar all by itself. You are introduced to the realities of finding a job on the outside (not impossible, but not necessarily easy, either) along with the importance of networking. I will leave it at that because the next two seminars I attended, and which are addressed in this chapter, focus on these subjects a great deal.

- *Writing a resume, cover letter, etc.* This class was accompanied by a couple of nifty workbooks which can help you write a resume that might actually land an interview, as opposed to the horrible ones that you will probably write without help. I say that from experience, because I brought with me a resume that I thought was pretty good, but after being reviewed by one of the instructors I learned that it was in all actuality quite terrible. Attendees spend a lot of time (a whole day out of the four day package) learning about business documents and how to write them. In addition, you learn how to interview and how to sell yourself. Marines, like most military folks, tend to be pretty humble and it is difficult to get them to talk about their accomplishments and the great things that they have done during their careers. Lastly, the fine art of salary negotiation is covered, which is something that is completely foreign to military personnel who have been paid based on rank and time in service for their entire careers.

All things considered, the TAP workshop was a tremendous wake up call for all of us in the audience. At the time it was required (and on the last day I received a neat little stamp on my check out sheet that boldly proclaimed *TAP COMPLETE*), and despite the negative connotation being "mandatory fun" it was truly invaluable. I learned more about the rest of my life in that class than in any single period of instruction that I had attended prior.

*   *   *   *   *

Lessons learned:

- ☐ I can't say it enough: start early! You are eligible to attend TAP/TAMP/TRS up to two years before you get out, and if you do you will be a lot better off than those of us who waited until it was nearly too late. The insights you receive are fantastic, but more importantly the class details what you need to do to successfully complete the transition process.

- ☐ Make sure to get the whole week off for the course. Even though it is required, there are often times when you "absolutely" have to get back to work and miss a brief or two. Believe it or not, you aren't that important. After all, you're getting out. Let some hard charger run your shop for a while so you can devote the time and energy needed to make the best of the whole course.

- ☐ Bring your medical record! If you don't you will miss out on a great opportunity to prepare for the medical side of transition, including making the best of your disability evaluations.

- ☐ Take lots of notes. You will be provided a pile of handouts and workbooks and the like, but if you don't take notes they end up being pretty useless. A good idea is to write the name of the presenter and their contact information (phone number, office location, and email address) in the corner of the handouts that they provide. This will make it easy to call on them later when you have a question, and I guarantee that you will have plenty of questions.

Back to Class part 2: The 25+ Retirement Seminar

The 25+ Retirement Seminar was the second of three transition courses that I was fortunate to attend. It is a week-long symposium that focuses primarily on training us – the slightly older and soon to depart active duty crowd – about the finer points of changing careers. Specifically, this course is intended to provide training about jobs seeking at a more senior level than the previous TAP classes, which were focused on younger folks who did not make the military a career. Consistent with the title of the course, the student body was comprised with career Marines and Sailors who had served over a quarter of a century in uniform, which for my class was a truly distinguished (at least we liked to think so) group of about forty men and women from the officer enlisted ranks.

Unlike TAP, the curriculum in this seminar did not meet the requirements mandated by the Department of Defense for a certified transition class. As such attendance was voluntary, but it proved to be well worth the time spent. TAP was a broad array of briefs and classes that centered on the mechanics of transition and is intended to educate the nation's newest veterans on the rights and entitlements that they had earned through their service. Since all of those subjects were thoroughly covered in the TAP classes the 25+ Pre-Retirement Seminar could focus on what each and every one of us was most worried about: how to get a job after we got out.

The course spans an entire week and it began with an introduction on the first day by a retired Marine named Dan from the Marine Corps Community Services (MCCS) Personal and Professional Development center located on base. We were shoehorned into a smallish classroom in a building that was new sometime around the Cuban Missile Crisis, but the air conditioning worked so we didn't really have anything to complain about. After Dan went over the schedule and the administrative details (like where the heads – bathrooms – were located and more importantly where we could find some coffee), he introduced Chuck. Chuck would be our teacher, mentor, and confessor for the succeeding days of the course, but the first day belonged to Dan.

Dan's portion of the class covered some of the same topics as TAP, but from a more senior perspective. For example, one of the guest speakers was a businessman from the local area who discussed entrepreneurship and the exciting possibilities of owning your own business. "When you own your own business," he observed, "you are realizing your own dreams. When you work for somebody else, you are helping them realize theirs!" True enough. The concept of being an entrepreneur was more in line with our "older" class, because most young men and women getting out after a few years weren't going to be in the position to go into business for themselves. The education level and practical experience garnered over a few decades in uniform, however, lend themselves to entrepreneurship. That was certainly some food for thought.

One of the most interesting and useful parts of the first day centered on a couple of sheets of paper held together with a standard government issued staple in the corner. Starkly white with black text (in true government fashion; no fancy graphics or glossy paper for us!), the title grabbed my attention right away:
How Prepared Are You to Become a Civilian Again?

Great question! I read on.

"How prepared do you think you are for the rest of your life? There are many things to consider as you prepare to leave military service. Think over each of the questions below and circle the answer that is most applicable to you. The more "Yes" answers you have, the better prepared you will be.

Hmmmmmmmm. How ready was I?

"1. Do you discuss you upcoming retirement freely with your spouse, children, friends?"

Yep. So far so good!

"2. Do you know what community, state, and federal resources are available to help you make the transition from military to civilian life?"

Feeling a bit perplexed, I wasn't so sure that a solid "yes" was the best and honest answer. I circled "yes" anyway because I wanted to make sure my score at the end of the questionnaire was a good one.

"3. Do you have a support system - friends, family - away from your work place?"

Whew! Another easy "yes"!

"4. Have you thought about meaningful off-duty roles that will prepare you now for civilian career opportunities?"

"5. Do you have a lawyer with whom you are comfortable?"

"6. Is your will up to date?"

"7. Do you have a psychologist, religious adviser, or other professional to whom you can turn for sound personal advice?"

Gulp. The questions were getting harder, or at least less easy to convince myself that I could continue to happily circle "yes". I didn't realize that consulting a shrink, a lawyer, or a priest was part of transition. Needless to say, I wasn't as prepared as I thought, but the exercise of completing the questionnaire did admirably serve to focus my attention.

Not long after being humbled by a simple 25 question questionnaire another lecturer took the stage. He was a youngish looking guy with a nice suit, and the initial impression was that he was another businessman here to tell us what we needed to do with our lives. His introduction, though, changed that errant perception.

It turns out that he was recently one of us who had made the transition to the other side of the fence a few years ago. He was also a graduate of this very seminar and was standing before us to spread the gospel of hope and positivity; he was the "after" that we all wanted to become. Dapper, smart, and articulate, he told us his story, which in a nutshell was that 1) transition is confusing and dismaying at times and 2) once you transition, life can be pretty good. Transition is the tweener time bookended by getting out on one end and getting a job or starting a new career on the other. Not to worry though, he said, because we were in this course. He credited his success to the lessons that he learned in the same seats that we were keeping warm; all we needed to do was pay attention and do everything that Dan and Chuck said.

Not long after his pitch we finished for the day. Happily, the remainder of the week would be held at the old Officer's Club, which was much more spacious and comfortable than the hobbit-like warren we occupied on the first day. An added piece of happiness was provided as well when we were each provided our very own copy of the book *"What Color is Your Parachute"* by Richard Nelson Bolles, which is probably the single best book about career change written (aside from the one you are reading, of course), at least from the civilian perspective. It was a good start to the week. We learned a great deal and received some useful free stuff to boot. Not bad.

Promptly at 0800 (8:00 AM for the non-military readers) the next morning we all piled into the O'Club and got ready for Chuck to show us the way forward into our collective futures. Before I go into the fine course he gave us, let me give you a little of his eclectic and interesting background.

Chuck enlisted in the Marine Corps back in the 1950s. He served his country for a period of four years on active duty and then got out. One thing that perplexed him then and still does today is that his transition from the Marine Corps was not as genteel or helpful as it should have or could have been. His departure from the active ranks of the Marines was more of a "don't let the door hit you on the way out!" than "thanks for your service, and good luck!" It always bothered him because he believed that the Marine Corps should have done more.

Chuck had a very successful career despite the failure of the service to prepare him for life on the other side. He was a salesman and later an executive in the medical devices industry, and after retiring from that line of work he opened his own practice as a career consultant. He has helped literally thousands of people prepare for interviews and snag successful jobs, including servicemen and women who were transitioning from all branches of the military. Several years ago, during a Marine Executive Association meeting (MEA is a great networking association that focuses on finding employment for transitioning and transitioned military folks, and we'll talk more about it later on), Chuck was asked if he could formalize the help he had been providing those in transition and put together a seminar for more senior folks, like me and my forty or so new found friends. He devoted a significant amount of time and diligently created the course that we were attending.

Fast forward again a couple of years and there I was, sitting on the edge of my seat learning lesson after lesson on what transition was like. Each and every transition seminar is fantastic, and they are variations on the theme of transition and job hunting. Chuck's seminar focused on the hiring process, and most telling was his perspective as a businessman. He started by handing out a workbook of sorts which contained the entire slide package for his classes along with space to take notes. This proved to be very useful over the next few days, and my only regret is that I didn't take more notes. He used anecdotes from his experience as an employee and employer as well as a wealth of statistical data and research to teach us the ins and outs of how to conduct a successful job search.

There are four specific topics from Chuck's seminar that were more in depth than the other seminars. Here they are in no particular order:

1. *The importance of professionalism.* Chuck has interviewed literally hundreds, if not thousands, of job candidates. One of the things he does in his practice is to act as a professional interviewer for companies across the United States. He performs initial interviews for professional "C" level (CEO, COO, etc. – the Executive Leaders of the corporate sector) candidates; interviews that, if successful, would get them in the door with major companies at the uppermost echelons. Chuck shared with us what it is like to interview senior people. Some of the vignettes were hilarious, some were a little uncomfortable, but all were lessons in how to put your best foot forward when interviewing. It isn't just your resume and a new suit that makes an impression, but little things like cleanliness of your fingernails (engine grease under the nails is only acceptable when applying for a job as a mechanic), the condition of your shoes (ever heard of polish and a brush?) and your breath (is roasted garlic for lunch a good idea before an interview?) His perspectives really showed that it takes a lot of hard work and diligent effort to make an interview go well. Likewise, it only takes a little laziness or inattentiveness to make it go poorly. To make a long story short, if you put the work in ahead of time and you will do fewer interviews and land a job. Don't do so and you will become a professional interviewee who never receives a job offer.

2. *Clothes.* The indefatigable Mark Twain observed that clothes make the man, and today I am sure that he would include women in that statement. In this case it is absolutely true. Too many of us have terrible wardrobes from decades ago or have a skewed perspective of what businesspeople really dress like (what? I can't wear my GI-issued khaki tie with a blue shirt?) The first impression is critically important in a job interview, and if you look like an idiot things probably won't go well when you try to dazzle the interviewer with your brilliance. All they will see is a fashion disaster that they don't want representing their company.

Chuck doesn't just wax eloquent with anecdotes in the realm of haberdashery. He brings in the experts. At the request of the seminar coordinator, the general manager from the haberdashery Jos. A. Bank gives a lengthy presentation on attire. Far from a sales pitch (and Chuck didn't get a kickback), it was instead an in-depth education ranging from how suits are made (which proved to be pretty interesting) to the importance and differences between fashion and style (fashion being the trendy thing that is in this year, and style being timeless; for example, four button suit coats with wide lapels were *fashionable* a few decades ago, but the two button coat never goes out of *style*). The presenters went into great detail on the quality levels in clothing as well as how to dress, which surprisingly has a lot more to it than just slacks + shirt + tie + jacket. Colors matter (I knew that) and textures do too (texture? Huh?) Belts should match your shoes. No bling; that nifty but obnoxious aircraft carrier tie-tack is probably not a good idea. Best of all, Jos. A Bank had a sale going on that very weekend that followed the class. I went shopping and after a personal consultation I like to think that I am now, indeed, a much more sharply dressed man.

3. *Resumes, cover letters, and other job related documentation.* Each seminar has a different take on resumes, and this course was no different. Chuck preached the merits of all of the various resume formats, but focused on the chronological resume over the functional or combination formats. In his words:

"I have a worksheet for the chronological resume that makes it easier to start. We have to start somewhere and filling in the blanks is easier than saying 'let's write a resume, but what kind of a resume do you want?' Initially I took this approach [while teaching the seminar] and I had 40+ Marines and Sailors looking at each other. They honestly didn't know where to start. We are all good at filling in the blanks and each person in the class knows the chronology of their own career. So if you fill in the blanks with your entire career we have a starting point. The

chronological format is easy for the class because they all have more than two decades of material to work with. When they finally decide on what they would like to do, then we can start discarding irrelevant information. But we had a lot of information to start with; at this point we can make the determination of what type of resume do I want to produce. Resumes are a very personal thing; the resume that you submit to an employer is the one that you decide is the best portrayal of you on paper. It is YOU in the absence of the real and physical you."

Chuck's point is a very valid one. The audience, which included me and dozens of my newest and closest herd-mates, had little to no experience writing resumes. That inexperience made the *chronological* resume a logical place to start. We will devote no shortage of pages on resumes in future chapters, but in a nutshell the chronological resume is just that: a lineage of your career that starts with today and stretches back into the past. How far depends on how much grey hair you have; if you are fresh out of college, then how you did in high school is relevant. Not so much for the "experienced" crowd. In our case, the last ten years are the most important. The *functional* resume is based on your skill sets and is not tied to a timeline. This is good for situations where qualifications and certifications are important, such as the healthcare field (for example, a specialist in podiatry would probably address their ability to get around a foot and ankle). The *combination* resume is just that, a combination between both of the other formats with the occasional other bit thrown in.

Cover letters are likewise important, because after all, you want to get a job, don't you? A mimeographed copy of the same resume sent to a multitude of firms won't get you very far, and especially if there is not a cover letter to go with it. The cover letter is a more specific introduction of you to the company to which you are submitting your resume. If you don't have a cover letter, or if it is obviously a generic one, you are guaranteed *not* to make a good impression and land a job interview. Other items are business cards, thank you cards, references, and more. All in all there is an extensive list of things about which I knew very little but that Chuck educated us all about. We will be looking at all of those things in following chapters.

4. Negotiating salary and benefits. This is important because it is something that all of us uniform are really terrible at. We come from a background where our salary and benefits are the same for all of us; after all, anyone can use the internet to look up exactly how much money anyone in the military receives in salary and benefits. If you want to see how much someone like me made in a year, Google "Military Pay

Chart" and look up Lieutenant Colonel (pay grade O-5) with over 26 years of service. While there is complete transparency in the military, there is not so much in the civilian world. In the corporate world one can be fired for telling everyone how much you make. There is a *BIG* difference between the civilian world and the military in regards to disclosure of salary and benefits.

Getting back to negotiating, Chuck breaks it down in easily understandable chunks that we can use to negotiate our salary and benefit with a potential employer. Little things like 37% of people who ask for something get it, while 100% of those who don't ask for anything receive nothing. Another gem is doing your homework: how much is the position worth? More specifically, how much is the position worth where you want to live? The salary for a job in the Midwest is simply not the same as one in New York or San Francisco. You really need look into the firm's background in order to determine what is right for the job, for you, and for your family. He also goes into great detail about benefits, perks, and the like. Do you get a company car? Parking privileges? Mileage reimbursement? All of those things that I had not thought of were laid out in a logical and thoughtful manner. There are literally dozens of resources just a few keystrokes away on the web. Try an internet search for the average salary and benefits for the type of job you are looking for. Search several sites and average them together, and that will give you a benchmark from which to negotiate. After all, the person with whom you are negotiating does this for a living, so you had better be diligent or you will end up making less with fewer benefits than you could have bargained for.

I learned a tremendous amount about transitioning from Dan and Chuck, and I am truly in their debt. If you are on the West Coast, then start breaking down doors to get into the course. If not, don't worry. Since it is such a successful program that fills a tangible need, the 25+ Retirement Seminar is being formalized and will be coming to a base near you soon if it is not there already.

*　　*　　*　　*　　*

<u>Lessons learned:</u>
- ❏ Find out if a senior level retirement seminar is available in your area. The successful implementation of Dan and Chuck's hard work here at Camp Pendleton has resulted in bases far and wide either adopting their program or developing their own. Also,

make sure to sign up early as there are only so many seats per class.

☐ The class taught us first and foremost to calm down and get organized as you begin your search for a job. It's easy to say "calm down", but the prospects of finding a job in today's market makes it an intimidating task. Being organized will make it a lot easier.

☐ Do your planning in a logical order. Don't try to do everything at once. You may want to make a timeline with all of your tasks laid out and with each entry having a start and finish date. Highlight the important tasks. Some of these tasks should be to create a resume and cover letter (each one should be personalized, but you should create a solid base document first), write down a list of personal and professional references, craft a networking plan, practice interviewing skills, conduct research on employment possibilities, and put together your professional interviewing wardrobe. Only plan spend about 10% to 15% of your time contacting employment agencies and headhunters because that is the percentage of jobs that they tend to fill, and if your timeline and plan is solid you won't need them anyway.

☐ Be comfortable in talking about yourself at an interview. Your interviewer really wants to know two things about you (1) What are your qualifications for the job? and (2) what are your accomplishments based on your qualifications? Being comfortable in an interview comes from rehearsing thoroughly for the interview and being able to clearly articulate your accomplishments and qualifications.

☐ Follow-up on all leads. Networking is where most jobs come from, and one of the follow-ups that you do after a networking engagement may lead to a position that you are seeking to fill.

☐ Searching for work is the worst job in the world. The sooner you get going on all aspects the sooner you will get a job and a paycheck, so don't procrastinate.

Back to Class part 3: The Ruehlin Transition Seminar

The third course that I was fortunate to attend during my transition was the Ruehlin Associates Career Transition Seminar (called just "Ruehlin" for short). The reason that I say that I was fortunate to attend is because enrollment is limited to around 15 participants (with spouses encouraged to attend), and the target audience is the most senior of the courses I attended. Not strictly limited to military people, it is also designed for senior government employees from the civil service who are retiring. Their target audience, as shown on their website, is centered on that select group of senior people:

'Many activities offer the seminar to senior officers (O-5 and above), senior enlisted (E-8 and above) and senior civil service (GS-14 and above) who are within a year or two of retirement, or who are on a known countdown. Nearly everyone who attends the course says, "Should have had this five years ago!" That might be too early, but the point is valid...people make gross errors and waste a lot of time because they miss opportunities or find that they have been "shopping in the wrong mall." We believe 12 to 18 months out is a good target.'

The blurb on their website was on the money. I wish that I had been able to attend the course at least a year earlier than the short seven months remaining to my separation date. Even though I attended the session relatively late in the proposed timeline it was still worth every minute that I spent in the course. The Ruehlin course is different from the TAP/TAMP and 25+ Pre-Retirement courses, however. The course is not offered through the base education or career center, but instead is a special opportunity offered by larger units and commands and in every branch of the military. It is not a government or military symposium, but instead a private enterprise that specializes on assisting with the transition of senior military and civil servants. In short, it is a professional course put on by a top-notch company that specializes in transitioning senior people with a strong emphasis on securing a new career. It is a job that Ruehlin and Associates are very good at.

My personal opportunity to participate in the seminar came up as I made my plans to depart the service known to my command. I had heard about the course and the positive experiences of many who had attended it, but in typical hard charger fashion I didn't pay any attention and as a result was really ignorant of the great opportunity that the course presented. Despite my ignorance, I made it onto an email list of interested parties (i.e., those on the way out or those smart enough to ask if they could get on the list well ahead of their retirement date) and was soon assured a spot at the table for the next course. Since it is only offered a couple of times per year at my command I considered myself very fortunate to have made the list. As I would learn, my good fortune was truly immense because as with the other courses I learned lessons that paid off immediately in addition to those that I will be putting to use for the rest of my life.

The focus of the Ruehlin seminar is similar to all of the other courses because it is designed to prepare people like me who are leaving the service after hanging up their uniforms for good. Ruehlin is very different, however, with its finely tuned focus and rigorous execution on finding a new career. Where TAP focused on the mechanics of transition and the 25+ centered on what the business world is like, Ruehlin pinpoints the process of getting a job. The other two courses did fantastic work on more of a macro level, which dovetails nicely with Ruehlin's laser-tight emphasis on the employment process.

Soon after I was selected to attend the course a plain brown envelope arrived in my mailbox. A little puzzled, I opened it up and out fell a green booklet and a letter. The letter was an introduction and welcome aboard for the upcoming session, and the book was a little homework exercise that proclaimed in bold capital letters:

CAREER PLANNING
And
MANAGEMENT

That got my attention. Very authoritative! So did the last bit at the bottom of the page:

IMPORTANT
PLEASE READ THE ENTIRE PACKET AND COMPLETE ALL OF THE QUESTIONS PRIOR TO ATTENDING THE SEMINAR

What I found inside was a series of assignments unlike any I had seen in a long time. There were about a dozen sections in the book and each contained a worksheet of sorts. They weren't like calculus word problems or anything particularly difficult to complete, but instead were simple exercises designed to pull a little bit of information from the respondent (me!) about him- or her-self. They all had a common theme, though, which quickly became evident. One section focused on my career, and not just what I had been doing in the military but what would I like to do next? Another section delved into education, and another looked at organizations and affiliations that I may be partial to. It also had a memo for the spouse, which was not just a nice touch. It brought into distinct focus that transition is not a solitary activity; everything that I would do from now on would be inextricably linked to my spouse, which is a great and often forgotten point. So, with a little trepidation and a couple of sharp pencils, I sat down to fill out the blanks and learn a little about myself.

A few days after completing the exercises in the workbook it was time to go to class. It began at 0730 on Monday morning continued on through Friday. The dress code was listed as *business casual*, which may as well have been top hats and tails for all I knew. After a quick search on the internet, I found that the expectation was a collared shirt and slacks with jacket and tie optional. Sweet! Not a problem, since I had all of those things, and thanks to my haberdasher friends from the 25+ Pre-Retirement seminar, they even matched. I, at least, *looked* like I knew what I was doing.

The course was conducted at a conference room on the base, and upon my arrival I stepped into what I supposed to be a business meeting of short-haired professionals approaching middle age. Everyone seemed to be somewhere in their forties. We all were dressed pretty similarly in the uniform yet non-uniformity of "business casual", with business suits, sports coats, and button down shirts as far as the eye could see. There was a woman with us as well, and she was as smartly dressed as the men. I saw a few faces that looked familiar, and we chatted a bit waiting for the class to start.

Promptly at 0730 a thoroughly professional gentleman closed the door and we began our shared journey through the seminar. He was our facilitator, and like us had completed a full career in the military, retiring as a Navy Captain after three decades of service. He shared with us that after he retired he found a job in a large corporation that was related to his military background, but that he also found the transition to the corporate sector disappointing. After working for the company for a while he realized that it really wasn't for him. He then joined Ruehlin and Associates in the mid 1990's and had been actively leading seminars ever since.

He was very experienced and a thoroughly smooth and professional facilitator. He was aided in the course by a very good PowerPoint slide package that he very professionally and smoothly presented. In addition to the personal instruction he handed each of a large red book titled *What's Next?* This would be our notebook, hymnal, and Rosetta stone all rolled into one; it was a comprehensive, well written, and very useful book that took the information presented in the daily seminar to the next level. In fact, it is such a useful reference that I still keep it on my desk at home and refer to it often as I work on my own resume or pursue job opportunities.

One of the first things he shared was John Ruehlin's story. He retired from the navy as a Rear Admiral, which is no small feat in and of itself. What he found upon retirement, however, was that the lofty office of admiralship did not seamlessly transfer to comparable civilian employment. Despite his impressive accomplishments and mountains of experience he had garnered through his successful career he discovered that he couldn't find a job that inspired him. He felt that he was unprepared to enter the private sector, and went through a very humbling period of months and months as the impact of transition fully settled in. After an eternity of failing to land the right job, he had a chance encounter with a fellow beach-goer while he was attending a cocktail party on the Atlantic coast. They chatted, and the result of the conversation was a phone number that John could call, because his new found friend knew somebody who was looking for somebody like him. After mulling it for a while, John followed up and called the number he received from his beach encounter, and as a result ended up in a very senior position with a multi-billion dollar bank.

The story is important, because it frames the entire course. John Ruehlin learned several things in his troubled transition, and those things became the central themes that we would be learning about and focusing on for the week:

- *First and foremost nobody in the private sector really cares what you did in the military. They care about what you can do for them in the business world.*

- *Transition is just that: a transition or change from one phase of life to the other. To be successful at it you must be fully prepared to move on.*

- *Getting a job or starting a new career takes a lot of work, and the best way to be successful is to treat it that way.*

The course did an exceptional job of addressing each of those themes. They were not presented as *pro forma* blocks of instruction, but instead where more like the strands of a rope which are carefully woven together through the weeklong course. Each of the themes deserves a much more detailed explanation:

- *First and foremost nobody in the private sector really cares what you did in the military. They care about what you can do for them in the business world.*

That seems like a pretty brash statement, but it is true. While in uniform we are all in a very homogeneous environment in which we are surrounded by people just like us. In the civilian world that is simply not the case; everybody is different! Despite their differences, civilians can broadly be broken down into two groups: social people and corporate people. Social people are friends, acquaintances, or pretty much anyone you meet outside a work context, while corporate people are those who can either offer you a job or know someone who can. Social people will be interested in your service and will love to hear your sea stories, but corporate people are listening through different ears. Corporate people want to know two things about you: can you make them money or can you save them money? If the answer to one or both of those questions is yes, then there is a job with them in your future. If not, then you are just another military dude or dude-ette with a bunch of stories to tell.

The problem is that you really can't tell the two groups apart most of the time. So what do you do? Stop telling sea stories? No, because the military that has been your life for years. What we learned to do was to leverage our experiences and desires into any conversation with the goal of connecting with the corporate people, or networking. Networking is the most likely way that you will get a job. Research shared during the seminar showed that well over 75% of jobs were found through interpersonal contacts while only a tiny proportion are found in the classified ads in the newspaper or by blindly firing off resumes. Networking is a central and constant theme throughout the course, and it proved to be very effectively taught.

We worked on our ability to network through a series of academic exercises and roleplaying during which we developed short sales-type pitches that we could use when the opportunity presented itself. Up to this point, most of us responded to the question "What are you going to do when you get out?" with "Get a *real* job..." While that sounds witty, we learned that it was probably the dumbest thing we could say because it instantly discounted us as viable employees to corporate people, and that was certainly no way to find employment. To overcome saying something stupid we learned how to craft a "thirty second sound bite", also known as an "elevator introduction" or "elevator pitch", which is intended to be used when you have a brief amount of time, for example the interval it takes an elevator to move between floors, to introduce yourself, present your credentials, and articulate what line of work you would like to go into. A more in-depth version is the "two-minute opener", which expands on the three components of the elevator introduction. This one is used at job interviews when you are asked about yourself or when you have a conversation with someone and they would like to know more about you.

- Secondly, transition is just that- it is transition from one phase of life to the other. To be successful at it you must be fully prepared to move on.

This is a bit more philosophical, but it is also critically important. Our facilitator told us anecdote after anecdote about people who were just like us that had a miserable time because they never could fully make the change from military to civilian life. Examples are the hard charger who cannot let go of the lingo; dropping the "F" bomb in every other sentence at a job interview is a guaranteed way to remain unemployed. Another is refusing to embrace little things like fashion by wearing horribly outdated or inappropriate attire to an interview or networking opportunity. You don't have to look like you stepped out of GQ or Glamour, but you shouldn't wear the polyester leisure suit you wore to your senior prom either. One of the most common problems, however, is clinging to the past. Your career was a great one, but you will be hired for what you can do in the future for the company, not what you did back when you were in the military. The course does a remarkable job of putting your career into a context that it can be a positive and integral part of building your future career instead of being the anchor that keeps you from moving forward.

- Thirdly, getting a job or starting a new career takes a lot of work, and the best way to be successful is to treat it that way.

In the first morning of class we were all introduced to our newest job title: each and every one of us became the Director of Marketing for the company that was ourselves. We learned that in order to get a job or start a new career we needed to be able to let the world know we were available and potential assets to businesses, and that nobody besides ourselves was going to make that happen. Ruehlin had a well-organized and effective program to teach us how to accomplish this in a few short days, and I what I learned fundamentally changed how I viewed my life after my career in the military. We learned to critically assess ourselves in order to determine our strengths and weaknesses. Based on those, we analyzed what we would be good at and more importantly, what we wanted to do in the future (which turned out to be an epiphany because I was so used to doing the same line of work that I had never seriously considered anything outside the defense industry). We learned the ins and outs of building a network, including little things like what our business card should look like (don't hand out the card from your last job in the military because you will come across as too cheap to buy your own), the aforementioned introductions, and tips such as what to do when somebody give you their business card (which is to write down a little about them so that you will remember who they are and why they gave you the card).

The meat of the course was spent on building high quality resumes. We learned how terrible ours were (mine was still pretty bad, but getting better thanks to the seminars) and how to write effective ones that would result in a job offer. We learned how to write the many types of business correspondence, such as cover letters, thank you notes, references, and responses to job offers as well. We learned how to write the three basic types of resumes – chronological, functional, and combination – but focused mainly on the combination style. Writing a good resume proved to be a lot harder than I had anticipated. It required a lot of introspection, a lot of research, and a lot of analysis. Anybody can write a love letter to themselves that says how great they are, but that won't land them a job.

We also spent no small amount of time on the mechanics of getting hired. Resumes will get you an audition, but it's your performance gets you a spot in the band. We learned about the etiquette of the interview (be early, but not too early; smell nice, but not like a gigolo on the prowl; dress like you want to get a job; professionally, not like a surfer dude fresh off some tasty waves) and the importance of the little things, like sending a thank-you note to show appreciation to the interviewer for his or her time. It helps to do some research on the company that you are interviewing with, too. If you can show your interviewer that you know more about his company than he does good things will happen.

The course was not just lectures and slide presentations, either. The facilitator took us through a series of practical exercises where we practiced our elevator pitches and how to interview, and he capped the week off with an hour-long one-on-one session with each participant. He had the same offer for each of us: an hour of his time to talk about anything we wanted. In my case, he scrutinized my resume (which had greatly improved thanks to his instruction and mentorship) and we talked about my future. He pointed out something which I had not really considered: why should I immediately go back to work? I had an opportunity to pursue higher education, so why not pursue it? After all, I was going to be receiving a pension, which wasn't enough to live on in San Diego, but the GI Bill and other benefits offer some fantastic opportunities outside the traditional career path. His candor and professionalism made quite an impression, and thanks to him I was able to look at my future from a different perspective that fundamentally changed the direction of my life.

I was truly fortunate to be able to participate in three different transition courses, each of which provided a different perspective on the same important subject. Ruehlin's seminar taught us in great detail how to go out and get a job, which is a skill that every one of us in the class needed to learn. More importantly, though, the course demystified the job search process and provided us with the tools to go out into the next great adventure. In the words of a Marine Colonel and recent Ruehlin course graduate:

"[T]he Ruehlin course was like the end of the Wizard of Oz—it pulled back the curtain on retirement. Now it's not a mysterious scary thing; it's just a short fat guy pulling levers, or more accurately, an old bald guy getting organized to do a bunch of planning and networking, which like all field grades I'm pretty good at doing. It's still a challenge, but now I know what I need to do and am much better prepared to attack post-USMC life vice my previous level of uncertainty..."

Well said. And right on the money.

* * * * *

Lessons learned:

☐ The Ruehlin course is not offered everywhere, nor is it offered by all commands. You may have to do some sleuthing around to find where it is being offered, but if you can find it the course is absolutely worth the time and effort.

☐ This is not a substitute for TAP/TAMP/TRS, but like the 25+ Pre-Retirement course it is optional. Although all three of these transition courses teach the same basic subject, their differing perspectives and areas of focus make each one incredibly valuable. You cannot take advantage of enough educational opportunities, and the Ruehlin seminar is a certainly a great one. It is not the only one, however, so make sure to take it in conjunction with as many other programs as possible.

☐ The focus of the course is on landing a job, more specifically landing a job while you are still on active duty. They introduce the concept of the "Hot Window" for employment, which is the period of the last few months before your last day in the service. It is the hot window because employers are not looking to fill positions much farther out than that, and the closer you get to your last government paycheck the more desperate you are likely to become. To land a job interview and a follow on job offer in that window requires a lot of work, and the course shows you how to do it.

☐ Successful transition requires a lot more than taking off one set of clothes and putting on another. There is a significant change in perspective required as well, not to mention a ton of work. Many separating military people take the first job that they are offered, and in many cases it proves to be disastrous, or at least unsatisfying and unfulfilling. You have a golden opportunity as you prepare to leave active duty because you can actively prepare for your next career while being supported to do so by your current line of work. It isn't the same in the corporate sector; job hunting while on the clock at a civilian company would likely get you fired. You are crazy if you don't take advantage of all the opportunities available to you, including those courses above and beyond the required TAP/TAMP/TRS, such as the 25+ and Ruehlin seminars.

Chapter 7: *Hello checkout sheet!*

This is the first chapter of many that will drill into the trials and tribulations of actually leaving active duty: the triumph and the tragedy that is the administrative side of transition.

There is one thing that all military people do routinely regardless of their branch of service. It is a common practice that crosses the rank gap and has no deference to gender. That thing that we all do is a process known as *checking in* and *checking out*. Since I was transitioning out, the spotlight will be focusing on the checking out bit because it is the final act of the play that had been my career and life for over a quarter of a century. Before I go into detail about checking out, however, we first have to take a gander at the history of the magical check-in/checkout process.

Just as Yin has its Yang and every accounting equation must balance, so must checking in marry up with checking out. So what gives? What is checking "in" and "out"? Simply put they are mirrored process that you go through whenever you leave one place and report to another. Just as a pilot needs to make the number of takeoffs equal to landings, servicemen and servicewomen have to balance the credits and debits of their career moves by going through the checkin/checkout process as they change units. This is a little different from the corporate sector because the military orders you to new assignments every two or three years or so, and along with those orders usually comes the requirement to pack up the family and move someplace new. I am not going to be talking about the moving of the family part, but instead about the leaving one job and showing up at another job part.

Once you join the military your ride on the hamster wheel begins. For Marines it starts with your first true check-in, which is an introduction to the yellow footprints at one of the Marine Corps Recruit Depots or at the Officer Candidate School. Some period of time after checking into the happy land of Drill Instructors you are afforded the opportunity to depart from their fatherly or motherly mentorship either as a gleefully motivated graduate, ready to take on the world with little more than a K-Bar fighting knife and an invincible attitude, or as a washout who could not withstand the rigors necessary to become a Marine. Either way, you will go through the process of checking out and moving on to your next duty station or going home.

Assuming that you earned the coveted Eagle, Globe, and Anchor you will take a little well-earned leave (vacation for my non-military friends) and then head out for your first duty station. This is invariably the place where you will learn about your Military Occupational Specialty (MOS), which is milspeak for the job you will be doing in uniform. Upon arrival you will put on your snappy Service Alpha uniform (the equivalent to business formal: coat and tie, but festooned with ribbons and badges) and report in to the base reception center. From there you will be directed to your unit, and when you get there you will start the formal process of checking in. It is a lot like the movies; there is generally a grumpy corporal or sergeant who disdainfully guides you to your barracks and tells you where the chowhall is, and where and when to report in.

Although you are at your new assignment to perform your duties, you can't get started until you go through the truly byzantine bureaucratic process known as "Checking In". It is part harassment package, part Easter egg hunt, and part searching for pirate gold. You have to sign for your room, which means you need to find the Marine in charge of the keys. You need linen, so off to the barracks manager to sign for some. You need your field equipment (helmet, flak jacket, sleeping bag, backpack; that kind of stuff) so you need to go to the consolidated supply warehouse. The list seems endless. The best part is that you are usually on your own to do it, but with the expectation that it will be done yesterday.

When you leave the process is reversed. You have to turn in your equipment (and it had better be clean!!), you need to return your linen, return your barracks key....again, the list is long and painful. And again the expectation is that you can somehow find Marty McFly and borrow the Delorean from Doc Brown for a trip back in time to knock it all out. Once you get it done, however, it is time to climb the next rung on the Marine Corps ladder by heading for your next unit. Guess what happens when you get there? You got it: you check in! Welcome back to the hamster wheel.

The cycle of checking in and out is a thread that runs through a Marine's entire career. It many ways it is a signpost along the career highway, with the hopes and challenges of arriving someplace new following the satisfying departure from a rewarding and dynamic posting. Each stop along the way is an adventure all its own. Like Gump's box of chocolates, you may not know just what you are going to get when you arrive but it will be something interesting nonetheless.

So why is it such a big deal? As I have said, military types have been doing this for centuries, so you would think that they have the process down to a science; after all, hundreds of thousands of Soldiers, Sailors, Airmen, Coast Guardsmen, and Marines check in and out every year. You would think it would be easy, but also in typical military fashion, that which seems so simple is of course made difficult. You can't do everything in one place. You can't do everything with one person. Each thing you need done is in a different part of the base, or in a different building, or maybe on a different base. Some places have hours of operation that are convenient to everyone who works there but are terrible for you, or they have only one person responsible for their task and he or she always seems to be on leave.

Leaving a job in the civilian world is a significantly different experience than leaving military service. Generally speaking, on the outside you can leave your job in one of two manners: happily or unhappily. The happy way of leaving is with an office party with a nicely decorated cake, some kind words, and a thoughtful (but not too expensive) gift from your cube mates to speed you on your way. The unhappy way is finding yourself wedged between two security guards as they hustle you and the dented cardboard box that contains your precious belongings out the door. In either circumstance you generally get to leave the company with a minimum of fuss and hassle, and it all happens in one day.

Not so fast or easy in the military world. Following the sacred military tradition of making simple things remarkably difficult, every departing Marine must run a perplexing gauntlet of clerks, administrators, and senior leaders on his or her way out of the gate. He or she must obtain the mark of consent from a dozen or two different entities before the labyrinthine process of checking out is complete; marks that range from elaborate signatures that would make a calligrapher swoon to stark and brazen ink from a well-worn rubber stamp. The signatures and stamps are coveted because without appropriate imprint you will remain forever in the purgatorial no man's land inhabited by the lost souls who could not obtain those vital marks on the most important of all documents to the soon-to-be departing: the checkout sheet.

The checkout sheet is indeed a glorious scrap of parchment because, much like a pirate's treasure map, it holds the key to that which you most strongly desire: your departure. Like a treasure map it divulges the often hidden locations of important places that otherwise would remain forever hidden, or at least forever ignored because the only time you really need to go there is when you are checking in or checking out. The checkout sheet is crucially important because it is the crucial key to receiving your final orders to the outside world; without completing it you can be stuck on hold and denied the ability to leave despite your desire to grow your hair and rediscover the joys of sleeping in late during the week.

The checkout sheet is usually provided by the administrative section of the unit you are leaving. Its purpose is to make sure that you hit all of the wickets on the way out the door; very important wickets like turning in thousands of dollars' worth of military equipment and completing crucial paperwork that ensures that you receive the benefits and entitlements that you have earned during your service. So, in and of itself, the checkout sheet is actually a good thing because it ensures that you do everything you are supposed to do before you hit the road. Unfortunately, just because the checkout sheet is important to you that doesn't mean it is particularly important to anybody else, which is a painful lesson to come to grips with. Your eagerness and urgency to get it completed has little to do with the desire of others to assist on your way out the door, so a word of warning the soon to be departing: make sure you allot ample time to knock it out. A smart guy once told me that a crisis on my part did not correlate to a crisis on his, and that just because I was in a hurry didn't mean that he needed to be. Important and accurate advice, as we shall soon see.

What does a checkout sheet look like? It is invariably similar across the spectrum of units and services. It is a sheet of paper that lists all of the agencies, offices, and people that you need to visit in order to depart your unit. More importantly, it has a place for each of them to make their mark, which is eminently important because without the proper notation by the functionary behind the counter your visit will be in vain. For those with nimble fingers and an eager pen beware! Don't think that just forging a random set of initials will let you slide by. That has been tried by many who have gone before you and as a result most places have acquired nifty and unique little rubber stamps (and variously colored ink pads) that must be used on your checkout sheet for it to be deemed authentic. Forge at your own peril, because to be caught will get you in big trouble and result in a trip to purgatory as your transgression is sorted out.

Equally as bad as forging a set of initials or two is the possibility of losing your sheet. In every command that I have ever served the process of checking in and out is manual; there is no automated system that saves a record of your progress. Lose you sheet and you are out of luck. Have a good time starting all over!

As you can see from my checkout sheet (above) it is a well-worn document, or at least it is now that it's completed. I obtained my checkout sheet from the administrative section of my unit, in this case 1st Marine Expeditionary Force Headquarters Group (try saying that three times fast) located aboard Camp Pendleton, California.

To get my mitts on a checkout sheet you I had to prove to the nineteen year old administrative clerk that I was indeed departing the unit, and for that matter, military service. Fortunately, the major muscle movements of personnel administration are done over a centralized computer system, and since my retirement request had already been approved, the young Marine only had to check the system to confirm my impending departure. He reached behind the counter and pulled out a single piece of paper, and with efficiency borne of experience he whipped a yellow highlighter over numerous lines of text. "These are the places you need to hit, sir," he explained, "when you are done you need to take it to IPAC (the Installation Personnel Administrative Center, where my friend the retirement counselor works) and they will cut you your final set of orders." With a cheerful "thanks, and see you around!" to the clerk I left the admin shop with a virginal sheet, ready to be filled with the scribblings and stamps of those who stood between me and my final day on base.

The sheet itself was an innocuous looking bit of poorly Xeroxed paper. It is a copy of a copy that was a copy of a copy, and as a result it was faded and tough to read. I filled out my administrative information at the top, stuff like my name, rank, and section (HQ for headquarters, in case anyone didn't know that) and headed out to get as many signatures and stamps as I could in the shortest time possible.

As usual, it wasn't that simple. It never is. The ease with which you get those spots filled varies widely. Some are easy, and some are hard, and some are downright painful. As I have said before the checkout process goes on every day at every base and in every service, but still it remains anything but a smooth and streamlined proceeding. As a result, some signatures or stamps are easy to get, but for others, well, not so much. The first place we'll take a look at is the most difficult stamp to obtain: the one you receive from the supply warehouse after turning in all of your field gear.

For those who don't know the way that Marines are equipped to train and fight is with a comprehensive set of personal equipment that ranges from a "lightweight" (ha!) Kevlar battle helmet to protect your noggin to steel reinforced combat boots to protect your feet. You have body armor reminiscent of a turtle's shell that is festooned with pouches to hold everything from a notebook and a pen to hand grenades and ammunition magazines for your rifle. You get a sleeping bag to keep you toasty when it is cold outside and a poncho to keep you dry when it rains. Need a jacket? You get one. Gloves? Here you go. Cup for your coffee? You even get one of those. All told you receive several thousand dollars' worth of personal equipment that you will use when you train and fight, and for the record it is hands down the best equipment that Marines have ever been issued. It is also a whole lot of gear. So much gear, in fact, that by the time you make it through the line you are staggering beneath such a mountain of green, brown, and black accouterments of war that even mighty Atlas would shudder at the heap that you shoulder on the way out of the warehouse.

And when you are done with it the Marine Corps wants it back. All of it.

Therein lies the rub. In the typically complex way of the Marine Corps you aren't actually issued all of the stuff you need at one time or from one place. You receive your basic equipment from a centralized warehouse that issues and recovers the personal stuff that I just wrote about, which are the items that every Marine needs. That equipment is enough for training and is a good baseline for the fight, but when you deploy it isn't sufficient. Iraq, for example, tends to be about a billion degrees in the summer and parts of Afghanistan approach arctic temperatures in the winter. In order to equip Marines for the conditions they will live in while deployed to fight they are issued supplemental equipment that does *not* come from the central supply warehouse.

That would be too easy.

Instead, each deploying unit is issued a set of specialized combat equipment tailored to where they are going. For my final vacation getaway to Afghanistan I was issued cold weather gear to keep me warm in that distant and frigid land. Lots and lots of cold weather gear! Three full jacket and pants ensembles of varying types (one for rain, one for warmth, one in a fetching white and grey camouflage pattern to make us look like a lumpy snow bank should we need to hide ourselves in the arctic tundra), lined and waterproof boots (comfy AND toasty!), cold weather socks, long underwear, fleece undershirts, gloves, mittens, and my personal favorite: booties to keep our toes snug when we weren't mucking about the countryside in our boots. By the time we got all of the cold weather gear we were ready for an Antarctic expedition; all we needed were a few dogsleds, a case or two of Spam, and some snow under our feet. And just like our previously issued fighting equipment it was all top notch stuff, not leftovers from the Korean War, which is nice (I say that because many years ago when I was conducting cold weather training we were issued musty old 1950's vintage canvas "cold weather" protective clothing that was anything but). At any rate, this pile of gear added to your other pile of previously issued gear becomes a mountain of equipment that would fill a small garage.

But we're not done yet!

You now have your fighting equipment and your environmental clothing, but you need to be issued the tools of the trade, such as your rifle, your pistol (if you rate one), and all of the other bits and pieces that make you into a warfighting machine. Your weapons shoot bullets, and those bullets are loaded into magazines. Ten ammunition magazines for your rifle. Three for your pistol. You need night vision goggles to peer into the darkness, and a bracket to mount those goggles to your helmet. Along with dozens of other items, you pick these things up at your unit armory and add them to the growing Everest-esque mountain of gear that you need to fight.

Enough, you think? Nope, not yet!

You still have to draw your unit specific equipment. Every unit has a different mission to accomplish, and as a result each unit has some unique equipment required to do so. My last unit was a specialized fire support and liaison outfit, so we needed special radio headsets, helmets, night vision equipment, thermal targeting sights, ruggedized computers, and other nifty items to ply our trade in combat. The pile keeps growing.

Now you're finally done! All you need is a flag to plant on top of your equipment mountain and your Edmund Hillary impersonation will be complete.

So off you go....training, deploying, fighting, coming home, and doing it all over and over again. Time passes, and soon enough it is time to start turning all of that stuff back in. The problem is that it all looks the same: some of it is brown, some green, some black, and all of it needs to go back where it came from. Were I a more organized person that would be no big deal, because I would have been smart enough to take the itemized receipts that the various supply clerks handed and file them away for the day that I would be turning the stuff back in. Well, I'm neither that smart nor that organized. Without a thought of the ramifications down the road I took the receipts provided long ago by supply clerks and jammed them into my pockets, where they were either laundered into oblivion or thrown out with the gum wrappers and lint that always seems to collect there.

So there I stood, eager to divest myself of the mounds of gear that clogs my garage, but unable to really remember where it all came from. I gave it my best shot, and soon enough I had a backpack and a couple of seabags stuffed with all of the equipment I seem to remember receiving at the main supply warehouse. After grunting and straining to get it all into my car, I zorched over to the Centralized Issue Facility (CIF- another exciting acronym) where I unloaded my car and again grunted and strained to get it all over to the checkout counter.

Standing at the entrance to the warehouse is reminiscent of Frodo's trip into Mount Doom, complete with the unsettling feeling in the pit of your stomach that you are stepping into the great unknown with an outcome that is far from certain. Entering the dark maw of the musty and cavernous building, I saw that it was going to be no quick and easy task. Lamentably, between me and the counter stretched a long line that serpentined back and forth. And back. And forth. Apparently I was not the only one interested in returning my gear that day. I searched the faces of those in front of me and saw the blank and resigned expression that every Marine knows: the "it's gonna be a while" look. Too bad there was nary a Snickers bars in sight.

Capitulating to the timeless fate of Marines immemorial, I lugged my stuff up and joined the line. Slowly, inexorably, like a drugged caterpillar the line inched through the twisting lane. A Marine is called to the counter, so he or she reaches down, seizes the straps, loops, and handles and drags the agglomeration up to the counter. The Marine's departure from the front of the line starts a sine wave of stooping Marines, each grabbing their gear and lunging forward, with the fleeting feeling of progress supplanted by return to resignation as they wait. Painful minutes stretch into infinity, and moments before my last hair turns grey it is my turn. Finally!

Up to the counter I struggled with my jumble of lovely drab and earth toned equipment. The clerk, a civilian contractor, asked for my ID card and we got down to business. As I have said before, it was not my first rodeo, so I made many of the basic preparations in order to avoid the things that get Marines into trouble at the supply counter. I had cleaned my equipment (nothing dirty is accepted because it is issued to you clean, and you are expected to return it that way) and disassembled it by removing the camouflage cover from my helmet, taking all of the pouches off of my protective vest, and separating the components of my sleeping bag. I tried to keep it organized with all of the pouches in one pile and clothing in another. So off we went: "Helmet, Medium," said she, and after she inspected the one I handed her to ensure that it was indeed a medium helmet she moved on to "Cover, Helmet, Medium...."

Hello, checkout sheet!

Dozens of items later my pile had shrunk, but it didn't completely disappear. It was smaller to be sure, but the pile still remained. Reduced from mountain to molehill, my equipment load had lessened, but unfortunately we weren't done during that initial visit. "Flashlight, Tactical" she droned, but my tactical flashlight was absent! I rooted through what was left to no avail. "Um, I don't have it," said I, hoping for a pass. No such luck! "You can come back when you find it. Jacket, Combat, Desert?" After much rooting through the pile I came up empty handed. My forlorn look was met by her steely gaze and flat reminder that I could bring my errant jacket in with my missing flashlight. I asked about the other stuff, and her steely stare softened. "You didn't get it here," said she, "and we don't want it." D'oh!

Off I went, with a bag of stuff I errantly thought I needed to turn in and a homework assignment to find the stuff I forgot. All things considered, though, it wasn't nearly as bad as it could have been. I seemed to remember putting the flashlight in the pocket of my "Jacket, Combat, Desert", but where the jacket was currently hiding was anybody's guess. As for the other stuff that the CIF didn't want, well, I had a few other stops to make and I was pretty sure that one of the many clerks who had issued it to me would recognize and reclaim it. All I had to do was make the circuit from the CIF to the armory to my unit supply section a few more times. Before too long the pile was gone, and as the items were turned in the magical stamps and signatures appeared on my checkout sheet.

Two trips and a found jacket and flashlight later, my checkout sheet was emblazoned with the stamps of success from the CIF, the armory, and my unit supply section. I had bested the supply monster and scribed its mark onto my checkout sheet. Things were looking up! Now there remained only a few dozen more places to check out from, and finding them would continue to be an adventure.

Some of the requirements on the list were easy to get, but others proved to be annoyingly difficult to obtain. Being a creature of habit (and in no particularly huge rush) I started with the fruit that was hanging lowest and closest; that fruit being the various offices and buildings around the in and around the headquarters where I worked. A quick gander at the checkout sheet revealed that I needed to visit about a half dozen offices that were just down the hall and up the stairs from where I was standing, so off I went.

The operations section ensured that all of my required training was complete (not that I needed any training on the way out the door) and to my great relief the legal section confirmed that I wasn't pending a court martial or anything else that could land me in the brig. The Substance Abuse Control Officer (SACO) confirmed that my most recent urinalysis was clear of drugs (good thing they don't check for gin and tonic) and the Family Readiness Officer happily stamped my sheet after a friendly chat. Things were progressing nicely.

So much for the low hanging fruit. Time to work my way up the tree.

I tracked down the Uniform Victim Advocate. I don't know what that person does but without obtaining the red squiggle from the official pen of the UVA office I would be stuck. So, after a quick "Hello! Can I get your autograph?" followed by the scratch of a pen on my sheet and a "Sure, have a nice day!" I left none the wiser as to the purpose of that particular office. I am sure that whatever they do there is very important, but my desire to get more signatures on my checkout sheet precluded me from trying to learn more about just what it is that they do in in the UVA shop.

From there I wandered across the camp to the armory and supply sections, where I waited until the time listed on the handmade sign that flapped in the lazy breeze (*at lunch until 1300* read the note taped to the window, *come back then*). After queuing up with a half dozen or so other hopefuls who were clutching checkout sheets of their own, the Marines on the other side of the glass drifted back from the chowhall or, more likely, the Subway sandwich shop that was only two blocks away. Once the window opened for business it only took a few short minutes to rack up several more precious stamps and squiggles on my sheet from the bored Marines who were the keepers of the sacred stamps and pens.

Higher up the tree I climbed in search of signatory fruit. I chased down a security specialist to turn in my "secret" access badge in order to get him to ink the paper to prove that I had done so. I snuck into the Commanding General's wing of the headquarters building to garner the mark of the Chief of Staff, and after peering around his doorway he invited me into his office and added his John Hancock to the list. I drove across base to turn in the gas mask that I had (thankfully!!!!) never used outside of an annual trip to the training chamber. I sat in the dentist's chair for my final checkup and was poked and prodded next door at the Aid Station for the start of my final physical. I met with the system administrator and turned off my email accounts and confirmed that I did not have any government issued electronic equipment in my possession. I met the mail clerk and completed a forwarding address form even though I had never received any mail there and I knew that I never would, but a checklist must be followed and the mail clerk, to his credit, was adamant.

On and on it went. Days turned into weeks, but before the weeks could turn into a month I finally obtained each and every stamp, mark, and squiggle needed to complete my quest. If I was Blackbeard the pirate I would have been chortling over a chest of gold with a bottle of rum in each fist having found the "X" that marked the ending spot on a treasure map, but I was more gleeful than he could possibly be when I had collected the last set of necessary initials. My checkout sheet was complete! With a happy heart and a smile on my face I drove down to the Installation Personnel Administrative Center and met with the holder of the sacred pen that would scribe the final signature on my checkout sheet: the retirement counselor. We'll talk more about obtaining that last and final signature in following chapters, but for the moment I was done chasing down clerks and turning things in.

*   *   *   *   *

Lessons learned:

☐ Checking out takes time. A lot of time, and the time is not yours but instead belongs to the people on the other side of the checkout counter. Unless you are a general, admiral, or a commanding officer you must get in line with everyone else. That isn't bad, though, because you meet a lot of great people along the way.

☐ Make sure that all of the prep work is done. Bring everything you need to turn in and make sure that any required documentation is done ahead of time so that you don't have to go back several times to get the stamp.

☐ Be nice! The Marines and Sailors that are on the others side of the counter are doing their jobs. They will be much more friendly and forthcoming if you are friendly to them first. The golden rule certainly applies.

☐ Follow the rules. Show up during the times listed for checking out because the Marines and Sailors who man the checkout counter only do so during those times, and if you show up and throw your rank around then you are taking them away from their other duties. And you will look like an arrogant jerk.

☐ Keep the receipts! You would think I would have learned that ages ago, but I didn't. I even tried to keep a folder each time I showed up at a new unit to organize all of the pertinent paperwork including receipts for equipment. Needless to say, I failed in the attempt. So, if you are checking in somewhere soon, be smarter than I was and save your receipts.

☐ Do a little research before getting in line. Had I made a few phone calls or emails I could have found the list of gear that I was expected to turn into the CIF. The same goes for the armory and your unit supply. It will also save your back from the strain of lugging extra gear all the way through the line and then back to your car because you brought it to the wrong place.

☐ Make sure your equipment is clean and complete. There are a lot of little straps and widgets that can get lost, and you will be buying replacements and cursing up a storm unless you have everything squared away. A few minutes with a scrub brush will save hours of waiting in line.

☐ Allocate a lot of time for the process. You will forget or lose something and will be making more than one trip to the turn in counter. In addition, there will be a lot of people like you in line ahead of you. It is not a speedy process. Be forewarned.

Chapter 8: *Final (?) Physical Exam. Or is it?*

Checking out of the Marine Corps was certainly an adventure. It was like a search for pirate treasure and Easter egg hunt all rolled into one, only not as exciting. After all there were no Easter Bunnies or scowling pirates, and the lack of chocolate eggs and chests of gold doubloons was sadly depressing. Getting the final signature, however, made every line I queued in and every frustrating hunt for the holder of the magic checkout stamp well worth it.

One of the enchanted stamps I picked up along the way was held by the Medical Officer, whose duty it was to ensure that I was poked, prodded, specimened, and examined from the hairs on my head to the tips of my toes. To obtain the necessary medical mark on my checkout sheet I headed over to the Regimental Surgeon's office, where I would endure the last physical examination I would be subjected to while on active duty.

I had heard many stories about the mysteries that surround the "final physical" from friends who said that it was no big deal as well as others who opined that it was a vexation far worse than they could possibly have foreseen. Personally, I was hoping for an experience more on the "no big deal" side of the scale. Just like everything else, however, it turned out to be not quite what I expected. I had been subjected to myriad physicals throughout my career, ranging from halfhearted glances from bored medical technicians to the exams in which modesty plays no role whatsoever. A big part of being a Marine (or a Soldier, Sailor, Coast Guardsman, or Airman for that matter) is being physically fit and ready to fight, and our medical folks do a great job of ensuring that we are ready to go at a moment's notice.

Before you are ready to fight, though, you have to be examined to ensure you are fit enough to serve. Your relationship with physical exams begins with a battery of tests that begin before you ship to recruit or officer training (to make sure you are healthy and strong enough to make it through the rigors of bootcamp or Officer Candidate School) and continues once you get there. Wanna be a pilot? Special exam for you! Paratrooper? Exam for that, too. Been a year since your last exam? Time for another one! Been deployed? Step up to the counter and say "ahhhh..." It never ends.

Until your final physical, that is. The term "final physical" is a bit of a misnomer, though. It is no mere single trip to the doctor's office, but instead a long and bumpy road that leads to the aid station, the Naval Hospital, and various clinics I had to visit to get that single, vitally important stamp from the Medical Officer. The ride was good, it was bad, it was funny, and it was sad, but most of all it was thorough. And it was a lot longer trip than I thought it would be.

My journey began at the Regimental Surgeon's office, where I learned about the complexities of mother of all examinations. It is the mother of all exams because it is no simple or cursory survey, but instead the inexorably thorough inquisition of one's bodily health and mental condition that left nothing uninspected.

As I learned from the helpful doctor, the depth and breadth of the exam is for good reason. My final physical served as the last chance for me, the soon to be departed from active duty, to avail myself of military medicine and fix those things that had heretofore either been unfixed or ignored in typical macho tough-guy fashion. While the thought of military medicine may make the reader shudder, it really isn't bad; in fact it is very good, because military health care providers are well resourced and have had a *lot* of real world practice over the past decade or so of war. The perceived problems with military healthcare stems from poor management and performance that occurred many years ago, and those deficiencies have long been corrected. The point of the final physical was to get me into the best shape possible before shoving me out the door, whereupon the Veteran's Administration and private sector would take up the responsibility for my health and wellbeing. It was my decision, however, as to how much effort I wanted to devote to the process. I could do as much or as little as I wanted.

"It's up to you, sir," he said, "but you'd be foolish not to take advantage of everything you can. It's free, and you have the time to take care of anything that may crop up."

A wise man, that surgeon.

"You would be smart to contact every health care provider that you have seen in the last few years. They will re-evaluate your condition and record it in your health records. That will help you in the long run, especially with your disability claim," he continued.

Disability claim?

Visions of walking canes, wheelchairs, and blue parking spaces rattled through my head.

He saw my look of horror and chuckled.

"You've been in for a long time," he said as he flipped through my medical record, "your knees are bad, your ankle is bad, your feet are a mess...." He trailed off as he continued to review my case. "You are going to be rated with some disabilities, and it is important that the ratings are done correctly. Don't worry about it. It's a rough life being a Marine, and you are going to be evaluated to make sure that you are taken care of. Here's my number. If you have any problems, have them give me a call."

To quote Indiana Jones: *It's not the years, it's the mileage.*

With a firm handshake, I left his office with my records in one hand and a newly printed checklist in the other.

The checklist was very thorough. It ranged from lab work (shots anyone? A vial or two or seven of blood for testing?) to audiograms for my artillery-assaulted ears (What? What did you say?) to an EKG to make sure my ticker still ticked and a chest x-ray to look at my ribs or my lungs or something else in the region that was equally important. How was I going to get all of this stuff taken care of?

In true Navy fashion, I had not walked ten feet before a motivated and professional petty officer saw my distress and took pity on me. He beckoned me to the counter that separated us. "Hi, sir! Lemme see that," he said as he pointed to my checklist, "We'll get you squared away."

And he did. With the dexterity of a court stenographer and the panache of a Tiffany's salesman he typed, telephoned, cajoled, and printed out appointment after appointment for me. Within ten minutes he had teed up meetings with specialists and medical providers across the base. Not only did he hit the standard requirements, but also those specialty clinics and providers that I had seen over the last few years: orthopedics for my feet, physical therapy for my knees, optometry for my eyes, audiology for my ears....you name it. With a smile and a cheery "here you go, sir!" he handed me a sheaf of appointment reminders and turned back to his duties.

That's why Navy medicine is great; the Sailors really bent over backwards to make sure I was taken care of. I have never seen anything like that at a civilian HMO, that's for sure! I looked over the appointment reminders and was surprised at just how long it was going to take to knock this final physical out. All told it was going to take more than *three months* to complete all of the necessary examinations and appointments, and that was if I didn't miss any of them. Three months! Yikes. Navy medicine may be helpful, but it isn't particularly speedy, especially for those of us getting our outprocessing physicals. Oh well. Fortunately I had the time.

So, with a feeling of great relief (and a little trepidation, to be honest) I walked out of the Regimental Aid Station and set out on the journey that would be my final physical.

Despite my optimism, the impression that I could knock it all out in a single doctor's visit was crushed by the freight train of medical reality. Fortunately, my ignorance was remedied by the surgeon and I now had a plan (and a checklist!) to take care of the necessary medical requirements needed for a complete transition. The good Navy corpsmen and regimental surgeon had educated me and set me up for success. It was my responsibility to follow their lead, and off I went. First stop: the base hospital.

I had several appointments at the hospital, which makes sense because hospitals are where most medical providers hang out. I also had a few non appointments to make; a "non" appointment being a visit to a walk-in clinic. Appointments are good because you are inked into the doctor's schedule, and as long as you show up on time you will be taken care of sooner or later. It may take a while, but you'll be seen. Non appointments, on the other hand, are again much like Gump's box of chocolates because you never knew what you were gonna get. You may get lucky and find an empty clinic staffed with bored providers who are eager to break the doldrums of a lazy afternoon by bringing you in for a checkup. Or maybe a stuffy waiting room packed with dozens of exasperated people who are there to see the same provider that you are, leaving no choice but to wait. And wait. And wait.

My plan was to hit the appointments (making sure to arrive fifteen minutes early!) and stop in the various clinics between the scheduled stops. My first consultation of the day was with orthopedics, so I headed over to get my knees, feet, and ankles checked out. One of the interesting things about being a Marine is that you tend to use such things as knees, feet, and ankles a lot, and as a result they tend to get broken, sprained, and worn out along the way. In my case, almost three decades of tromping around coupled with four tours in combat zones had taken their toll.

I signed in at the orthopedics desk, found a seat in the waiting room, and waited. After a few minutes (and within ten minutes or so of my scheduled appointment) my name was called. The very nice Navy doctor sat me down in the examination room and looked over her notes. After exchanging some pleasantries, she got down to business.

The purpose of the visit was not to find anything new, but instead to ensure that all facets of my previously treated conditions were properly annotated. After reviewing my case, she brought everything up to date and assured me that everything would be properly recorded in my record. She had treated my ankle and feet previously, so that is where she focused her examination. After she was done poking and prodding my hooves, I asked her about my knees. It turns out that neither she nor anyone in her clinic had examined them; that was the responsibility of different clinic. She couldn't re-evaluate what she hadn't evaluated in the first place, so I had to find the original provider.

D'oh – another appointment on the calendar.

After she was done, she directed me to the registrar that was in charge of appointments. The registrar had access to the scheduling system and could set up an appointment with the clinician who had seen me for my knees a few years before. Ok, thought I. Easy enough.

Wrong again.

The registrar, who was a civilian that had been doing the job for a looooooooooooooooong time, asked if she could help. I explained that I had been treated for a knee injury and needed to make a final follow-up appointment. She turned to her computer and with a few efficient but furious keystrokes she looked at me and said that she had no record of my treatment.

No record? Huh?

I recounted my trips to the sports medicine clinic and the treatment that I had received.

"Ah," she said, "That is Sports Med, not Ortho. You have to talk to them." "Not ortho?" I meekly asked. "No!" was her testy response. Needless to say, after I left the registrar's office I immediately called sports medicine to make an appointment. Fortunately they had one available, but unfortunately it was over a month away. Good thing I had a little more time between that day and my EAS.

I then headed off to various other appointments, the excruciatingly boring particulars of which I won't subject you to. What was of note, however, was the kindness and flexibility that many of the walk-in providers exhibited when I attempted to squeeze in and get a signature on my medical checkout sheet. Some were more receptive than others, and fortunately I had picked a slow day at the hospital. There were few full waiting rooms, so I was able to see the right practitioners and garner the necessary signatures without too much hassle. My hat is off to the audiology department in particular, though, because I showed up just after their posted walk-in hours had ended. The petty officer behind the desk looked up when I poked my head in the door and asked if he could help me. I had hurried up to the clinic after my previous appointment but arrived in his lunch hour. He took pity on me, and beckoned me into the office. Whew, I thought. Great!

What I didn't realize was that his wife and young child were waiting to go to lunch with him. Once I saw them, I apologized and turned to leave. "No problem, sir! I'll catch up with them. It won't take but a minute." His lovely wife and toddler headed out to the car and the good Sailor took care of me. I felt like a complete jerk, but his professionalism and dedication to his duties were such that he could not in good conscience turn away a patient – even one as inconsiderate and boneheaded as I was for intruding on his lunch hour. At any rate, less than ten minutes later I had completed my audiogram, which is the hearing test in which they put you in a booth with earphones on and you push a little button when you hear high and low pitched tones. Or you can just furiously press the button when you *think* you hear them, which is usually the case for former artillerymen. With the efficiency and politeness of a true professional he explained the results of the test, signed my checklist, and headed to lunch. I apologized again, but he told me not to worry about it because taking care of patients was his job, and lunch could wait. Man, did I feel like a total heel.

So, after spending a day here and a day there over the period of a few months I was able to knock out my final physical. Along the way I got to meet a lot of interesting people who all shared a common trait: each and every one was a dedicated professional, but in true Navy fashion, was unique in his or her own way. A young corpsman who had shredded some tasty waves earlier that morning talked about the beach as he drew seven vials of blood for lab work ("this'll sting a little, dude, uh, *sir...*"), and my x-rays were taken by a very pleasant technician who offset the drabness of her scrubs with bright red fingernail polish and a highly blinged-out iPhone. Another sailor talked about his upcoming vacation plans as he removed some stitches from my forearm, sharing his excitement about his mom's home cooking as he provided me with instructions about how to avoid permanent scarring from with my newly-healed incision. They were all great professionals, and they took care of me. And, more importantly, they signed my medical checklist, which allowed me to finish my final checkout from the Marine Corps.

My hat's off to them. Thanks, Navy!

*   *   *   *   *

Lessons Learned:

- [ ] Start EARLY. I began my outprocessing physical about four months before I went on terminal leave with the expectation that it would be a quick and easy thing to do. Not so much! Make as many appointments as you can as early as you can. It is important that you review your recent medical history (over the previous five years or so) and personally contact each clinic or provider in order to get on their schedule. I assumed that all of my appointments were set by the medical staff at the regimental aid station, but I was wrong. It wasn't their fault because they didn't know that my knees had been treated at sports medicine instead of orthopedics, but as a result I had to wait almost an additional month for my sports med appointment because I didn't personally make the call.

- [ ] Plan ahead. Take the time to write a list of all the things that are bothering you or that you have been treated for over the past few years. Most Marines just "suck it up" and refuse to show weakness by getting medical care, which is good when a Taliban terrorist is chucking hand grenades at you but not so good when you are about to get out of the military. If you do not have your problems recorded in your record then they do not officially exist. It is as simple as that. And if they do not exist, they cannot be evaluated for disability purposes or for future care in case they get worse. And they always get worse.

- [ ] Write down some notes about your medical history and add to them as you attend each appointment. This is important, because you will ultimately have a second set of physicals with the Veteran's Administration to determine your disability rating and future medical requirements. If you forget what the doctors tell you during their examination then you can't pass that information to the VA. The VA is not staffed by mind readers, so the lack of information may weaken your claim for benefits and prevent you from accessing free medical care for service-related conditions.

- [ ] Go into your initial final physical appointment with the notes that you have prepared as well as your complete medical record. You will get out of it what you put into it. Make sure to take the physical seriously, because if you blow it off then I guarantee that you will lose out on medical benefits or monetary compensation in the future. The time to be the big tough Marine ends at the hatch to the aid station!

☐ Don't be a knucklehead like I was. Only go to walk-in clinics during their appointed hours. Out of their professional sense of duty, the providers will forego lunch with their family or stay at work after hours to make up the time they lost while taking care of you. The best thing to do is to avoid putting them in that position by showing up during their posted hours.

☐ Be flexible. If you think that your physical will go with anything close to military precision then you are in for a very unpleasant surprise. I had to sit in waiting rooms for a long time to get all of the necessary checks in the necessary boxes, and I guarantee that you will too. I recommend making one appointment first thing in the morning and one right after lunch because if you are the first on the list then you will be seen promptly. If not, you run the risk of waiting because other consultations took longer than they were scheduled to. This will also allow you to hit the walk-in clinics after you get done with plenty of time before your next stop. Don't schedule more than one appointment in the same morning or afternoon or you will find yourself sprinting between floors in order to make it on time like I did. Save yourself the hassle and space them out.

☐ Go with the system. Parts of it will make no sense, like my ortho/sports med confusion. It is what it is, and when the lady at ortho says you have to go to sports med, then save your breath and go to sports med. It may not make sense to you, but they aren't likely to modify their decades old records and appointment database just because you don't like it. Trust me.

Chapter 9: Changes ahead: Medical and Dental Insurance

As a uniformed member of the U. S. Armed Forces I had been very fortunate when it comes to health care. No matter what malady I came down with or injury I suffered medical services were always available, and they were always free. Everything from bullet wounds to brain surgery to chipped teeth was taken care of. They are pretty nice benefits to have, particularly considering the occupational hazards that come with fighting the nation's wars.

I have never had to really think of healthcare as something outside the purview of my job, but with my impending transition from active duty to retirement it rose in prominence from "largely uninteresting" to "really important". The need to obtain health coverage was discussed at the various transition briefs, but I didn't really pay close attention because the actual date of my reintroduction to the civilian world seemed so distant. Time passed, though, and before I knew it my EAS was just around the corner. I could procrastinate no longer, and after spending some time rooting through the enormous pile of transition related pamphlets, booklets, and notes that I had amassed over the previous months I found what I needed: a handout from the transition class I had attended a few weeks before that had **"TRICARE: Transitioning from Active Duty to Retirement"** in big bold letters across the top.

Score!

I read the handout, and it had just enough information to point me in the right direction so that I could find a real person to explain it all to me. In my case, that person is a very nice civilian who works in the TRICARE service center at the Camp Pendleton Naval Hospital. She took pity on me when I showed up in front of her counter in my quest to ensure that I didn't enter civilian life unprepared and uninsured.

She also educated me on the ins and outs of health insurance. It turns out that there are several different insurance products that I could choose, and each had advantages and disadvantages when compared to the others. For example, although I would be eligible for healthcare through the Veterans Administration, my family would not. Needless to say taking care of me and not my family is a non-starter, so I had some decisions to make.

The first decision was which level of TRICARE benefits did I want? There are three to choose from. As a retiree my family and I would be automatically enrolled and covered in one of two plans: TRICARE Standard or TRICARE Extra. These plans don't have monthly or annual fees, but instead are "pay as you go" or "cost for use" plans. Even though they are free if you never use them it can get expensive if you actually need medical care. The difference between the two plans is based on providers; for Standard you can be seen my doctors outside your network of providers, but you pay higher cost shares than Extra, in which you select providers within the network and receive a discount. (To thoroughly understand the finer points of TRICARE and check out the most current information on benefits you should consult your local TRICARE office or check out their website at www.tricare.mil.)

The other available product is TRICARE Prime. For Prime you have to enroll and pay an annual fee of $547.68 (the rate for 2013-2014), which is incredibly inexpensive when compared to what people in the private sector have to pay for similar coverage. That said, it is a benefit that retiring military types have earned the hard way through at least twenty years of arduous and physically challenging service. As a result, many retirees have conditions (such as combat wounds, partial deafness, and early onset osteoarthritis for example) that could be classified as "pre-existing", and could potentially limit accessibility to a new healthcare provider in cases where VA medical care is unavailable or unwarranted. So it all works out.

After considerable research and long discussions with my spouse I made the decision. TRICARE Prime it would be. As with all things governmental, though, there were quite a few wickets to hit in order to enroll. The first and most important one is that you must enroll *before* your last day in the service in order to avoid any gaps in coverage. If you don't seek out the TRICARE office, fill out the paperwork, and write them a check for the first payment before your retirement date the level of coverage defaults to Standard or Extra. It can be quite a risk because the potential costs associated with medical care for you and your family can be staggering should something catastrophic happen when you are not covered by TRICARE Prime because you failed to write the check in time.

If you don't get around to enrolling, however, don't despair. You can still sign up, but you will have to wait until the following month for coverage to start. TRICARE follows what is known as the "20th of the month" rule, which means that as long as you enroll by the 20th of the current month your coverage will begin on the

1st day of the next month. Wait until the 21st, however, and your coverage begins on the 1st of the *following* month. Needless to say, it behooves you to sign up before you get out.

There are several factors to consider when you sign up for TRICARE Prime. As a Marine I never had to select a doctor; all I had to do was go to the Aid Station or hospital and I would be taken care of. As a retiree, however, the option of wandering into a Regimental Aid Station to be seen evaporated. I needed to determine who my doctor would be.

Noting my puzzled expression, the very nice TRICARE administrator took me through the process of selecting a provider. She checked to see if there was a clinic within 30 minutes of my home, because if there was one then that is where I would go for care. It turns out there was a clinic, but she quickly determined that its patient load was full and I would have to find another provider. She printed out a list of possibilities (including pediatricians for the kids), and after a quick telephone conversation with my wife we picked our providers. This is particularly important for retirees who are moving to a new home because they may or may not have access to a clinic or even a TRICARE provider. For those moving back to the country or out of the United States (because TRICARE is administered differently overseas) make sure to surf through the TRICARE website to see what options pertain to your situation.

So, after about a half hour with the most helpful and cheerful TRICARE administrator I completed the application process. She typed my information into her computer and presented me with a completed application, which I then reviewed and signed. I handed it back along with a check to cover the first quarterly premium. She gave me some advice, too. "Call the TRICARE toll free telephone number in about a month," she said, "to confirm that you are enrolled and that they received your payment. If you don't double check and something doesn't go through you are not covered. So do yourself a favor and double check!"

It was very sound advice. She had obviously been around government agencies for a while. I followed her advice and called a month later. To my happy surprise I was fully enrolled and everything was squared away.

So off I went, happy as a clam. And then I remembered that there didn't seem to be anything about teeth in the conversation or the paperwork. Hmmm...Sure enough, another lesson! Medical care is different than dental care, so if I wanted my family and me to have dental coverage then I would have to apply for that as well. And pay for it too. Retirement was getting expensive!

TRICARE does offer dental coverage, but for some undiscoverable reason it is called Delta Dental. I don't know why they call it that, but they do. Before transitioning, dental care was the same as medical care; all that the service member needed to do was go to the dental clinic and get any dental issues taken care of. For families, on the other hand, it was not nearly as simple because dependents are not allowed to utilize military dental facilities. They are required to pay for care out of their pockets or obtain additional dental insurance (hello Delta Dental!) to get their choppers attended to. If your family happened to already be using Delta Dental, there would be little noticeable change in service. However, in case your family has not been using the dental plan or you happen to be moving away to a new home, you will have to follow the same protocol as TRICARE enrollment and find an in-plan dentist.

The decision to enroll is time sensitive, because if you wait too long there are some significant ramifications in the terms of your coverage. If you enroll within four months (120 days) of your retirement date then the entire range of treatments are covered (with varying deductibles and whatnot) immediately. If not, you have to wait a *year* (365 days) for some expensive little things like crowns and bridges and implants and orthodontic work. Hmmm...you say. "I don't need braces, so maybe I'll just roll the dice and wait to enroll until I really need dental care". Maybe that works for you, but what about the kids? Your decision to delay enrollment may seriously impact their ability to get orthodontic work, or more likely it will seriously impact your wallet when you find that they won't be covered for a year because you chose not to enroll. It's probably a good idea to go ahead and sign up!

The cost is pretty reasonable, and the coverage is competitive with other dental plans. For an individual the cost is around $45.00 per month, and for a family of four it is around $150.00 or so. The actual rates vary by location, but these are good ballpark figures to work with.

Here is what your hard earned money gets you:

- *Exams and cleanings are fully covered.*

- *Fillings are 80/20 (meaning that Delta Dental covers 80% and you pay 20%).*

- *Endodontics, Periodontics & Oral Surgery (root canals, gum treatment & extractions) are covered 60/40.*

- *Dental Accident Coverage is 100/0*

- *Cast Crowns & Onlays, Bridges, Dentures, Implants, Orthodontics are covered 50/50.*

- *Deductibles are $50 per person, $150 cap per family, per benefit year (Oct 1 - Sep 30).*

- *Maximum out of pocket expense is $1,200 per person, per benefit year.*

- *Dental Accident Maximum out of pocket expense is $1,000 per person, per benefit year.*

- *Orthodontic Maximum out of pocket is $1,500 per person, per lifetime (good for kids with crooked teeth!)*

You can check out all of the particulars about Delta Dental at their website: www.trdp.org.

To get started you must pay the first two months' premiums up front, and you can enroll by mail, online, or by telephone. Very convenient! It helps if you ask the dentist that you would like to use if he or she is in the network before enrolling. It will make things a lot simpler because then you don't have to play "find the dentist". Ask around; everyone has a dentist they like, and if your friends are former military then the odds are that they are using an in-plan provider.

So get out and select a dentist, and get moving quickly if you want to ensure immediate and full coverage for you and your family. Don't wait for a filling to fall out or for a tooth to start aching because if you do then you will be out a lot of money that you could have saved with a phone call and a few minutes of your time.

*   *   *   *   *

Lessons Learned:

☐ Do some research. There is invariably a table piled high with flyers and pamphlets at transition courses and seminars so do yourself a favor and grab one of every one that is available. Then, over a cup of coffee or a cocktail, sort it all out and file it away because you never know when one of those bits of paper will prove worth its weight in gold. For me, it was the TRICARE transition flyer because it was like the Rosetta stone of post-service healthcare. It gave me the basic information I needed to find the right people and ensure that my family and I were covered. The internet is great, but having a sheet of paper with all the info you need is pretty handy.

☐ Don't let your retirement date pass without enrolling in TRICARE. Even if you don't want Prime, find out where your base TRICARE office is and sit down with one of the helpful administrators. They are pros who will make sure you fully understand your entitlement and the various programs offered. If you can't find an office, go to www.tricare.mil.

☐ If you are moving it behooves you to closely examine all of your options. This is particularly important for those folks going overseas because that gets complicated very quickly. So, if you are headed back to the family homestead in the Midwest or you are off to the Himalayas, make sure to get all of your questions answered before you pull chocks and hit the road; TRICARE administrators are difficult to find in Tibet.

☐ Talk it over with your family. They get a vote. Healthcare is a big deal; indeed a much bigger deal than I had thought. Make sure you make the best decision for you and your family.

☐ You are not automatically covered with a dental plan when you transition. It is not lumped in with the TRICARE medical plan, but instead is a separate and distinct insurance product. You need to sign up for Delta Dental just like you did for TRICARE.

☐ Time matters. If you miss the 120 day window you are assuming some risk that can end up being very expensive should you need emergency care or braces for the kids. Preventive care is free, too, so don't wait for your teeth to start falling out!

☐ Ask around. People generally like their dentists and are happy to share who they are. A quick call to their office will let you know if they participate in Delta Dental (and in my experience most of them do). Once you enroll, a stop by the office with your documentation will get you into the dentist's system and set you up for your first post-service appointment.

☐ **UPDATE:** in mid-November of 2013 DOD announced that it would be closing all 189 TRICARE service centers in the continental United States. In 2014 they were replaced with three regional call-in numbers: *East* 1-877-874-2273, *South* 1-800-444-5445, and *West* 1-877-988-9378. To determine which your region go to this website: www.tricare.mil/About/Regions.

Chapter 10: _(Almost) my last haircut_

So there I was...

Most great stories and nearly all tall tales start with those four words. This chapter is neither, but more of a cautionary tale about how reality often smashes my errant assumptions. In this case reality smashed my belief that I had completed my weekly visits to the barbershop because I was on my way out the door.

So there I was....standing at the customer service counter in the Separations and Retirements section of our base IPAC, holding in my trembling hands the folder that contained all of the papers, documents, and adminstrivia required for me to check out of the Marine Corps and start my life as a civilian. I trembled under the naïve assumption that once I had completed all of the requirements listed on my checkout sheet I would be able to take off my uniform for the very last time and explore the exciting new world of men's fashion and exciting new hair care products. My giddiness was suddenly crushed, however, by a sign on the bulkhead (Marinespeak for wall) that proclaimed in bold capital letters:

ATTENTION CUSTOMERS:
According to MCO P1020.34G, both
Males and Females must be within
grooming regulations and appropriate
Civilian attire or Uniform of the Day

It wasn't a new sign. In fact, it was a little dusty and curled at the edges, and it was hung in the typically austere fashion of all such signs in administrative offices across the Marine Corps: a plain black and white sheet of paper inside a plastic document protector and stuck to a colorless wall with some yellowing cellophane tape. It also wasn't alone. Glancing around, I saw that identical signs in identical document protectors were taped, pinned, or otherwise affixed to almost every vertical surface in the office.

Apparently they wanted Marines and Sailors to look like Marines and Sailors when they came to the office to conduct their transition related business.

That, in and of itself, is no surprise. However, I was a bit taken aback because I realized that I had indeed not had my last Marine Corps regulated haircut, and here's why:

Earlier we learned about the importance of the End of Active Service (EAS) date. It is your last day on active duty, and the day after your obligation to serve your country is complete (unless you have a reserve service obligation of some sort) and you are free to run amok and do all of the things that you couldn't do in uniform, like grow your hair and sleep in 'till noon. Totally makes sense.

Ahhhh, but not everyone leaves work on their last day and wakes up the next morning as a civilian. There are some benefits that can insert a few days between your last day at work and your first day back in the real world. Those benefits are known as *"Terminal Leave"* and *"Permissive Temporary Assigned Duty"*, or "PTAD".

Terminal Leave, which is technically titled as "retirement or separation leave", is referred to as "terminal" in the jargon of the service, as in:

"You out yet?"

"Nope, going on terminal."

It is simply an opportunity to use up whatever leave (vacation time for non-military readers) that you have accrued before you get out. This is actually a pretty big deal, because taking your leave instead of selling it back to the government offers some significant advantages. If you use your leave you continue to receive all of your other pay and benefits, such as housing allowances, stipends for food, medical care, dental care, and so on for as long as you are on leave. If you sell your leave back, which is the other option, you receive a prorated lump sum payment for your salary less any taxes you owe. In other words, you are handed a check (not really, because nobody gets checks anymore but instead your bank receives an electronic deposit) that totals the amount of salary you would have made had you taken leave, but with the huge difference that no other benefits or payments are included. Considering that a significant amount of the benefits package in the military comes in the form of untaxed money that is not part of your salary you stand to lose out on some money as well as medical coverage and such. So, needless to say, nearly everyone takes some terminal leave.

PTAD is another way that you can get some time off with pay before you get out. PTAD, military speak for the civilian world's *Paid Time Off* (PTO), is allowed in a number of instances and for a variety of reasons. Examples include time off for the parents when little ones arrive (great for when your kids are born while you are able to be there instead of being on the other side of the planet fighting the Taliban or Al Queda), for military families who are adopting children, jury duty, and the many other events in life that occur that require you to be absent from work yet should not require you to use up your leave to attend them. How it works is the service member is issued a set of orders that direct him or her to go forth and do what needs to be done and then to report back in when it is over. Paternity PTAD, for example, begins when the child is born, whereupon the father is granted ten days off to help bring the newborn into the family. During that time, he is free to care for his family without having to come into work or put on a uniform, which is good because he probably won't be at his best anyway. At the end of the ten day period he needs to come back to work and check back in, and when he comes back he must be within grooming standards and wearing his uniform. As an aside, paternity leave only applies to the father because new mothers in uniform receive 42 days of maternity leave after the birth of the child, and that can be extended if medically required. The benefits associated with parenthood are actually pretty good!

But I digress. Back to *my* situation.

In my case, I had a significant amount of leave on the books. Leave in the military accrues at a rate of 2.5 days per month, so you earn 30 days of leave a year. Nice! If you take it all, then you obviously have none left over, but if you don't take it all you build up a leave balance that grows monthly. The regulations state that you can maintain a balance of up to 60 days of leave, but any leave in excess of that number on the change of the fiscal year is lost. What that means is that if you have 65 days on the books on September 30th (the last day of the government's fiscal year), five of them are "lost" (meaning deducted from your balance with no payment to the leave holder) and the new fiscal year starts on October 1st with your balance reduced to 60 days.

Those are the peacetime rules. With a couple of wars going on, however, it can quite often be extremely challenging to take all of your leave. In my case, I had completed four deployments to Iraq and Afghanistan in the five years leading up to my transition, and as a result I had not been able to take much of the leave that I had earned. In fact, since leave accrues until the day of your EAS, I would have built up over 90 days on the books that I could take as terminal leave. Because there were literally thousands of people like me out there with excess leave, the 60 day annual limit on leave was temporarily increased to 75, and up until the end of the fiscal year you could technically carry a balance of 105 days. Since my EAS was on the other side of the October 1st fiscal year changeover I had to request for approval to use 95 days of terminal leave in order not to lose the time I had accrued. The request (which had to go all the way up to the Headquarters of the Marine Corps) was approved, and so half of the post-EAS time off equation was complete.

The other half of the equation consists of PTAD. As a retiring service member you are authorized to take 20 days of PTAD to facilitate house hunting, looking for a job, and other transition related tasks. PTAD is treated in the same manner as leave and every day counts, even weekends and holidays. That means that 20 days PTAD is 20 consecutive days on the calendar that may be taken in conjunction with your terminal leave. Pretty nice benefit! You still receive your pay and allowances and can take care of the millions of things that need to be done as you transition. For those moving away, they can take the 20 days of PTAD in conjunction with their terminal leave, which in effect allows them an almost three week head start on their new lives. Best of all, they get to start using new hair care products that much sooner.

Which brings us back to my coiffure related dilemma. Since I was not moving away, I was actually eligible for a little more time off because I would be allowed to take my 20 days of PTAD in five day increments. Locals, like me, can pick up their PTAD orders on Monday morning and then spend the rest of the work week looking for a job or a new home. Those orders expire on Friday at 1700 (five o'clock in the afternoon) which is the end of the work day. The weekend is then "liberty", which is naval terminology for time off that is not chargeable as leave or PTAD. The following Monday a new set of orders are waiting at IPAC, and as a result 20 days magically becomes 28.

But, unfortunately that's where the signs plastered all over the transition office come in. I would have to pick up my orders in uniform or in appropriate civilian attire. And within grooming standards, which meant I still had a few dates with my barber. D'oh!

Four weeks and three haircuts later I found myself standing awkwardly at the same counter. This time, instead of getting a new set of PTAD orders, I was there to get the last set of orders I would ever receive: my Orders to Nowhere (or actually to my home in the local area, which now that I was out of the military really was nowhere as far as they were concerned).

Again I had in my trembling hands the folder containing all the documents needed to complete my checkout. Reverently, I handed it over to the young Marine on the other side of the counter. She quickly scanned over my paperwork, and after a few moments she called to my friend the retirement counselor. He walked up and gave me a broad smile: everything was in order! I was about to officially leave the Marine Corps for the final time!

He had me sign for my final set of orders, and after stamping them "official" he provided me with several copies along with duplicates of my DD-214 (the Certificate of Release or Discharge from Active Duty). It was anticlimactic, but with the passage of my orders from his hands to mine it was all over. I was done. I was out. And it felt weird.

*   *   *   *   *

Lessons learned:

- ☐ Read the small print, or in this case, the signs that adorn the administrative office. I had never paid any attention to them because they never applied to me before, but once they did their significance rocketed to the top of the chart.

- ☐ Pay attention to when you are getting out. If you are not careful you will lose some of your leave when the fiscal year ends at midnight on September 30th, and once those days are lost you cannot get them back. Your administrative section can help you request a waiver ahead of time, and if you don't get one you will be out of luck if you try to go back and recoup those lost days.

- ☐ If you are taking local PTAD then you should expect to go in every week to pick up your orders. I had never heard of this requirement before, but I should have expected it because that is simply the way things are done in every other situation. As a result I had a few more haircuts to take, but that was no big deal considering I was able to extend my pay and benefits by eight days. What is a big deal is if you don't go in to pick up your orders you can get in trouble for Unauthorized Absence, which is the Marine way of saying AWOL. *That* will end poorly.

- ☐ Terminal leave and PTAD must be approved by your commanding officer, and in some cases by the service headquarters. It is not a right, but instead it is a benefit that may not be approved in some circumstances. The deal is that while you are on terminal leave and PTAD your unit goes without you or your replacement because he or she usually doesn't show up until your EAS. Your job will most likely go unfilled. Depending on what your job is or the situation in your unit that may not be acceptable, and you may deemed to be "too important" to let go. There goes your earnest desire to go on Terminal Leave and PTAD because they may be denied.

Chapter 11: The Big Day

Part 1: the last day (before turning into a civilian again)

New Year's Day is a time for change. You get to break out a new calendar and do your best to keep all of those resolutions that you made between tequila shots and glasses of champagne the night before. For me, January 1st of 2012 was particularly important because it marked an incredibly significant day in my life.

New Year's Day was the day that I became a civilian. Again. 27 years and 21 days after I raised my right hand to swear an oath to support and defend the Constitution of the United States I felt as though I was transported back to that cold December day in 1984. I was officially a civilian. Actually, I became a former Marine; "former" because once you become a Marine you are one forever. There is no such thing as an "ex-Marine". Ex-soldier, yes. Ex-Marine, no.

New Year's Eve was a party. It was a celebration with friends that marked the end of a tiring and, for many, a challenging 2011 and the bright beginnings of a new and shiny 2012. We rang in the New Year with a lot of noise and a lot of champagne; in particular an enormous bottle that was given to me by a great friend to mark my transition. My headache the following morning indicated that I had indeed made a dent in the river of bubbly that flowed from it!

Waking up the next morning was a little odd. I had been a Marine for the better part of three decades, and despite my newly found "former" Marine status it was striking that I no longer had any official tie to the Marine Corps. I would be receiving a pension, which is great, but no longer would I be watching the news with the same level of interest in world events as I had been. The probability that I would find myself in some pestilential third world hotspot suddenly became zero, and the odds that I would have to leave my family for months on end for a deployment disappeared. I had returned to the society which I had served for so long with the opportunity to enjoy the benefits that make it the greatest nation on the planet.

It was a little like being the teenager that enlisted while still in high school. I had the rest of my life in front of me, and I had the opportunity to choose what came next. It was another whole new life; I could do anything I wanted. Except maybe professional sports. I'll cede that option to the practical realities of starting life over at the age of 44.

I left my military career behind with a wall full of plaques and a head full of memories. Being a Marine was the best career that I could have possibly pursued, because it took me places that I would otherwise have never seen and challenged me to levels that exist only in the direst of circumstances. I have made lifelong friends and learned more about life than I thought possible at the ripe old age of 17 when I signed up.

So it is with a certain level of eagerness that I looked forward to the next great adventure. I was not certain where the road ahead would lead me, but I was excited to take the first steps in a pair of flip flops. Like me, my combat boots are forever retired from active service.

Part 2: the first day (of being a civilian again)

At the stroke of midnight on your EAS day you are instantly and irretrievably pitched over the fence that separates your military life from the one that follows. If you were like me, though, you probably don't remember that actual moment. I wasn't seeing too straight that night...

...and my head was *pounding* the next morning.

To add to the misery of my hangover was my first true OSM. What is an OSM you ask? It is a frenetic panic attack that overwhelms you when you realize that your life has utterly changed. It is the *Oh S*** Moment* when the gravity of it all hits you like a freight train.

Some people never really get past their OSM and their lives seem to be stuck in a rut which compels them to focus on who they were instead of looking forward to who they could become. I had my OSM soon after my EAS, and to get through it I made a few decisions.

First, I decided that I needed to stay fit. I had a closet full of new clothes and I didn't want to look like the Michelin man when I put them on. In addition, I had been exercising as a part of my daily work routine for a really long time, keeping on that familiar schedule was strangely comforting. And it kept me from busting the buttons from my shirt. It is far too easy to get soft and squishy if you aren't careful!

Second, I chose a completely different road to follow by pursuing Masters of Business Administration degree at USC. I discovered a new path, and the study of business replaced my study of artillery and the Marine Corps. I found a new obsession: starting a wholly new, challenging, and different career.

So when you have your own personal OSM, find something out there to pull you past it. If you don't latch onto something quickly, you are very likely to slide into a state of apathy that is tough to recover from. You can become soft and lazy if you aren't careful! Physical fitness and a mental challenge worked for me. Find something that will work for you as you restart your life. There is plenty of time for slacking off after you retire from your *next* career.

Part 3: Just what is a "Veteran", anyway?

Although you would think that is a simple question, it really isn't. In fact, it is startlingly perplexing – at least in terms of employment. And unless you are independently wealthy or capable of living on you pension, you are going to need to go find a new career, or at least a job or two until you find out what you want to do with the rest of your life.

Let's start by looking at a few ways a "veteran" is defined.

From the Merriam-Webster dictionary: *an old soldier of long service or a former member of the armed forces.*

That seems pretty straightforward. It is a logical definition of a veteran, but unfortunately it is too broad in terms of obtaining benefits from the government for your service.

From the Veterans Administration: *A veteran is a person who served in the active military, naval or air service, and was discharged or released under conditions other than dishonorable.*

That narrows the definition down a bit by stating that a veteran is a person who served in the **active** military. So, to be considered a veteran who can receive benefits from the VA you must have served on active duty. Service in the National Guard or reserve establishment does not meet the definition (unless you served on federal active duty orders – more on that in a minute). But what about the definition of a veteran when it comes to getting a job?

For companies holding government contracts there are explicit affirmative action requirements concerning veterans, including a ruling that was released in 2013 that broadened the definition of veteran status in terms of employment. Known as the *Affirmative Action and Nondiscrimination Obligations of Contractors and Subcontractors Regarding Special*

Disabled Veterans, Veterans of the Vietnam Era, Disabled Veterans, Recently Separated Veterans, Active Duty Wartime or Campaign Badge Veterans, and Armed Forces Service Medal Veterans rule, it is an update on previously existing regulations comes from the Department of Labor's Office of Contract Compliance Programs (OFCCP).

The rule establishes a veteran hiring benchmark of 8% (with the intention of having a contractor's roster of employees mirror the population of veterans in the nation's workforce) and levies an extensive list of data collection and reporting requirements on firms with government contracts of more than $100,000 and/or more than 50 employees.

So why does that matter? Certain categories of veterans are considered to be "protected", and are covered by a government contractor's Affirmative Action Plan. In short, 8% of a contractor's workforce should be veterans, and not just any veterans either – they must be "protected veterans". This means that it is very important for a company not only hire protected veterans, it must also report how many veterans are on the roster to the Department of Labor through the OFCCP – just like any other protected class (like persons with disabilities, certain minorities, etc.).

To be able to meet the benchmark objectives set by OFCCP for compliance a veteran must fall into "Protected Veteran" category as defined within the ruling. It is important for you, the veteran, to understand which category you fall in to, because it matters to employers and can be an advantage for you as you pursue a job. While the rule is a thrilling read, to help get straight to the point here is a quick breakdown of the requirements to be considered a protected veteran along with examples of documentation which proves eligibility:

1. <u>Disabled Veteran status.</u> A disabled veteran is one who is entitled to compensation from the Department of Veterans Affairs. A *Special Disabled Veteran* is one with a VA-assigned disability rating of 30% or greater (or 10% – 20% in case the veteran is determined to have a serious employment handicap) or was discharged or released from active duty because of a service-connected disability.

Documentation: The Department of Veterans Affairs provides a Summary of Benefits letter to the veteran which denotes his or her disability rating.

2. Veterans who served on active duty during a war or in a campaign or expedition. In terms of this regulation, the last war was World War II, although active duty service for more than 180 days between August 5 1964 and May 7 1975 counts to establish protected veterans status as a "Vietnam Era Veteran" whether or not the veteran actually served in Vietnam. All of the operations since 1945 are considered to be campaigns or expeditions, and to be considered a protected veteran a serviceman or servicewoman must have participated and received a campaign medal or badge as a result. This can be confusing, but in a nutshell if a veteran served overseas in places like Iraq, Afghanistan, Kosovo, Kuwait, Vietnam or Korea then that veteran is a protected veteran.

Documentation: The Department of Defense provides the veteran with a Certificate of Release or Discharge from Active Duty (DD-214), which contains the dates of service and lists all decorations and awards earned in section 13. If a veteran has a campaign or expeditionary medal, then they are considered protected. Service medals, except the Armed Forces Service Medal (below), do not count.

3. Veterans who served on active duty and were awarded the Armed Forces Service Medal. The Armed Forces Service medal is awarded for military operations that are not considered to be campaigns or expeditions, which essentially means non-combat or non-hostile operations.

Documentation: As listed above, if section 13 of the DD-214 lists the Armed Forces Service Medal then the veteran is considered protected. This is the only service medal medal that meets the requirement (the National Defense Service Medal and Global War on Terror Service Medal do not count).

4. Recently discharged veterans. Veterans who have been discharged for three years or less, regardless of whether they meet the requirements of 1, 2, or 3 above.

Documentation: The DD-214 lists the date of release from active duty/discharge.

Those requirements are all pretty straightforward. But what about people who served in the National Guard or Reserves? That is where things get complicated. While those who serve in the Guard and reserve are veterans of the service, they may not fall in the protected veteran category. Here is a breakdown of eligibility for Guard and reserve:

1. Traditional service. Guard/reserve personnel who serve out their obligations by only performing their weekend drills and annual training requirements are not protected veterans. Even though they serve on active duty during their initial training periods, this service alone is not enough.

2. Activated or mobilized for Federal service. Guard/reserve personnel who are ordered to active duty are considered to be protected veterans if they deploy in support of a war, campaign, expedition or an operation that qualifies for the Armed Forces Service Medal. If they are placed in federal service and do *not* deploy as listed above then they are *not* protected veterans.

Documentation: Section 13 of the DD-214, which lists the medals that the veteran was awarded, just as with regular active duty veterans.

3. Disabled veteran status. As with active duty, Guard/reserve personnel who are entitled to disability compensation from the Department of Veterans Affairs are considered to be protected veterans.

Documentation: The same as for active duty – the Department of Veterans Affairs provides a Summary of Benefits letter to the veteran which denotes his or her disability rating.

Although by law employers cannot require you to disclose your status as a veteran, it is to your advantage to do so. It is very important for you, the veteran, to know which category you fall into as you pursue your next career. Most large companies and many smaller ones have government contracts, and if you are a protected veteran you will receive preferred hiring consideration.

*   *   *   *   *

Lessons learned:

- ☐ Not everyone who has worn a military uniform is considered to be a veteran for VA benefits or for employment.
- ☐ Employers are prevented by law from requiring you to disclose your veteran status. It is to your advantage to do so, but if you don't want to, then that is your call.
- ☐ To determine if you qualify for benefits from the VA or if you are a protected veteran, refer to your VA Benefits Determination letter (generated by the VA) and/or your DD-214.
- ☐ Make sure all of your campaign and service awards are listed on the DD-214 before you get out – changing it once you are veteran is an enormous pain in the posterior!

Part II: Out

Chapter 12: *Reflections*

A few months before my retirement date I had occasion to go back to where it all started, well, where my life began as a United States Marine. As a resident of the greater San Diego area I am bounded by Marine and Navy bases and stations pretty much on every side, and during my years in uniform I had been fortunate to serve aboard many of them. One such base is the Marine Corps Recruit Depot, where I shed my civilianhood as a petrified teenager in a terrifying new world only to return nearly two decades later as a senior officer who helped run the joint. Oddly, during the course of my career I had gone from being an inmate within the mustard colored walls of that hallowed institution to one of the metaphorical fat men behind the curtain who made the whole thing run. Upon my graduation from bootcamp I had sworn to myself a solemn oath never to return to the wretched shores of San Diego and its terrible Marine Corps Recruit Depot, but like most youthful bents I disregarded it, came to my senses, and ultimately returned.

The Depot sits next to the San Diego International Airport, aka Lindbergh Field. Any Hollywood Marine (as MCRD graduates from San Diego are known) can tell you that it is endless torture to suffer the indignance of being a worthless recruit, marching around on the parade deck as jet after jet lifts off only yards away. Every airliner that takes off is the personification of the very freedom that the recruits have sworn to defend despite having relinquished such freedom when they arrived at bootcamp. It was such airplane that brought me back to the depot after I went on terminal leave but before hung up my uniform for good.

My in-laws had been in town for a visit, and as it was time for them to head home I took them down to the airport to catch their flight. With the kids in the back seat we headed down to Lindbergh Field, and as we drove past the distinctive training grounds I noticed that I was running low on gas. After a few hugs at the airport terminal security line, my in-laws headed for their gate to catch their flight and we hit the road. Never one to pass up the chance to save a buck or two on gas, I drove over to MCRD to take advantage of the PX service station.

We approached the gate and I saw a number of teenagers who were no different than I was a quarter of a century earlier. Having just graduated from bootcamp, they were waiting for a taxicab or a ride by the main gate. Each seemed accompanied by a small mountain of luggage that comes only from an all-expenses paid vacation to such an establishment; seabags (duffel bags for non-nautical types), garment and gym bags in the mottled green that matched the camouflage of their field uniform, and the ubiquitous black satchel that contained their orders and other important papers. Like a thunderclap, I was instantly transported back to when I was one of them: another young man eager to step out on the exciting journey into the rest of his life. Just as quickly as lightning passes, though, my reverie was broken by the Marine guard at the gate brought me back to reality by asking to see my ID card. Suspiciously eyeing my longish hair, he offered a salute and a thoroughly professional "good morning, Sir!" as he waved me through. It was not as though my life passed before my eyes, but my psyche was twisted with the realization that I was no longer looking forward to my life as a Marine, but instead was passing the baton to those who were.

I cruised over to the gas station and filled up. My kids had been there many times before, so when I asked if they wanted to see my old workplace they eagerly agreed. Besides, I needed to get my last active duty haircut (!) before my terminal leave expired. It seemed apropos that the last hair that I would part with in the service of my country should go into the same trashcan as the first, with the only real difference being that my hair was graying a bit and maybe just a little less of it would make it into the dustpan.

After getting my hair cut we headed out to see the sights. Our first stop was that small fitness area behind the "RESTRICTED AREA" sign that marked the hallowed grounds of the Drill Instructor School. I had served as the director of the DI School (the Marine Corps' premier leadership academy) some years prior, so I invoked the executive privilege that comes with being a Director Emeritus and we snuck over to cavort on the exercise area's pull up and dip bars. Even though I was still a senior officer on active duty (for a few more days until my terminal leave expired at least) and even though I was formerly the director of the school, I still got chills up and down my spine as I violated the admonition to stay out of the restricted area. Such is the power of the training that recruits endure on the path to become Marines; I still dreaded the thought of a drill instructor finding us where we weren't supposed to be and taking his revenge upon such dangerous rule breakers as me and my two rambunctious boys.

I breathed a sigh of relief when we left Drill Instructor School behind and walked up and down the arcade, which is the half-mile long open portico that is the distinctive hallmark of the base. The sights and sounds crossed the chasm of time; the place looked almost unchanged despite the years that had passed since first stepping foot onto the yellow footprints. On the parade field (or "grinder" as it is universally known) we saw a platoon of camouflage uniform wearing recruits frozen in mid stride, surrounded by a blur of Drill Instructors in their service uniforms who seemed to be everywhere all at once, issuing commands and correcting deficiencies. They were being evaluated on their ability to properly conduct Close Order Drill, or *COD*.

Again, the time machine between my ears kicked into overdrive and I was back on the grinder, younger, leaner, and utterly terrified that I would make a mistake and incur the painful wrath of my Drill Instructors. With a shudder, sat on a bench and pulled my curious kids close.

"What are they doing?"

"What kind of guns do they have?"

"Are they your friends?"

I answered their questions ("Close order drill", "M-16 Service Rifles'", "we are all friends") and watched the magic happen. It was cathartic to see the next generation of Marines being made before my eyes, and oddly enough it looked precisely as it did when I was there back in the mid-1980s. That is what makes and keeps the Marine Corps great: tireless dedication to duty, selfless passion for the institution, and absolute certainty that being a Marine is something momentous. Such things are the flint and steel that sparks the flame that burns in the soul of each and every recipient of the Eagle, Globe and Anchor.

As I watched them march by it was clear to me that the next generation was as good as mine. The passing of the torch ensured that it would burn bright and clear for the next year, the next decade, and indeed forever. The soul of the Marine Corps is made up from the soul of every Marine, and it rests deep within each and every man and woman who has earned the title. I observed a part of that soul being born, and was proud to be a witness.

To them I say good luck, but make sure to enjoy the ride. Too soon they will be sitting on a park bench watching the generation of Marines that follows them march into their own destiny, just as my sons and I did on that bright and sunny weekend. Despite the hardships, the terror of combat, and the boredom that accompanies standing watch in the middle of the night, I would trade places with any one of them and do it again.

To them, all of them, I say good luck and Semper Fidelis!

Chapter 13: The Gap

Soldiers, Sailors, Airmen, Coast Guardsmen, and Marines don't serve for the money. You can't put a price on the hardships, the time away from your family, the danger, or the camaraderie that comes with wearing a uniform in the service and defense of the nation. The pay is enough to live reasonably comfortably, but certainly no one is getting rich on their military paychecks.

Although you aren't becoming wealthy on payday you are getting paid for what you do. The government does a great job of ensuring that you receive what you are entitled to by dropping half of your monthly salary by direct deposit into your bank two times a month. Despite the fiscal challenges that the nation faces the thought of not paying the Soldiers, Sailors, Airmen, Coast Guardsmen, and Marines who keep the country safe makes lawmakers squirm and infuriates taxpayers. Suffice it to say that just like clockwork your paycheck will find its way into your bank account on the first and fifteenth of the month, unless those dates are holidays or weekends, in which case you get paid a few days earlier. That is always nice.

Those checks just keep on coming, at least until your last day in uniform. Then things get a little more complicated.

The military pay cycle is pretty simple. In employment terms, all military personnel are government employees who are paid a base monthly salary in addition to any additional benefit payments to which they are entitled. The base salary is taxed at the normal federal and state rates, but the benefits are not. Examples of benefits include things like *Basic Allowance for Housing* (BAH, which subsidizes off-base housing) and *Basic Allowance for Subsistence* (BAS, which is a meal stipend). There are many more, such as jump pay (for those who find falling out of perfectly good airplanes on a regular basis as part of their job description) and combat pay (that not-so-huge amount of extra tax-free money you receive for going to places where bad people shoot at you).

All of these things are added up, resulting in your gross monthly pay. Taxes and any other allotments (allotments being automatic withdrawals from your pay for things like Serviceman's Group Life Insurance or savings bonds) are deducted, and the result is the money that is due to you for your service. That amount is divided into two equal payments, which are in turn deposited into your bank account on payday.

It is important to recognize that the month is divided into two portions, with the salary and benefits for the first half of the month being paid for on the fifteenth and the second half of the month being paid on the first day of the following month. This is very important to remember as you transition, because if your last day in uniform falls towards the end of the month you would believe that your paycheck is due the next day, and that it will include all of your pay and benefits up to your EAS.

Well, in theory it's supposed to. As we have found with things related to with transition, it's not that simple.

Your last paycheck will not show up when you expect it to. It will almost certainly be delayed for a few days or weeks unless you are indeed very fortunate. Although each service has slightly different regulations concerning your final mustering-out pay, they all have the same basic requirements: the final paycheck must include all pay and benefits due to the separating service member minus any obligations that he or she owes the government.

This can be pretty surprising if you don't expect it. What obligations can you owe the government? The obvious ones are any fines that you incurred by getting in trouble, but if you stayed on the straight and narrow you should be good, right?

Not necessarily. The bean counters hold your final paycheck in their possession until all of the possible ways that you could owe money are double-checked and accounted for. These include but are not limited to charges for any equipment that you may have lost (remember turning in all of your gear to the Consolidated Issue Facility?) or adjustments to benefit payments (for example, it is not uncommon for your deployment related payments to be adjusted for months after you return from overseas, and any overpayments will be recouped by the government). Your final paycheck will also settle up any additional sums of money that the government may owe you for things like unused leave or unsettled travel claims. The long and the short of it is that your final settlement paycheck is not going to show up on the same schedule as you are accustomed to because all of the various accounts must be balanced before the check is cut.

If you are relying on that check to pay for necessities then you are in for a rude surprise. No amount of begging or complaining will make that paycheck show up any faster. You can help yourself, though, by making sure that all of your ducks are in a row as you check out. Make sure that all of your gear is turned in, for example, and include the receipt showing a zero balance with your checkout paperwork. Stop by your admin shop and make sure that your pay and allowances are correct long before you begin to check out, and be sure to deal with any problems immediately. You can't pull the wool over Big Brother's eyes. The government will get what's coming to it, and if you settle everything up fair and square as quickly as you can then you won't have to wait nearly as long for your final paycheck. It will make the bean counter's job that much easier and your final settlement check that much simpler for the government to write.

In my case, my final paycheck took 26 days from when my terminal leave expired and it showed up in my bank. Welcome to "the gap".

If you are not eligible for retirement, then that check is the last one that you will receive for your military service. If you are retiring, though, you will be receiving a pension (which is paid differently than active duty pay and entitlements). The retirement pay cycle is monthly, meaning that retirees receive a check once a month as opposed to the twice monthly system which active duty personnel enjoy. Your first pension check is due on the first day of the month after you retire, which means that you are not going to receive anything at all until a full month after you get out.

This can be quite disconcerting if you don't plan for it. When you retire you are going to have a month without a paycheck so make sure to be ready! Don't put yourself and your family in the sad position of having to eat sawdust and oatmeal until your retirement check arrives. Sock a little extra into savings ahead of time or mooch a few bucks from your relatives to bridge the gap, but make sure that you are prepared to go for a month without a paycheck.

And if you are getting out instead of retiring, be prepared to wait a while for your final paycheck to show up.

Don't say I didn't warn you.

*   *   *   *   *

Lessons learned:
- ☐ Your final paycheck will be held up as the accountants settle up all of your accounts. If you are relying on it to cover immediate expenses then you are in for a tough financial time. Plan ahead.
- ☐ The last payment will be reduced by any payments you owe the government and increased by any payments the government

owes you, so it may be significantly from your normal pay amount.

☐ Unlike the bi-monthly active duty pay cycle, your pension is paid monthly. The first retirement check shows up a full month after your retirement date, so you will have a gap between your EAS and your first pension check.

Chapter 14: More changes: A new ID card

It finally happened. The big day arrived and I found myself suddenly thrust back out into the real world. Crossing the threshold of transition is more than just a metaphorical exercise, however. There are still quite a few things that have to be accomplished before the process of becoming a civilian again is complete.

One important "little thing" is obtaining the official token of retirement: the blue identification card. Only retirees are eligible for one because it is the key to benefits after leaving active duty; benefits like health care, commissary privileges, and shopping at the PX. It is also the proof of military service which allows you to go back onto base. Unlike an active duty ID card, though, it doesn't require renewal every few years. Instead, it expires on your 65th birthday, whereupon I suppose you will have to drive your golf cart or hover car or whatever it is they use for transportation in the distant future down to the base Pass and Identification office and obtain a new one. 65, you see, is the magic age when retirees become eligible for Medicare, and for whatever reason that requires a new form of identification.

It is very important to get your retired ID card as soon as possible after the last day of your terminal leave has vanished into the night. Technically, if you don't, you are violating the rule of law because a) you are no longer on active duty, and the card misrepresents your status on the morning after your EAS and b) the Armed Forces Identity Card has a few features that your state issued ID or driver's license doesn't contain. It is not simply a laminated piece of paper. It is a "smart card" with a chip embedded inside that contains personal information, and it can also be used to gain access to government computers. Not that you can really do anything particularly nefarious with such access, but with your transition comes the end of your right to get on official computer systems.

In addition, the military ID card is a record of your official Geneva Convention status. Even though you are now retired, your status actually matters in case you are captured by the enemy. Although that is particularly unlikely to happen in southern California, you never know when it might be useful. In my case, I was Category IV, which meant I was a commissioned officer. When I was enlisted was a Category III. I know that because it said so right on my enlisted ID card. Again, not a huge deal, but with my retirement I became uncategorized. Had the US been invaded on New Year's Day *and* had I been captured *and* had the invader checked my ID card then I would have been thrown in a POW camp as an actively serving officer instead of being released as a harmless retiree. That in and of itself is reason enough to get my new card.

So off to the base Pass and ID office I went. It appeared to be a simple and straightforward process: all I had to do was to go into the office and turn in my active ID for a retired one. It was straightforward, but in typical fashion it wasn't so simple.

I showed up and signed in on the clipboard that lay beneath the tattered and yellowing notice that announced "SIGN IN HERE". I then sat down in a government issued plastic chair with about a dozen other people who were also waiting for new identity cards. I was halfway through perusing a three year old issue of <u>Consumer Reports</u> (*always* a good read) when my name was called.

I walked up to the counter.

"Can I help you?" asked the clerk.

"Sure. I need to turn in my active ID card for a retired one," I answered as I reached for my wallet.

"OK. Two forms of ID please. And your DD-214."

D'oh.

ID's I had. My DD-214 I didn't.

I failed to bring the single most important document that a separating serviceman or woman will ever receive. As we learned earlier, the DD-214 is the official source document that documents your military service. It shows when you entered the military, when you left active duty, and contains your eligibility for VA benefits, healthcare, and reenlistment (in case you can't handle civilian life and want to get back in). It is also apparently required to obtain a retired ID card.

Since I didn't have my DD-214 with me I shrugged my shoulders and resigned myself to another trip to the Pass and ID office. I should have known better and brought it along, but like a knucklehead I didn't. The thing about being on active duty is that you tend to take a lot of things for granted; after all, your information is in every computer data base imaginable. All anyone has to do is look at your ID card, input your social security number, and pull up your data. Unfortunately, once you retire the great big data eraser in the sky shows up and purges you from the system, as was the case for me on the first business day after my EAS:

03 Jan 2012 @ 0243 MOL LTCOL GRICE, MICHAEL D. was dropped from your unit

With that pithy little message I was erased. With my erasure rose the importance of the DD-214, because it was an artifact of my service that could not be summarily deleted. And without it, as I found, things were much more difficult, if not impossible, to accomplish.

So the next day I returned with my two forms of ID *and* my DD-214. I was even able to finish reading the tattered issue of <u>Consumer Reports</u> after I signed in and before I was beckoned back to the counter. With a cheery smile I turned over my small pile of documents, and within a few minutes I had a shiny new blue retiree ID card complete with a cheesy picture of myself that I would be looking at for the next few decades. No POW camp for me!

* * * * *

<u>Lessons Learned</u>:

- ☐ You need to turn in your active duty ID card immediately after your EAS. If you don't you are breaking the law, which is generally a bad idea. This also applies to your dependents because their status changes as well, so make sure that they update their ID cards as soon as possible too.

- ☐ Your DD-214 is the most important document you will have after you transition. I recommend that you keep a copy of it with you at all times when you are conducting transition relate business. Have the administrative shop that completes your transition provide you a few extra copies, and make sure that they are stamped "CERTIFIED TRUE COPY" at the bottom. That will ensure that you don't have to make extra trips like I did.

- ☐ Buy a binder or folio (which is a nifty word for a folder that has a zipper on it to hold all the stuff inside) and keep all of your working transition paperwork organized. That way you can whip out your DD-214 or whatever document you need at a moment's notice and avoid going back and forth to get things done. You will need other documents, too, like your checkout sheet, medical appointment reminders, etc., and having an organized notebook will help a lot.

Chapter 15: Albert Einstein, Don Draper and Supercuts: a new dilemma

Adapting to life after the Marine Corps has been interesting, to say the least. Not that I am truly retired, mind you. My permanent address has not changed to a fishing boat on Lake Placid, and I am still years away from heading to the local diner in time for the Early Bird Blue Plate Special.

Fishing and discounted dinners aside, one thing cropped up that I hadn't really paid much attention to but required some serious attention right away.

I stepped out of the shower, you see, and after toweling off my head I looked in the mirror and almost fell over. Where for decades I had sported a closely cropped Marine haircut (although not as closely cropped as most, to be quite honest) I now saw that I was doing a pretty decent impression of Albert Einstein after he stuck his finger in a light socket. I had hair going everywhere: straight up, sideways, backwards, you name it. It was downright frightening!

It snuck up on me. It really did. I had just started using a comb again for the first time in decades but hadn't been paying much attention as I "did" my hair every morning. I was able to part it after a month or so, which was pretty neat. It started tickling my ears, too, as it grew over them. Also pretty neat. I toyed with sideburns. Neat again! But it just kept *growing*.

Don't get me wrong. I'm not complaining. I am thrilled to have hair. Plenty of my friends don't, as they suffer from the relentless onslaught of middle aged baldness. Fortunately, I come from a family unfamiliar with the ravages of excessive hair loss, and now I am reaping the rewards of such a hirsute lineage.

Anyhow, as much as I enjoyed growing out my hair it was now becoming annoyingly unsightly. In addition to it being shockingly grey in places where it used to be solidly brown, my attempts to tame it with brush, comb, and hair gel (!) failed to bring it under control.

It was time for a haircut.

Where do civilians get their haircuts, anyway? I had been going to the same set of barbers for decades. It is a very simple process when you are in the military, and especially so in the Marine Corps. The uniform regulations state that a Marine haircut must graduate from zero (meaning no blocked cuts allowed) up to a maximum length of three inches on top. Not a lot of room to work with, but even so there are about a half-dozen varieties of authorized Marine styles: the "Mr. Clean" bald look, the fresh out of bootcamp "High and Tight" (shaved around the head with a patch of hair on top) the '50s inspired "Flat Top", and the "I really don't want one of those other haircuts" regulation haircut in low, medium, or high style (the low, medium, and high in reference to how closely you want it cropped on the side of your head). After my overly enthusiastic embracing of the High and Tight Flat Top as a young and motivated Marine I gradually came to my senses and embraced the rather sedate Senior Officer's Low Regulation haircut. Just enough on top to push over one way or the other, but not long enough for the Sergeant Major to question my gender ("Gee whiz, sir, when are you going to start braiding it?").

Anyhow, I digress. Week in and week out for years and years I had plonked myself in the fine Naugahyde splendor of the base barbershop and asked for a "low reg". A few minutes later, the barber's work finished, I looked in the mirror to see myself exactly as I had looked a week earlier after my *last* haircut. It didn't matter if it was in California, Japan, Iraq, or Afghanistan; the same ritual took place. "Hello. Low Reg." Bzzzzzzzzzzzzzzzzz. "Done." And that was that.

Now I was flummoxed by what to do. I feared going to a military barber because I knew what the outcome would be, so instead I cast my gaze to the local strip mall. Civilians get their hair cut too, and where else but at a hair-cuttery sandwiched between Men's Wearhouse and GNC? Why, at SUPERCUTS, of course.

So into SUPERCUTS I went. It was quite bewildering. There was a little seating area littered with magazines; not too different from the military side, except that the décor was nicer and there were no copies of _Guns and Ammo_ or _Soldier of Fortune_ scattered about. Instead, I could only find dog-eared issues of _US_ and _People_. Good thing I didn't have to wait long enough to read about how many kids Angelina and Brad adopted last week because I really don't care and really don't want to know.

A very nice young woman greeted me, and after explaining that I needed a haircut, I was introduced to another nice girl with an "i" at the end of her name. She was a "stylist" named Brandi or Candi or something like that. She was very different from the surly and generally grumpy barbers I was accustomed to.

She sat me down in the chair (which, to be quite honest, was not a real barber chair, but then again, she wasn't a real barber) and asked what I wanted. I explained again that I was newly retired and didn't want to look like Albert Einstein. As I talked I glanced around the shop and saw a pastiche of pictures: hair models with gelled spiky hair next to mullets next to wavy haired surfer dudes. I opted for something a bit more conservative. I asked for the "Don Draper" look from the television show *Mad Men*. After she got done howling with laughter she set to work.

"I'll thin it out here on the sides. You have a lot of bulk."

Bulky hair? Really? I guess that explains the Einstein look.

"How about the sideburns? How low do you want them?"

Decisions, decisions! How low do sideburns go? I jabbed my cheek with my index finger at about mid-ear.

"I'll get rid of the fuzzies, too."

Fuzzies? Nobody wants excess fuzzies, which I learned are stylist-speak for neck hair. Fuzzies be gone!

After ten minutes of snicking scissors and buzzing clippers she was done.

"Gel?"

Sure, said I. She worked it into my newly-shorn locks, and in no time I looked almost nothing like Don Draper but significantly less like Albert Einstein.

Victory!

I quickly paid at the register, and after turning down the generous offer to set me up with a bewildering variety of hair care products I left the shop with a freshly stamped "frequent customer" card. Just think...nine more haircuts and my tenth one will be free! At the current rate I'll be claiming my free shearing some time in 2015, but who am I to complain? I am retired, after all.

Chapter 16: *Trading tradition for a tuxedo*

Gentlemen's Quarterly, the unequalled guide to fashion, suavity, and panache unabashedly states that every man must own a tuxedo. I have had the great fortune to be able to ignore that bit of fashion advice for decades thanks to my military service and the associated collection of dashing uniforms that filled my closet as a result. I had been haberdashed to the fullest with military raiment for every occasion and could emerge from my dressing room equally ready for a gritty firefight or a formal black tie affair. Unfortunately, my dizzying array of uniforms didn't transition well to the civilian world, and the flexibility of a closet filled with every conceivable military fashion choice exists only as long as you continue on active service.

I had not really thought much about it, other than when I rummaged through my closet in search of the civilian clothes that hung amongst the uniforms I no longer needed but could not seem to part with. That is until November rolled around.

November is a big month for servicemen and servicewomen because it is the month of Veterans Day. The crisp height of autumn finds proud old soldiers marching side by side with their younger counterparts in parades that mark the service of those who have worn the cloth of the nation. It is the time for all of us to renew our promise not to ever forget the sacrifice that they have made to ensure our country remains the best on earth.

For Marines, however, November holds an even greater meaning. November is the month of the birth of our Corps, and each and every Marine who has ever served can tell you what day our birthday is. November 10th, 1775 is the date of the founding of the United States Marine Corps, and Marines continue to celebrate that momentous and distinguished day.

It is a day replete with elegant ceremony, pomp, and circumstance. Marines everywhere, regardless of clime, place, or situation will stop what they are doing and throw a birthday party. Events range from white tie formals that rival the cotillions of nineteenth century France to a pair of tired Marines sharing a dry MRE pound cake in a muddy foxhole between firefights. Whatever the situation, Marines will gather together and perform a timeworn ceremony to mark the day that we all grow a year older. In the case of my first November out of uniform, the Marine Corps turned a youthfully venerable 236 years old.

The formal events that mark the occasion are quite elaborate. They usually start with "preflighting", which is when Marines and their guests gather *before* the cocktail hour to get a head start on the evening. Preflighting usually goes in someone's hotel suite, and there you will find a few coolers filled with beer and the counters laden with cocktail fixings. After having a cold one or two it is time to head for the cocktail hour that precedes the event; time for another drink (for all of the teetotalers out there who are aghast at the thought of drinking before the cocktail hour starts, well, I'm sorry. Marines are known for doing many things well, and drinking is one of them). There is nothing quite as wonderful as sharing an evening with the ones that you love and the ones you will lay your life down for. It is a truly transcendent experience.

Cocktail hour ends with a bugle call to beckon everyone to their seats. Moments later the ceremony begins, and every Marine's heart quickens to the tap of a drum and the brassy keening of the band. Two by two an escort of Marines marches onto the scene, armed with glittering swords and a steely gaze, smartly coming to a stop in facing rows that frame the setting for the ceremony. They are followed by the Guest of Honor and Commanding Officer of the unit that is hosting the party, who march to their places at the head of the evening's parade ground. The nation's colors, reverently carried by a guard of Marines, are solemnly presented with every pair of eyes in the house is riveted on Old Glory as the national anthem is played.

Following the posting of the colors (when the flag is placed in its ceremonial position) a cake is brought forth, escorted by Marines dressed in their uniquely distinctive and elegant dress uniforms. The ceremonial adjutant draws forth a scroll on which is scribed a directive from General John. A. Lejeune, a legendary commandant of the Marine Corps whose service predates ours today by a century or so. Without the aid of something as pedestrian as a microphone, the Adjutant takes a deep breath and booms out the venerated message for all to hear:

"On November 10, 1775, a Corps of Marines was created by a resolution of Continental Congress. Since that date many thousand men have borne the name "Marine". In memory of them it is fitting that we who are Marines should commemorate the birthday of our corps by calling to mind the glories of its long and illustrious history.

The record of our corps is one which will bear comparison with that of the most famous military organizations in the world's history. During 90 of the 146 years of its existence the Marine Corps has been in action against the Nation's foes. From the Battle of Trenton to the Argonne, Marines have won foremost honors in war, and in the long eras of tranquility at home, generation after generation of Marines have grown gray in war in both hemispheres and in every corner of the seven seas, that our country and its citizens might enjoy peace and security.

In every battle and skirmish since the birth of our corps, Marines have acquitted themselves with the greatest distinction, winning new honors on each occasion until the term "Marine" has come to signify all that is highest in military efficiency and soldierly virtue.

This high name of distinction and soldierly repute we who are Marines today have received from those who preceded us in the corps. With it we have also received from them the eternal spirit which has animated our corps from generation to generation and has been the distinguishing mark of the Marines in every age. So long as that spirit continues to flourish Marines will be found equal to every emergency in the future as they have been in the past, and the men of our Nation will regard us as worthy successors to the long line of illustrious men who have served as "Soldiers of the Sea" since the founding of the Corps.

JOHN A. LEJEUNE,
Major General Commandant"

The honoring of tradition does not end there. With a flourish borne of tradition and practice, the adjutant proffers his or her sword to cut the cake. Two slices are produced, and are presented by the Commanding Officer to the Guest of Honor for the evening, and then the second piece is respectfully conferred to the oldest Marine present. In a tasty Marine Crops tradition the oldest Marine then passes the piece of cake to the youngest Marine (having left at least one bite, and with a new fork), who then takes a bite, symbolizing the passing of tradition from the old guard to the new. The birthdates of the oldest are read out as they sample their piece of cake, with the oldest receiving the muted respect that such long service commands and the youngest receiving the howling laughter and applause that accompanies the honor of being younger than the children of many Marines present. The sage meets the prelate, and they share a piece of tradition-laden cake. Not a bad tradition at all.

With the returning of the plates and cutlery the sequence is reversed. The cake is marched away to the tune of *Auld Lang Syne,* followed by the color guard after paying respects again to our nation's flag. The guest of honor and commanding officer follow the flag off of the ceremonial floor, closely accompanied by pairs of escorts. With a rousing rendition of *Anchors Aweigh* (to honor our naval tradition) and the *Marine's Hymn* (to honor all Marines and the birth of the Corps) the ceremony draws to a close. All that remains are remarks from the current Commandant of the Marine Corps (usually by video), the hosting commanding officer, and the guest of honor which are traditionally presented just before dinner is served.

The best remarks are those that are meaningful, thoughtful, endearing, and brief. Having been to countless balls during my 27 years in uniform I have felt the thrill of excitement that a great and motivating speaker brings to the ceremony as well as the mind numbing drudgery inflicted by those who even with the best of intentions drone ceaselessly on. And on. And on. (The longest in my experience approached the hour and a half mark before departing the podium and allowing us dive into our wilted salads.)

Once the remarks are completed and the guest of honor is presented with a token of appreciation for his or her words of motivation and wisdom the formal ceremony is complete. Marines and guests cheerfully turn to those who share their table and break bread together in a respectful and joyful atmosphere more reminiscent of a wedding than a military ball. After dessert (which of course includes the birthday cake) the bars reopen and the ceremonial parade ground becomes a dance floor, on which the metaphorical rug is cut to shreds in the hours that follow. It is a birthday party, wedding, prom, and Sadie Hawkins dance all rolled into one, Marine Corps Style; and it is the best party you will likely every attend. Just ask Justin Timberlake and Myla Kunis.

So that brings us back to my personal predicament. November arrived after Halloween just as it always does, and with the approaching 236th birthday of the Marine Corps I was placed on the horns of a dilemma. What ever would I wear? It was a conundrum that I had not faced since high school! Fashion choices...a suit or a tuxedo? Get a haircut and wear my uniform (which, as a retiree, I was still allowed to do)?

The decision was further confounded by circumstance as I was honored to find myself invited to attend the 11th Marine Regiment's Headquarters Battery Ball as the guest of honor. Yikes! I thought back to all of the balls that I had attended what they meant. I had squired lovely ladies and escorted my bride in my Dress Blue and Evening Dress uniforms, and had broken chunks of ration cake with my fellow Marines in the field and on the decks of amphibious ships at sea. Those birthdays all shared one central theme in my life: that the day of celebration was a mile marker on the autobahn of my career. This ball, however, fell as I left the highway and steered to the offramp, and somehow it didn't seem right to wear my uniform.

So I followed the advice of Gentlemen's Quarterly and purchased the evening clothes that I would wear that night and indeed for every future formal event until they box me up and bury me somewhere at the end of my days. On that, my 27th consecutive celebration of the birth of the Marine Corps, I traded in the tradition of wearing the cloth of the nation for a new set of clothes. As I departed the ranks of serving Marines I joined the citizenry of the nation I had defended for so long, and it seemed somehow fitting to wear a Tuxedo to mark the occasion.

After all, you can't wear your uniform forever and like ZZ Top says: *everybody* likes a 'sharp dressed man'.

Chapter 17: Choosing a path ahead

So there you are, sitting at the kitchen table with a cup of coffee in your hand and the rest of your life in front of you. You have made the decision to hang up your combat boots and get out of the service. What you have not decided yet, though, is what to do next. You stir your coffee, look out the window, and ask yourself *"so now what?"*

It is a great question, and you probably don't have a truly great answer for it. In many ways leaving the military puts you in the same position you were in when you graduated high school or college: the world lies before you with prospects to go in pretty much any direction you choose. Which path is the one you want to take?

There are many possibilities. You can go back to school, get a job, move back in with your parents, or become a hermit. For the first time in years it is a choice that no senior officer or NCO will make for you. So what are you gonna do?

Contrary to popular belief it is unlikely that you will be able to find a porch to sit on for the remainder of your days, unless you are retiring to a cabin in the middle of the mountains and plan on living on whatever you can grow, catch, or hunt yourself. The retirement benefits, if you receive them, aren't *that* generous. You are going to need to supplement your well-earned but meager pension or find a new line of work to pay the bills.

What if you are just getting out after a hitch or two? Finding the retirement portico is probably decades in the future, so you need to find something to do until the rocking chair becomes your retirement throne.

So, back to the question: *now what?*

There are two common paths that people leaving the military generally take. They either go back to school or find a job. Many vets, like me, end up doing both at the same time as they work their way through college or graduate school. Regardless of which path you take you are ultimately going to end up back in the employment market. That is what we will be working on next: finding a new career and landing a job.

Despite what you may have heard, you can find employment after you get out despite today's tough economic conditions. It isn't easy, though. There is no magical job fairy that sprinkles you with sparkly guaranteed-career dust. There are opportunities, though, but it takes some dedicated and serious work to take advantage of them.

How long has it been since you wrote your resume? How about a cover letter? Have you had any experience being interviewed for a job? What kind of skills can you show to a potential employer? What do you want to do?

Well, the time has come to answer those questions, and the only one who can answer them is *you*. You have made your decision to leave the military and with that decision the reality of the situation hits you right between the eyes like a mallet on a croquet ball: you have to go get a job.

The military is a tough profession. It is rife with conflict and stress and danger; anyone who finds wearing a uniform an easy way of life isn't doing it right. The hours are long if you are lucky enough to be at your home duty station, and the deployments are even longer as those in uniform find themselves shuffled off to distant parts of the planet for months or years at a time. It is a truly arduous line of work.

The one thing that military folks are not fighting for, however, is their paycheck. As long as they are in the service they will receive their pay and allowances. Unless they do something very wrong or fail to meet promotion requirements they can stay in until they decide to leave or have to retire when they hit their service limitations. In practical terms they cannot be fired; although they may be relieved from their specific duties but they still are employed as they move on to another military job. Unlike the civilian world there is rarely an existential crisis that finds military personnel wondering when or if their next paycheck will arrive. Sure, they move around from job to job and from base to base, but always within the context of continued employment and service within the Department of Defense.

It continues on until the day arrives when your next job is not assigned to you by a bureaucrat in Washington. On that day you realize that your next job is the one that *you* find for yourself. And that day is a big one.

Gulp.

It is both shocking and remarkably intimidating to suddenly be thrust in charge of your future. Even though you have attended (or will attend) various transition assistance programs and seminars and have started thinking about the future, it doesn't really sink in until you arrive at the realization that after your EAS you are on your own. Don't worry, though. We'll get there, starting with the process that you will need to follow in order to take advantage of your military experience and leverage it into finding a job, and who knows? Maybe even a new and exciting career!

Too many people leave the service with the unfounded expectation that there are jobs-a-plenty out in the civilian sector and that corporations are foaming the mouth to hire veterans. After all, who has greater leadership skills and management expertise than someone who has led their peers and subordinates into combat or supervised teams of highly trained people as they employ or maintain millions of dollars' worth of equipment? Which firms wouldn't want to fill their plants and factories and businesses with former military professionals and to save them from themselves and make their organizations into run like little armies?

The answer to that is pretty simple. Almost none of them.

The cold hard truth about the business world is that while companies do hire veterans, they hire them to fill the needs of the company and *not* the needs of the veteran. Companies exist to do one thing and one thing only: to make money. If they don't make money, they go out of business. Sure, there are nonprofit companies that aim to accomplish other things, but they need money to be able to meet their lofty goals. The coin of the realm, if you will pardon the pun, is the mighty dollar.

If you cannot show to a potential employer how you will 1) meet a need in the company that only you can fill, 2) help them make more money, or 3) help them save money, they really don't need you.

It is quite a shocking realization to learn that no matter what your skills are, no matter how many deployments you made or how many medals you have on your chest nobody on the outside really cares. Sure, they are respectful of your service and sacrifice and will gladly buy you a drink, but they are not going to put you on the payroll unless you can show how you can add value to their firm.

This is why it is critically important to do a couple of things before you start heading out into the job market. Here are the most crucial things that you MUST do before you start job seeking:

1. *Get over yourself.* You have served your country and you have gone places and done things that civilians will never experience. The reality is, though, that if they want to hear all about the military and what it is like to serve they will go to the movies. You need to move on from being Colonel Highandmighty or Sergeant Major Highspeed. I guarantee you will never find a good job if you cannot let go of your

military past. Employers want to hire you for what you will do for them, not for who you used to be.

2. *Figure out what you want to do.* This is not as easy as it sounds. I strongly recommend that you find the time to sit down for a few uninterrupted hours and really analyze what you would like to do with yourself now that you are out of the military. Ask yourself a few questions, such as: where do you see yourself in five years? Ten? What are you good at? Do you want to find work in the areas you are familiar with, or do you want to strike out in a totally new direction? We will be doing some exercises to help you figure this out later in this chapter.

3. *Start planning.* Now that you have an idea of which direction you would like to steer your ship you need to chart a course. What companies are doing work that interests you? Are they hiring? Do you need to get some specialized training or education in order to pursue those goals?

Once you have worked through these three points you will be much better prepared to start looking for a job. We'll cover that later, but first let's get started on figuring out what it is you want to do next. That starts with the realization that the path to your future leads past the guards at the base's main gate and back into the wilderness of the civilian world.

One of the things about transitioning from the military is that you cross a very bright line from being in uniform to being out of uniform. One day you are lacing up your combat boots and saluting the flag while the next you are suddenly faced with deciding, on your own, what shoes you are going to wear after sleeping in well past reveille. It can be a jolt. One of the most jarring bits is realizing that you have crossed the line into the civilian world and that there is no going back. With that realization comes the need to start your next career.

Before you can find a job or a new career, however, you need to determine where you want to go. For a lot of reasons it isn't as easy as it seems! Where do you even start?

That's easy. You start by getting out four sheets of paper.

Take two of those sheets and set them aside; we will be using them later. A real challenge facing military personnel is not just what they want to do in the future, but also to determine what they are suited for. What is really a good career choice for the way ahead?

It isn't that people don't have an idea of what it is they would like to do next, but that they often don't know how to get there. How do they start a new and rewarding career? We'll go down that road together, starting with your two blank pages. At the top of the first sheet write, in big capital letters:

THINGS I AM GOOD AT

Now start listing things at which you excel. Not just work, but hobbies, sports, or anything else that you (or others) feel that are your strengths. Maybe you are a great aircraft mechanic. A terrific infantryman. A woodworking hobbyist. A mountain biker. Whatever it is that you feel you are good at needs to go on the list.

Now pick up the second sheet. On this one, write in big capital letters:

THINGS I AM BAD AT

This one is more difficult than the things that you are good at because it requires a certain amount of reflection and honesty about your abilities and talents. Once you begin, though, it is surprising how quickly it is populated. Maybe your penmanship is terrible (like mine). Maybe you can't type. Really take a candid look at yourself; are you indecisive? Maybe a little too decisive? Are you overly aggressive or passive? Are you an introvert who finds cocktail parties excruciating? Afraid of public speaking?

Take the lists with you for a day or so. Don't expect to write everything down at one sitting, but instead jot down bullets as they come to you. Sleep on it. When you get up the next day take a look at the lists again over your breakfast and coffee. I guarantee that you will have a few more things to scribble down.

Remember to be honest with yourself, particularly with the second list. The more thought and effort you put into writing down what you are good and bad at the more likely you will be to find a solid fit between your next career and a satisfying future. A big part of starting anew is finding out what you are really suited to do; not just what you want to do or are good at, but something that will be rewarding and meaningful and that you will enjoy.

That isn't to say that you can't go out and be whatever you want to be, but we live in the real world and not everyone is independently wealthy or capable of living on dirt, rocks, and rainwater. You need a new career. As you depart the service you have a whole new life to live, and the best way to live it is to have an idea of where you really want to go.

We started with four sheets of paper. By this time it should have been a few days and you should have one sheet filled out with a list of things that you are good at and another with a list of things you are bad at. Go ahead and put those two sheets aside for now, but don't lose them. We are going to need them soon (and if you think of anything to add to either list, go right ahead and write it down).

Now take out the two blank pieces of paper. Our previous lists evaluated our skills, and today we are going to look into ourselves and evaluate what our desires are. These are not the same things as skills, though.

Here is why.

Everybody has had a job that they hated. Maybe it was delivering newspapers in the snow and rain, and maybe it was working in an office. You may have been very good at whatever that detested job was, but just because you were good at it doesn't mean that you want to do it for the rest of your life. This can be a true epiphany; it was for me. Recognizing that being good at something does not mean that it is the only thing that you can do with the rest of your life. There are other possibilities out there.

So, as you probably have guessed, you are going to pull the first sheet of paper out and write this at the top in big, bold, capital letters:

THINGS THAT I LIKE TO DO

List out those things that you really enjoy. Not just work or professional items, but everything that you truly take pleasure in doing. Maybe it is fishing. Perhaps you love writing. Maybe you love the outdoors. Or the indoors. Or watching football. Whatever you put on it is for you because the list is *yours*. Take some time and write things down that make you happy.

As you have probably also guessed, the next sheet of paper should have this written at the top:

THINGS THAT I HATE TO DO

Go ahead. Vent. It is good for the soul to actually put on paper those things that you absolutely despise. It doesn't only have to be things that you abhor, so go ahead and include the things that you just don't like. After all, you are in the driver's seat of the car that will take you through the rest of your life, so why not make it a sweet ride free from the stuff you don't enjoy? Think beyond the context of work: Do you hate crowded places? Cigarette smoke? Broccoli? Whatever it is, write it down.

Take a few days to compose your lists. Keep them handy and write things down as they pop into your head. Sleep on it. Take a few days to think about it before we move to the next step. After all, it is the rest of your life that we are talking about, so go ahead and take your time. Write as much as you can! The more you vent the better you will feel, and also the more you write the more effective this exercise will be for your future.

The purpose of the four lists is to put on paper those things that are important enough for you to think about and write down; the actual act of putting pen or pencil to paper is important because it forces you to put some focused thought into your future and record how you feel about the next segment of your life.

At any rate, you should have four lists sitting in front of you:

THINGS I AM GOOD AT
THINGS I AM BAD AT
THINGS I LIKE TO DO
THINGS THAT I HATE TO DO

Now here comes the fun part.

Take the **THINGS I AM GOOD AT** paper and place it next to **THINGS THAT I HATE TO DO**. Put the other sheets aside for now.

Starting at the top of the **THINGS I AM GOOD AT** sheet, look for any matches in the **THINGS THAT I HATE TO DO** list. If there are any matches, then cross them off the **"GOOD AT"** list.

When I did this the first time it was a startling exercise because I had never really thought about my talents and skills from the perspective of whether I liked to do them or not. On my **"GOOD AT"** list, for example, was curriculum management for military training and education courses. I have a lot experience setting up and running training programs, classes, and programs of instruction. I had so much experience and success in the training realm that I was regarded as being an expert on the subject. That said, on my **"HATE TO DO"** list I had written down *bureaucratic administrative paperwork*, and that is exactly what curriculum management is all about. Although I love to teach, I had never really considered that I did not like to do the tasks associated with developing course content and managing curricula. By performing this simple exercise I came to the realization that I really didn't want to pursue training administration as a future career despite having many opportunities to do so.

Now move on to the **THINGS I AM BAD AT** and **THINGS THAT I LIKE TO DO** lists.

This pairing takes a little more consideration. Just because you are bad at something doesn't mean that you can't get better at it. For this part of the exercise start at the top of the **"LIKE TO DO"** list and compare it to the **"BAD AT"** list. It may sound odd, but maybe you like skiing and have never had a chance to hit the slopes enough to improve your schussing beyond the bunny hill.

If there are any matches, then ask yourself this question:

"I really like writing (or woodworking, or gardening, or school, or whatever) but I am not good at it. Is it something that I am willing to dedicate my energies to becoming better at in the future?"

This is important because it may be a doorway into a new career path or other life choice. Maybe you can go to school to learn how to be better at whatever it is, or perhaps you will find an apprenticeship or some other program to enter that field. Or, if you really want to become a better skier, moving to a state like Colorado or Utah may be a good idea.

However, if you are not willing to dedicate your energies to get better, then you should cross it off the **"LIKE TO DO"** list.

So now your lists should be a little shorter. Time to take the next step.

Place your **"LIKE TO DO"** and **"GOOD AT"** lists next to each other. Now look for matches. What do you like to do that is also something you are good at? Circle those matches in big red marker.

Now line up the **"BAD AT"** and **"HATE TO DO"** lists. Any matches here? If so, circle those as well.

Here is the last step: Line up all four sheets on the table, starting with **"LIKE TO DO"**, then **"GOOD AT"**, then **"BAD AT"** and **"HATE TO DO"**. These four sheets of paper represent the spectrum of possibilities that you can pursue, based on your thoughtfully created lists.

What strikes you on the **"LIKE/GOOD"** side? Do any of those circled items jump out at you? Is there something that gets quickens your pulse? That may be a path to a rewarding future. How about the **"BAD/HATE"** side? Is there anything there that makes you nauseous? You probably ought to steer clear of those.

This is really an exercise in thinking about your future. All military people, whether they serve three years or thirty, depart the service with a set of skills and talents that they have dedicated themselves to. Just because you were really good at your job in uniform does not mean that it is the only thing you can do for the rest of your life. If you are not careful you will become myopic and it will significantly impact your future; if all you see yourself as is an infantryman then you will have a hard time finding a job in the civilian world.

A common problem that I see with many veterans that I work with is that they are fixated on who they *were*, and not on who they could be. Their military past so rigidly defined their persona that they have difficulty getting past their short haircuts and affectation for military jargon.

There is nothing wrong with being incredibly proud of your service and the Marine, Sailor, Soldier, Coast Guardsman, or Airman that you were while in uniform. To start a new career, however, means that you must be willing to accept that you are no longer in the military and that you are able to follow a new path in life. You may have been the greatest artilleryman on the planet but if you want a job in the corporate sector you need to recognize that there are no artillery companies in the civilian world.

Hopefully this little exercise uncovered some opportunities that you can pursue in the future, and it showed that you are capable finding a new and rewarding career for your life after the military.

If nothing else, it gave you something to do for a couple of days.

All it cost was four pieces of paper.

But now that we have some ideas of what you would like to do (and not do), we need to look at the second part of the equation: Where do you want to go?

This is important because it is equally important as what it is you would like to do with the rest of your life. As a separating service member you are in a pretty good position to decide where you want to live; you can stay where you are or the military will relocate back where you first entered the service from at no cost to you. However, if you decide to go someplace else the government will compensate you for the amount it would have cost to send you home. If you settle someplace closer, though, you don't get to pocket the difference (as we discussed earlier).

The reason this is important is because aligning your future career aspirations with where you and your family would like to live is critical. Transition is a very stressful time, and there are a lot of resources out there to help you move to your post-military home and help find employment. Unfortunately, those resources dry up pretty quickly once you are out and you cannot go back and undo the decisions you made as you transitioned.

There are three big considerations that come into play with your selection of where to end up once you become a civilian again:

1. *What will make you and your family happy?* You have likely been moving around where the military has ordered you to go, and as a result your family has made sacrifices along the way. Your final move should be somewhere that both *you and your family* want. Family input is critical; after all they have supported you in your vagabond career so now it is time to listen to them.

2. *Is where you want to live consistent with your new goals in life?* You have more of an idea of what you want to do in the future, but can you do it where you end up? If you want to be a great skier then you may want to make sure you end up someplace with snow covered mountains, or if your life goal is to become a captain of a fishing boat then there had better be some water nearby.

3. *Can you afford to live there?* Your military relocation benefits will greatly assist you in getting to where you want to go, but once they run out you are on your own. You really need to assess your financial situation, career goals, and family desires and make sure that you don't make a stressful time even more so by putting yourself in a fiscally challenging environment.

These are big considerations because they all involve compromise. To be successful it is imperative that you balance your career goals with your family and finances or you may find yourself in a tough spot without the ability to go back to the military for help.

Take some time to think about it. *Really* think about it. Where do you want to go? Sounds like time for another list, so take out a sheet of paper.

This time, though, is different. Give the sheet of paper to your family. Ask them where *they* would like to live, and after they write down *their* two cents compare it to your goals and your family's financial situation.

You may be surprised at how all of these things shape your perspective on life after the military, so take the time to really examine where you want to plant the family flag and what you want to do after you plant it. It should be a place that you can really and truly call home.

After all, you have been serving your country for years. Isn't it time to get a little of the American dream for yourself and your family? You've earned it, and the best way to make sure it really is the dream that you hope for is to make sure that your career goals, family, and finances are aligned. If you do, then you will make your family happy as you set out on the path to the rest of your life. If you don't, though, there will be a lot more stress in your future. And who needs that?

∗   ∗   ∗   ∗   ∗

<u>Lessons Learned:</u>

- ☐ Starting over once you get out is not easy. It takes work, and you will waste a lot of time and suffer from some pretty significant blows to your ego if you think that the civilian world owes you something for your service. They don't. If you want a job or a new career, then you have to get out there and earn it.
- ☐ Facing a future outside predictable certainty of the military is daunting. Having a plan for the way forward will greatly reduce the uncertainty and anxiety that comes with transition. Plan for your next career with the same rigor as you planned missions in the military: with a focus on the endstate that you wish to achieve. The hard part is figuring out what that endstate is, but by examining what you like and don't like as well as what you are good and bad at you can reduce the uncertainty and refine your goal.
- ☐ What you want to do is as important as where you want to do it. Make sure to involve your family in the decision of where you plant the family flag after you hang up your uniform.

Chapter 18: *It's time for a new career, but where do you start?*

Now that we have looked what we would like to do in the future we need to figure out how to get there. A huge step down that path is learning how to find a job, or at least how to present yourself in the best way possible so that you are competitive in the job market.

In the military you started out just like everyone else. You were a recruit or an officer candidate with short hair and very little knowledge or experience about the military. As you progressed through training and headed out to the operating forces you learned what was expected of you and how things are done. Over time you met people and developed a professional reputation which helped you obtain desirable and rewarding assignments. By the end of your military career (whether you served three years or thirty) you had developed a solid reputation and a tremendously helpful network of peers, juniors, and seniors.

Once you take off your uniform, however, your reputation largely goes with it. The civilian world and corporate sector will be thankful for your service but they will have no idea what you did because military service is a mystery to them. While your military network will still be around it won't help too much because you aren't looking for a job in the military. You just left, remember?

So the long and the short of it is that you are starting over. Nobody is going to hire you just because you formerly wore a uniform. You need to do the same things you did as a young recruit or officer candidate; you need to begin the process of building a new network and a new professional reputation.

We'll start with the basics. There are a lot of things you will need to do, and it can seem overwhelming if you try to do them all at once. You need to build a resume. Craft a cover letter. Research and decide where it is that you would like to live and work. Discover a rewarding new career. Meet people who can help you. Learn how things are done in the corporate sector. It's a lot, so let's take a look at the very first and simplest thing you can do to get started.

During your transition you have undoubtedly passed through some of the courses we looked at earlier, and in between classes you had an opportunity to get to know your peers and instructors. You have also probably attended some job fairs or professional association mixers where you, the job seeker, found yourself in a room with people who know a thing or two about the employment market. If you were paying attention you probably saw people chatting here and there, and at some point in the conversation they exchanged business cards.

They are networking, which is another way to say getting to know someone new. The difference between socially saying hello and networking as a job seeker is that you are now building a set of contacts that will hopefully be helpful in your search for a new career. To be successful in the job market you need to network, and in order to network effectively you will need to get some business cards. Cards are important because when you are hunting for a job you are competing with a lot of other people, and as you network you will be meeting men and women who can help steer you towards a new career. They are not going to remember your name or even who you are if you don't give them something to carry away with them; after all you are going to be one of the many people that they meet on any given day. I guarantee that you will not get a call from someone who does not know your phone number. Help them and you by giving them a card. *Your* card.

Not all business cards are created equally. There are services that will print them up for free (with an advertisement for the printing company on the back, of course) or you can print them on your home computer. If you don't have any (or if you only have cards that have your old job and contact information on them) you can use those services or print your own until you can have some quality cards of your own made up.

To get an edge over the competition go ahead and spend a few dollars to create a high quality and professional looking business card. Anybody can get free ones or print their own, but that telegraphs that you are either too cheap or too unmotivated to increase the quality of your business cards above the bare minimum. Remember that the card represents you. It is all that the person you handed it to has to remember you by, so make sure that you leave a good impression.

I recommend that you go to a stationery or paper store that also produces business cards. You will be surprised at the incredible variety of products available, with myriad colors, shapes, fonts, and cardstocks to choose from. Take a look at the catalogs from the perspective of how you want to be represented and remembered. A good rule of thumb to follow is to be conservative because that is what is expected in the business world. Conservative means white or off white with colors like "bone" or "ivory" or "linen". A scarlet card with gold letters may make your heart glow with its familiar Marine Corps colors but it will not help you build a network in the business world because it will show that you cannot let go of your past. Remember, you are out to make a whole new set of first impressions.

Select a font in a size that is conservative (no wingdings or comic serifs) and isn't obnoxiously big or unreadably tiny. Put only the information relevant to you and your job search on the card. Avoid quotations or sayings that may put people off; "If you ain't infantry you ain't squat" may be pithy around the barracks but is actually insulting when you are looking for a job from a non-infantryman in the corporate sector. And none of them are infantrymen.

Pick a cardstock that is heftier and stronger than the cards you can get for free. They feel cheap. You want something that presents you as a serious and high quality *person*, and a solid card is a good way to start.

Next, decide what you want printed on your card. I recommend that you go with the basics at first with just your name, contact telephone number, and email address. Don't put your military call sign or nickname because it comes across as being a bit amateurish to people who don't understand why people call you "Smasher" or "Flash". It is more formal to put down your whole name, but it is OK to put down what you prefer to be called. If you are named Patrick but go by Pat feel free to go with it.

After your name include your best contact information. After all, that is why you are printing these things up in the first place: to be contacted. I recommend that you list your mobile phone number instead of your home phone because having your four year old answer a call from a prospective employer may not end well in your quest for a job. Also make sure to update your voicemail greeting in order to make it sound professional. If a potential employer hears *"Yo dude! I'm not here so leave your digits and I'll buzz you back!"* it is a strong bet that the caller will hang up before leaving a message. Also include your email address, but like the voicemail you may need to update it in case it is incomprehensible, odd, or inappropriate. Email addresses like *"drunkdude@whatever.com"* will not get you a job. I promise.

So get out there and have some cards made up. Carry them wherever you go because you never know when an opportunity to network will come up. Have a few in your wallet or purse. Throw some in the glove compartment of your car. Have extras in your briefcase. Always keep spares around, because you never get a second chance to make a first impression, and your best first impression comes with a strong handshake and a professional business card.

*　　*　　*　　*　　*

Lessons learned:

- ☐ You are starting over. The network you fostered during your military career is not necessarily the one that will get you into the corporate sector, so you need to start getting out and meeting people.

- ☐ The expected token of exchange in the networking world is the business card. I personally recommend that you go to a stationary shop and have a set professionally done with only your name and contact information printed on the card. This is for two reasons: first, you are looking for a job, and it is not the best idea to use the card from your current job to find a new one, and second, handing a professional looking and feeling card with your name, phone number, and email address saves both you and the person you are interacting with from writing that info down on a cocktail napkin. Anybody can print out a flimsy card on their computer, but remember that the first impression is the most important. Do you want to be remembered as the cheapskate with homemade cards or the kind of person who puts some effort into finding a job?

- ☐ Avoid military "-isms" on your card such as call signs, rank, Military Occupational Specialty, etc. You are selling yourself as a future employee, not a former service member.

- ☐ You need to do three things before your first interview: get over yourself, figure out what you want to do, and start planning. We will talk about these in greater detail in later chapters.

- ☐ Take a deeeeeeeep breath. It's going to be OK. Trust me.

Chapter 19: Getting a job, part 1: Networking, Job / Career Fairs, and Social Media

Networking

One sure fire way to learn more about the employment market is to talk to people who know something about it. As we learned in the last chapter, in the civilian world such a conversation is known as networking, and such conversations happen all the time. On one side of the spectrum are purely social mixers and cocktail hours and informal meetings, and on the other side are rigidly formal events. One organization that does great work in between the extremes of formality is the Marine Executive Association, or MEA. What is the MEA, you ask? I'm glad you did, because it is a great resource for transitioning servicemen and women because it leads to something we all need: jobs.

The MEA is a networking organization where people who are leaving the service can meet others who are transitioning as well as business people who need high quality and motivated people to join their organizations. It is informal (after all, there is no rank after you get out) and informative, because most of transitioning military types really don't know that much about civilian employment.

Here is the write-up about the association from their website (www.marineea.org):

"The Marine Executive Association is a national, volunteer, non-profit organization of former and current active duty Marines who provide assistance to Marines transitioning from active duty to reserve/retired status, leaving the Corps at the end of obligated service or moving from one civilian career/job to another. Transition assistance includes: Resume review; Job hunting and interview tips and techniques; Job posting by employers to the MEA web site; Resume posting by Marines for employer download; and resume and interview coaching by volunteer Marine. The MEA provides a weekly E-Mail list of all jobs that have been posted during the previous week and resumes posted for employer download, review and screening."

The association is open to all services, and in a recent meeting that I attended there were Air Force, Army, and Navy veterans there too. Transition is the great equalizer; we no longer wear uniforms and military rank, position, and MOS no longer matter. We also share the same concerns and have the same need for employment, so inter-service rivalry goes right out the window. We're all in the same boat now.

In southern California, the MEA-West runs the show under the management of a retired Marine colonel named Steve. The meetings are monthly occurrences. On the third Wednesday of the month the attendees gather to socialize and have a drink at *Iron Mike's*, which is the Staff Noncommissioned Officer's club located in Camp Pendleton's South Mesa events center. After a half hour or so at the bar, we migrate over to a meeting room where the evening's guest speaker will talk to the crowd about what it's like on the other side of the fence. Our speaker for a recent meeting that I attended was Kim Shepherd, the Chief Executive Officer of the Alfred P. Sloan award winning placement firm *Decision Toolbox*. She gave us tremendous insights into the business world, with a strong emphasis on how to evaluate yourself in order to find what you are really interested in doing in your next career. Kim was followed by a group of business leaders from the Los Angeles area who were interested in helping veterans learn more about the corporate sector. They are a group of great Americans who want to help vets find jobs, and they shared some great ideas and recommendations to help veterans make it from job seeker to job finder.

One of the great aspects of MEA meetings is that attendees get to hear about opportunities from corporate professionals, and the insights that they share are priceless. It isn't every day that an industry leader takes the time to mentor a pool of job seekers, but it happens at every meeting of the MEA. Since roughly 80% of jobs are found through networking, getting to know the right people is certainly in your best interest as you transition!

After the guest speakers are finished we all introduce ourselves. This is a chance to give your "elevator pitch", which is a thirty to sixty second sound bite about yourself and what you are looking for. You never get a second chance to make a first impression, and standing up in front of a room full of people gives you some practice so that you will make a good one when it counts. It also lets the employers in the room know if you are someone that fits their needs, and I have personally witnessed vets get job interviews on the spot after the introductions are finished. Such is the power of networking!

The introductions are the last part of the structured meeting. Once they are completed the formal part of the meeting is done it is a little like a high school dance as job seekers work their way across the room to meet up with businesspeople who have pitched the opportunities available in their organizations. It is also when old friends catch up and new friendships are forged, or in other words, the networking tree grows a little stronger and new branches sprout.

It is a great opportunity to get out there and see what the job market is like. Once you get plugged into MEA-West (or MEA-East, I suppose) you will begin receiving emails from the head of the organization. He sends out dozens of emails each week, and each one contains anywhere from one to ten or twenty job opportunities. Many of these opportunities are first listed in Steve's emails, and a *lot* of veterans have found employment through the MEA. One former Marine who left active duty in the 1990s shared that every job he has taken since taking off his uniform has been through MEA networking, and he is far from alone. Even in this tough employment market there are jobs out there. Networking with the MEA will help you find them, so find out where and when the next meeting goes and belly up to the bar!

Job and Career Fairs

Since my transition I have participated in more career and job fairs than I can count, and I have also had plenty of conversations with others who have made the circuit of job-seeking events. Many of those I chat with are frustrated, and some of them have reached the point of "job fair fatigue" that they are giving up on attending them.

A lot of their frustration comes from an unclear set of expectations for what job and career fairs are about. Not all job fairs are the same, and not all career fairs have the same goals, opportunities, or areas of interest. Just like everything else in life, job and career fairs are different, and if you don't recognize that going in then you, as a participant, will likely become frustrated and disillusioned.

There are many different types of fairs, and each of them provides a different service and experience for the transitioning military or veteran participant as well as for the companies and organizations that attend. The underlying goal for fairs is universally the same – to provide avenues to employment for vets and those in transition – but how that goal is achieved varies with each and every fair. There are three basic types of job or career fairs: open fairs, niche events, and company sponsored engagements.

The first type of job and career fair is the most common. These events are usually held on military bases in conjunction with the transition assistance office, and they are generally large in size and very general in terms of the companies and organizations that attend.

Often held in conjunction with transition assistance programs or seminars, their targeted group of participants is primarily transitioning military personnel. I have never seen one that turns veterans away from the door, but it is important to recognize that the companies that are participating in these events are primarily looking for transitioning military personnel to fill jobs that are entry level in nature. These tend to be well attended by job seekers and participating companies to the point of being quite crowded in many instances. It is important to recognize that these events are great opportunities to go meet representatives from numerous diverse companies and organizations in order to learn more about opportunities and to see if there is something out there that you would like to pursue. It is also important to recognize that it is not the place to start handing out resumes with the expectation that a hiring manager has been waiting all day for you to show up so that they can hire you.

Think of these open events like a high school dance, except you are going without a date. You can socialize with a lot of potential dance partners and maybe spend some time cutting the rug with one or two, but you are not going to fall in love and get married on the dance floor. It's a meat market, and the employers are there to see who is out there, share what their company does, and to hand out business cards. They are not there to interview people for jobs.

Unfortunately, I have had many people in transition lament that they handed out resume after resume at such an event and nobody ever called them back. As a result, they become frustrated and cynical about job fairs. That is too bad, because these types of fairs are great for those in transition to see what is out there. If you recognize that up front, then you will have a great opportunity to learn more about companies, industries, jobs, and possible careers. If not, then you risk missing a great opportunity to network.

The second type of event is one that is focused on a specific niche of transitioning military personnel and veterans. These engagements focus on a subset of candidates that will meet with companies based on the focus of the event. One subset that is in constant demand is the group of junior military officers – those young company grade lieutenants and captains who have completed their obligated service and are now entering the corporate sector. These men and women are prime candidates for jobs in management and sales. Another example is the first termer segment – even younger men and women who are leaving the military after one or maybe two enlistments.

These folks are perfect for entry level positions in the manufacturing, transportation, security, and retail industries.

Regardless of the which group of veterans the fair focuses on it is important to recognize that if you are *not* in that particular group then the engagement would be a waste of time for both you and for potential employers. Do yourself a favor and do some research to determine if a particular fair is focused on a particular group – and if it is, make sure that you are in it before you attend!

The third type of career or job fair is one in which a specific company, group of companies, or an industry hosts an event that focuses on their specific area.

Industry specific opportunities are usually centered on providing insights for veterans and transitioning military into what businesses within the industry specialize in, such as manufacturing, oil and gas production, financial services, and healthcare. They are usually held outside the realm of military bases at either a hosting company's facility or a hotel or conference center. There is usually no cost for transitioning military or veterans to attend, and often there are industry-centered orientation and training seminars offered during the event. Since the seminars are hosted by companies or groups of companies, there are usually hiring managers present with job opportunities in hand that they want to fill with the veterans who participate in the seminar.

As someone in transition or as a veteran it is important that you manage your expectations. Job and career fairs are set up to get two groups together – the group of job seeking vets and a group of employers. The bigger they are the more impersonal they are, and you can easily become frustrated if you go to one with a pocket full of resumes the expectation of walking out with a job offer. My advice is to use these engagements as intelligence gathering opportunities in which you can learn more about opportunities and to network with potential employers that you can contact at a later date.

Social Media

One of the challenges that every transitioning servicemember faces is creating a network outside of his or her military circle. Earlier in this chapter we talked about networking engagements and the need to connect with new people. Meeting people one at a time is not particularly efficient, however. The most efficient and effective way to network is to join the information age and use social media to get your name out there.

Another reason to engage in social media is that every hiring manager that I have spoken with, *every one of them,* says that the first thing that they do when they consider a candidate is to get on the internet to see what's out there. Universally they indicated that they check LinkedIn, Facebook, and Google to see what an individual looks like online.

HR folks are looking for several things when they turn to social media. First off they want to see if you have a social media presence. If you do not have any accounts anywhere then that in and of itself is suspect. Are you hiding something? Do you not know how to use the internet? Are you in the witness protection program?

The second thing they look at is whether or not your social media is consistent with your resume and cover letter. For example, if you list that you have a bachelor's degree on your resume, then it should be listed on your LinkedIn profile. Your chronological history should be consistent between your resume and your LinkedIn profile as well. In short, your professional presence on LinkedIn should reinforce the skill set that you present on your resume, and if it does not then you will likely not be called in for an interview. Consistency is important.

The third thing HR professionals review is Facebook (and Instagram, twitter, and any of the other social media engines) in order to see what you look like in your personal life. *"Wait a second!" you say. "My personal life is my own business and an employer has no business looking into it!"*

Wrong. Anything that you put out on the net is fair game. If your LinkedIn profile makes you out to be the perfect candidate but your Facebook page makes you out to be a potential liability, then you will not be called back for an interview. It is that simple.

An example that one recruiter shared with me is particularly relevant. A candidate had submitted his resume, been interviewed, and been extended an offer letter to join a different company. He quit his job the week before he was supposed to start at the new firm, but before his first day he was informed that the offer was rescinded. Why, you ask? Because the HR professionals performed their due diligence and thoroughly reviewed his Facebook page before he started, and they discovered a single objectionable post from another person that he *"liked".* It was enough for him to lose the job he was seeking and to go crawling back to the job he had just quit.

The rule for job seekers on social media is that it is incredibly important. If you are not on LinkedIn, then you are at a serious disadvantage because that is the tool that over 350 million people use to present professionally represent themselves. Think of it this way: your competition (i.e., others seeking the job you want) are on LinkedIn, and if you are not they will get the call instead of you. Some simple rules of thumb for LinkedIn are:

- Post a current picture. If you are still on active duty or serving in the National Guard or Reserve, then a picture in uniform is OK. If not, then post a picture in business formal or business casual attire. Nobody is going to hire someone who can't let go of their past, and if you have been out for a few years and the photo on your profile is of you in uniform, then it shows you are too lazy to post an updated picture. I recommend that you get a professional portrait done – it looks much more professional than an iPhone selfie.

- Use the summary section like a generalized cover letter. Present yourself as the kind of person that any company would like to hire. Don't use ALL CAPS (seriously – it makes you look like an idiot), avoid acronyms and military lingo, and keep it professional.

- Post descriptions of the jobs you have held in the chronological section that non-military readers will comprehend.

- List your education, and include any relevant certifications you may have earned while in the military (PMP, Six Sigma, Training Certificates, etc.).

- List only organizations and interests that are not controversial. If you are a proud member of the American Bow hunting Association and you post it on your profile, you will alienate those who find hunting objectionable. It can hurt your chances.

Finally, HR professionals turn to Google. They will enter your name (including variations, like "Michael" or "Mike" in my case) to see what pops up. One veteran friend tells a compelling tale of his presence on the web: there is a person with his exact full name that robbed a store in Florida some twenty years ago. Whenever his name is Googled, the first thing that pops up is the story of the robbery, and it created quite a stir at a job interview when the interviewer asked when he got out of jail. He now brings it up early in the job seeking process so that the HR folks are not surprised. The moral of the story is to Google yourself and see what pops up – you may be surprised!

Social media is very important. Ignore it at your own peril, and remember that your presence on the web should present you in the way that you want an HR professional to see you – if you got liquored up on Friday night and posted selfies of yourself doing shots of tequila then you are not going to get offered a job. I guarantee it.

*   *   *   *   *

Lessons Learned:

- ☐ Networking *works*. In today's economic uncertainty there are literally millions of resumes flying around, and the stories about people who have submitted hundreds of resumes without finding a job are frequently in the news. The vast majority of employment opportunities are found through someone you know, so increase your chances by getting out there and meeting people.
- ☐ Help yourself as you network. Carry plenty of business cards to hand out, and make a point of meeting as many people as you can.
- ☐ Carry a resume. We will spend a lot of time later on about how to prepare a resume, but attending a networking meeting where employers are actively seeking to hire without your resume (and personalized business cards) is a bit like going to a nightclub in your pajamas; sure, you're there but you aren't particularly well set to participate. Many employers are looking to immediately fill positions and the guy or gal with a quality resume in hand will get the job before the one who doesn't. Don't be that person with empty hands when an employer asks for your resume!
- ☐ There are countless networking organizations out there. MEA is just one, but there are commensurate organizations for all branches of the armed forces, for federal employees, and civic organizations. They are all tremendous resources that you can tap for free, and you will certainly meet some great people along the way that will help you along the path to employment.
- ☐ Develop an "elevator pitch" that succinctly introduces you to networking contacts. Keep it short; no more than 30 seconds in length and it should contain the important nuggets about

yourself that you want to convey such as who you are, what your talents are, the industry or area in which you would like to work, and how soon you are available to start. I recommend that you weave your elevator pitch into the conversation instead of blasting away with a 30 second monologue – just make sure to include all of the pertinent elements as you converse. Stay away from intimately personal or controversial topics, though. Steer clear of advertising your political affiliation or views on social issues. Keep it professional, and practice it frequently so that it comes naturally to you when you meet someone as you network. It is your verbal business card that leads to an exchange of real business cards if it is compelling enough.

☐ Job and career fairs are great opportunities to learn more about opportunities. They are not job interviews. Don't become disaffected or disillusioned because you have unrealistic expectations!

☐ The larger the career fair, the less time you will be able to get with a particular company or recruiter.

☐ Network, network, network. Meet and talk with as many employers as you can. You can never learn enough about the corporate sector, and the representatives from companies are there to share with you what their companies do and the types of jobs that are available.

☐ Always give company representatives your business card, and make sure to get one from them as well. Write some notes on the card to remind yourself about the conversation – in particular any details about the person you spoke with. They will meet with dozens or hundreds of folks daily and will never remember you, but if you contact them and can refresh their minds about your conversation it will make a very positive impression.

☐ Don't go to a job fair if it is focused on a group of veterans that you are not a part of – if it is for first termers and you are retiring, then don't bother to go. You will just waste your time.

☐ Social media is a double edged sword – your virtual presence is out there for everyone to see, including potential employers. You are building yourself as a brand, and if your brand is not professional in every aspect then you are putting yourself at a disadvantage.

☐ Get on LinkedIn. If you are not on LinkedIn then you are going to be viewed as suspect by HR professionals.
☐ Be careful on Facebook, Instagram, and other social sites. Anything you post or like is fair game for hiring managers, and if you are not careful it may cost you a job.
☐ Google yourself. See what pops up – you may be surprised!

Chapter 20: Getting a job, part 2: Resumes, Cover Letters, and the CV

Earlier we addressed the importance of making a good impression. Not just in life, mind you, but also in the context of embarking on a new career. By now you should have some most excellent business cards that you can hand out while you are networking, but that is only the beginning of the path that leads to a job. If you are diligent, your networking will pay off – I promise! The way it pays off is the next step in the job search process: when a prospective employer asks to see your resume. If you want to get the job that they are offering your resume had better be pretty tight, because if it is not then you won't make it to the next step of securing a job interview.

Your resume is the core of your job-seeking business correspondence. It is your opportunity to sell yourself to a potential employer. We'll discuss other forms of job seeking correspondence such as cover letters and thank you notes later, but for now let's get a bit more familiar with how to build a resume.

Getting a job is like going shopping in reverse. When you go to the grocery store you are selecting the products that you want and need to feed your family. As you go down the canned foods aisle looking for a can of baked beans, for example, you are presented with a whole lot of choices. There are brands like Bush's and Van de Camp's and Heinz and Hunts and flavors that range from tangy BBQ to wicked hot Jalapeno. Lots of choices! You, as the customer, get to examine the dizzying display of cans and pick the beans you want.

I hate to break it to you, but you are but one can of beans out of thousands on the shelf that is the job market. There are a lot of other cans out there selling themselves to potential customers who may hire them, and in order to break yourself out of the generic bottom shelf and into the highly desirable gourmet section you will need to differentiate yourself from everyone else. That is where your resume comes in.

Your resume is essentially the "professional you" distilled down into two pages or less. It is your one shot to sell yourself to an employer and get yourself through their front door for an interview. In the current economy there are literally thousands and thousands of other people out looking for work, and they have all been firing off resumes to try to land a job. The competition is pretty fierce, so you really need to break out of the pack.

But how do you do it?

I'm glad you asked. Before we get into writing resumes there are a few things you need to do first. Let's start with those.

A few chapters back we went through the four-sheet exercise to determine what you really want to do with your life, so now let's take that a few steps further. You know what you want to do and where you want to do it, so in order to find a job that meets your goals you will need to do some research in order to find the best opportunities.

Start with the internet. I recommend that you go to an employment website such as monster.com or careerbuilder.com and punch in both what you would like to do and where you would like to do it. Within a nanosecond or two, and for free, you will have a list that shows dozens to hundreds of opportunities that fall within your search criteria. I recommend that you spend an afternoon surfing the web and looking at the possibilities that are out there; not because you are necessarily going to apply for any of those jobs but instead in order to get a feel for what's possible.

Look at the lists critically. What industries are hiring? Where are they located? What are the prerequisites? You can drill down and learn about the specific requirements for jobs similar to the ones you would like to find. This is important, because the research that you do now will help you build a resume that fits the bill for the job you want, moving it from the "ignore" pile to the "call for interview" stack.

Also play around with the terms that you put into the search engine. Try different variations on the job title and keywords. Be creative and use a thesaurus if you need to. The point is to get a feel of the job market in the area that you are looking to enter.

The other thing you need to do is contact some real live people. You are leaving the military, which means that you have plenty of compadres who you can tap into. Although they themselves may not have much to offer in terms of experience in the outside world, they all have families and friends who don't wear uniforms. If you want to go into financial services, who better to reach out to for information than your bunkmate's uncle who happens to be a banker? The great thing about networking is that you can get access to people who would not speak to you if you cold-called them, but are happy to share a cup of coffee or lunch with a peer of their son, daughter, or a family friend.

Another way to get a feel for the area is to read the local newspaper. Read it from the front page all the way to the end to get a sense of what is really going on. Is local unemployment up or down? Are there any new businesses or manufacturing plants opening up? What is the engine that drives the local economy? What industries are in trouble? What is the crime rate like? Where are the nice and not so nice places to live and work? Do some serious homework.

Let's get back to talking about resumes. We have covered some of the basics of business correspondence already but now we need to get down to the serious business of crafting one.

Before we get started, though, we need to answer the question: What is a resume, anyway? More important, what is a *good* resume?

A resume is the document that condenses your skills, education, and experience into a short one or two page document. The purpose of the resume is to introduce yourself to a potential employer in such a way that you are viewed as compelling enough to bring in for a job interview.

It is probably the most important single document you will produce during your job search. Without a resume potential employers will not even know you exist, and with a great one you will be much more likely to get an interview. The problem is that there are a lot of really average to poor resumes out there because people don't follow some of the simple rules that lead to a good one.

While there is no guarantee that a good resume will result in a job interview and the sweet new career that you want, I can certainly guarantee that a bad resume will keep you out of the running. So what can you do to get out of the "bad" resume pile and into the "good" one?

The first thing you must recognize is that your resume makes the first impression you with the company where you want to work. You may have met someone who asked you to send them your resume, but it is very unlikely that they are the actual hiring manager or decision maker who will present you with an offer. That person will know you only by the document that you send in, so your paper had better be focused, well written, and error free.

Let's talk about the error free bit first. Remember that this is your first impression, and if it contains grammatical or spelling errors you are telegraphing to your potential employer either that you have poor skills with the English language or are too lazy to proofread your resume. Nobody is going to read your mistake-laden resume and think "Oh boy! I really want to hire someone who can't spell!!"

A way you make sure your resume is error free is to proof read it yourself and to have others proofread it as well. I recommend that you print out your resume and read it as though you were a teacher grading an exam. Don't just read it on your computer screen. You may miss things because people tend to overlook grammatical errors that are not identified by their word processing software (such as the misuse of "there" and "their"). Get out a red pen and critically examine it. You will be surprised at the errors you find. Make sure to double check your contact information as well: I accidentally misspelled the city I live in on my first resume and overlooked it because I did not scrutinize the header, which was where I had placed my contact information. An interviewer caught it and pointed it out. I felt like a complete moron because I had read and reread my resume a dozen times but skipped reading the header without consciously realizing it.

Your resume must be well written. That is easy to say but very difficult to do, particularly in light of the requirement to keep it short. You need to be able to distill your whole professional life, including your education, work experience, training, and skills into a few pages. Much easier said than done! Mark Twain, the quintessential American 19th century writer, put it best when his publisher sent him a telegram asking to write a couple of pages in a couple of days:

> From the publisher: *NEED 2-PAGE SHORT STORY 2 DAYS.*
> Twain replied: *NO CAN DO 2 PAGES 2 DAYS. CAN DO*
> *30 PAGES 2 DAYS. NEED 30 DAYS TO DO 2 PAGES*

We will get much more deeply into how to craft a well written resume in following chapters as we delve into the different types and methods of writing them. One thing to keep in mind as well is that your audience, the hiring manager, is a civilian who likely has no knowledge about the military. Things like your military occupational specialty code, rank, and duty assignment are likely Greek to him or her. You will need to translate military-speak and jargon into simple English; otherwise the reader will be confused and your resume will rocket into the trashcan. The point is that it is a lot harder than you think to reduce your life down to a few pages and still get the message of why you should be hired across to the hiring manager.

Your resume must be focused. This goes hand in hand with the stricture that it must be well written, but you will find these two concepts at odds as you compile your resume. You will want to tell the employer why you are the right person and support it with a lot of vignettes and experiences, but you don't have the space to drone on about how great you were at you whatever it was that you did. You need to be able to strip it down to the essence of what you are trying to say without all of the fluff, and you need to be able to do it so that it reads well.

You shouldn't need Twain's 30 days to write a two page resume. Although it takes time and practice to write a good resume, you will get better and faster at writing them as you go because you won't be creating just one. That would be too easy! You will be creating several because different industries and employers will have different resume requirements. There are three basic types of resumes – *chronological, functional,* and *combination* – and each format is uniquely distinct. We will dive into all three resume formats in much greater detail later, but here is a quick overview of each type:

The most common resume is also the easiest to write. Known as the *chronological* resume, it is in essence a brief sequential history of your professional life. It is appropriate for situations in which you may not know the specific job you are going after, and also in cases such as job fairs or networking events where you have the opportunity to hand out a bunch of resumes to corporate recruiters. It is the broadest of the three types, which is great for most networking opportunities. It is not the best format for companies seeking very specific skills or talents, though, because it is too general. It is also not great for someone with little practical experience or a limited employment history because the format relies on both of those areas to be effective.

The second basic type is the *functional* resume. The functional resume presents your skills in a sorted fashion that shows what you are good at and what expertise you offer to the company. This type of resume is useful in areas where specific skill sets or talents are required to land a particular position. These resumes are very common in the security, health care, and scientific fields because they articulate your strengths, talents, and abilities in the focused and specific areas that jobs in those industries require.

The third and most flexible type is the *combination* resume. This incorporates both chronological and the functional components into a single resume, which provides the potential employer with insight into your experience over time as well as your specific skill sets. It is the toughest to write, though, for the reason that Mark Twain complained about to his publisher: now you have to bring together two resumes and combine them into a single two page document.

One thing to keep in mind is that fewer and fewer companies are accepting paper resumes. Most use applicant tracking systems which either use *resume scanning* to disaggregate the text from your resume into searchable elements based on the *position description* (PD) or they will employ a web-based interface in which you import your resume one piece at a time. Regardless of which automated method a company uses, the introduction of automation makes it very important that the words you use in your resume are the same as the words that describe what the company is looking for. Here is a little more on applicant tracking systems:

Nearly all large companies use them. The reason why is simple; when you are a Johnson and Johnson sized company with over 3,000 open positions it is impossible for recruiters and HR folks to physically read the dozens or hundreds of resumes they may receive for each position. To make the process more efficient, the companies use automation. The problem for a job-seeker, though, is that each company is different and there is no single automated program in use.

Regardless of the program, however, there are only two basic types of systems: those that use resume scanning and those that require you to input your information manually.

Resume scanning is just that – the system scans in your resume, converts it into an electronic version, and then searches it for keyword matches. The advantage to resume scanning is that it uses our entire resume as submitted, so the rules for writing resumes are just as important as if you were handing in a paper one.

Data input is different. For these systems, you essentially complete you resume online by typing it into text boxes one section at a time. More sophisticated systems will do this automatically (like the LinkedIn Resume Builder), but most require you to type in the information one character at a time (or copy/paste). Either way, your resume is going to be virtual, and once it is in their system it will be successful only if you write it in a manner that ensures that the key words they are looking for are contained in your resume.

Determining what key words are needed for a particular job can be tricky. A rule of thumb is that if a requirement is listed in the PD, they you had better have key words that match. For example, if it lists "Four year college degree required" then your resume had better contain the words "Four year college degree".

Resume Format #1: The Chronological Style

There are as many opinions about resumes as there are people who write and read them. Just type "Resume" into Google and you will find literally millions of results. Clicking a few of the resulting links will take you to sites that proclaim that resumes are dead and that the "new" business world uses social media to find employees, while other sites say that traditional resumes are the key to finding work at established and respectable companies. I am writing about are the things that I have learned and the techniques that I have employed to get jobs after leaving the military, so keep that in mind as we talk about resumes. I have used all three types in my pursuit of employment, and all three have resulted in job offers. Social media is great, but the majority of employers who are hiring veterans are still using the old tried and true methods: networking, cover letters, resumes, and face to face interviews.

Each of the three resume formats has its place depending on the circumstance and type of job you are pursuing. In this section we will take a look at the style that is most commonly used in the business world: The chronological style.

The chronological form of a resume is the simplest of the three to put together. In simple terms it tells the sequential story of your professional life and career to the prospective employer, who then decides whether or not you are worth bringing in to meet in person.

There are pros and cons to the chronological format, so let's look at each in turn:

Pros

- It shows the relevance of your work experience over time. It is actually a "reverse-chronological" resume because you list your most recent experience first and work backwards from there, but everyone just calls it the chronological style for simplicity's sake. Since it shows your most recent work first you can highlight your current skill set and talents up front and show how you have garnered experience and developed those skills.
- It is fact based. Since you list your experience on a timeline you can show when you learned your skills, where and when you received relevant education and training, and articulate your experience to show how you have grown professionally.
- It is a universal format that is understood across industries and around the world.
- It can add credibility by showing what organizations you have worked in and the duties you performed in them throughout your career. This can also be a con, however, because you must

remember that civilian hiring managers may usually have no idea about military units or service jargon, so you need to be able to put your experience into terms that they will understand.

Cons

- This is not a good format in cases where you have little or no experience to show. For example, if you were in the military for one enlistment this format will probably work to your disadvantage because you don't have that much to show for experience over time. In that case, a functional resume (which we'll talk about next) is probably a better format to use.
- It is also not a good format in cases if you have large time gaps in your experience base. Since it is a timeline, having gaps of a year or two here and there may raise a few eyebrows.
- Likewise, if you have frequently switched jobs then this may not be the best format to use. Jumping from job to job telegraphs to the employer that you may be a risky person to hire.
- It also may not be a good format for people looking for specific jobs in specific industries that require specific skills. The combination or functional formats are much better suited for those circumstances.

So let's get to it!
The chronological resume consists of four essential elements:

1) Your name and contact information, including your telephone number and email address. As I wrote earlier, make sure that your telephone number is one that you can control (i.e., your mobile phone) because you don't want your preschooler answering the phone when a potential employer calls. It may be cute, but you probably won't get the message that they called. Also, make sure your voicemail greeting is professional sounding or it will not result in a job offer. Trust me. Likewise, make sure your email address is not offensive or controversial, and don't use your military email account. Instead, sign up for a free Gmail or Yahoo email address and use it solely for job search purposes. I don't recommend including your home address on your resume, though, because you cannot control where it will end up. Identity thieves are everywhere.

2) A summary statement. This is a thumbnail sketch of who you are in terms of your experience. Not everyone agrees that you need one, but I include one in my resume to get the attention of the reader as quickly as possible. After all, the hiring manager is reading lots of these things and if you don't grab their interest quickly your resume will land in the trash can.

3) Your experience over time. This is the meat of the resume. Here is where you need to show what you are made of and what you have done in such a manner that the employer will like what they see. It is a remarkably difficult task to be able to strip down a lifetime's worth of experience into less than two pages, so be ready to spend some time on this section. I recommend that you include no more than ten years' worth of experience (for those with more) because anything beyond that timeframe is pretty dated, and the most relevant experience is the recent stuff anyway. The format I use lists my job title first along with the associated dates, and then put a few bullets underneath that show what I did in that job. It took me a lot of practice to write my military experience down in such a way that a non-military person could understand it. Also, pay attention to how the bullets are formed. They follow the "action verb" format, meaning that they show that I did something followed by the effects of what I did. This resonates much more than using the passive tense.

4) Your education and other pertinent info. The education bit is self-explanatory, but what about certifications, awards, or other things that you have done that reinforce your work history or differentiate you from the pack? This is where they go. For my resume, I included significant awards that I have received, associations I am affiliated with, and applicable qualifications and certifications. Things not to include are your hobbies, marital status, family information, or anything not related to the job you are seeking. Those things can be distractors for the reader and may actually turn them off; if you write that you are an avid hunter and the reader is an animal lover then you are in for trouble. Also, you only have two pages, so don't waste space!

The chronological style is the best resume type to start with. You will use elements of it for the other two formats as well, so you won't have to reinvent any wheels.

The internet is full of samples that you can check out. Here is what my chronological resume looked like as I left active duty, so feel free to follow the style I used or branch out on your own. For what it's worth, this particular two page resume resulted in a job offer in the defense industry:

Michael David Grice

123.456.7890
Mike.grice@email.com
TS/SCI Security Clearance

Career Summary:

Combat proven officer who has led men and women in very diverse environments and in supremely challenging circumstances. As an award winning leader I have been hand selected to command specially and highly trained units with hundreds of Marines and Sailors in humanitarian operations as well as fighting in two wars. Thoroughly experienced in professional military training and education. Recognized and respected expert in leadership, fire support, planning, logistics, and aviation command and control. Widely respected and sought out subject matter expert in Field Artillery and fire support employment, training, doctrine, and theory.

Professional Experience: *United States Marine Corps, 1984-2011*

Commanding Officer, 1st Air Naval Gunfire Liaison Company   **2009-2011**
- Competitively selected to command and lead a unit of over 250 Marines and Sailors, including active combat operations in Afghanistan and contingency deployments with the U. S. Navy.
- Developed the operational design for Marine Corps integration with the Afghan Army that was adopted and implemented by the Commanding General of Marine Forces in Central Command
- Ensured the welfare of hundreds of people and managed over $45 million in equipment

Expeditionary Fire Support Branch Chief, Expeditionary Warfare Training Group   **2008-2009**
- Improved the content and effectiveness of five programs of instruction and dozens of classes
- Hand selected to represent Navy and Marine Corps positions for executive level briefings

Special Operations Command Central Asian States Current Operations Planner   **2008**
- Deployed to Kabul, Afghanistan as an expert in security and planning operations
- Supervised the support and reporting requirements for over 150 special operations people in seven central Asian countries as they conducted training and counternarcotics deployments
- Integrated Czech and Romanian Special Operations soldiers with US Forces in Afghanistan

Executive Officer, 5th Battalion, 11th Marine Regiment   **2007-2008**
- Supervised the acquisition of over $100 million in equipment and the training of over 600 people on new equipment and procedures as the organization transition from cannons to rocket artillery
- Professionally mentored dozens of leaders in a chaotic and supremely challenging environment

Brigade Platoon Commander, 1st Air Naval Gunfire Liaison Company   **2005-2007**
- Led over 100 highly trained Marines and Sailors during two tough combat deployments to Iraq
- Innovatively developed procedures that integrated sister service attack helicopters into the Marine Air Command and Control System that were adopted as standard by the Army and Marine Corps
- Personally led a team of specially trained Marines on over 120 combat missions in Ramadi, Iraq
- Handpicked to represent the Marine Corps at executive level decision briefs and conferences

Director of the Drill Instructor School, Marine Corps Recruit Depot, San Diego   **2004-2005**
- Specially selected to train and mentor the school's instructional staff of a dozen senior enlisted leaders and to oversee the training of over 200 Drill Instructors and 60 supervisory officers
- Completely reviewed and revised the Drill Instructor Course program of instruction resulting in an updated and modernized course that met all Training and Education Command requirements
- Conceived and implemented a training program for company commanding officers that ensured consistency in supervision at the line management level

Figure 1: Chronological Resume Example

Michael David Grice   2

Executive Officer, Third Recruit Training Battalion, MCRD San Diego   2002-2004
- Completely revised all administrative policies resulting in a marked increase in unit efficiency
- Created a mentoring program that enhanced the professionalism of young officers
- Personally supervised the reassignment or discharge of over 1700 distressed recruits

Commanding Officer, Battery E, 2d Battalion, 11th Marine Regiment   2001-2002
- Hand selected to lead over 100 Marines and Sailors on a Marine Expeditionary Unit (Special Operations Capable) deployment including humanitarian assistance operations in East Timor
- Commended for pioneering innovative training procedures that resulted in the most highly trained non-lethal riot control unit and artillery battery forward deployed to Okinawa

Honors:

- Recipient of the Leftwich Trophy for outstanding leadership
- Military decorations for heroism and meritorious service
- United States Army Field Artillery Association Order and Ancient Order of Saint Barbara
- United States Army Cavalry Order of the Golden Spur
- Hogaboom Leadership, Chase Essay, and Geiger Aviation Writing Awards

Affiliations:

- Fellow, Marine Corps University's Lejeune Leadership Institute
- Adjunct Faculty, Marine Corps University Command and Staff College
- United States Army Field Artillery Association
- Marine Corps Association
- Marine Executive Association
- Boy Scouts of America

Publications:

- Over three dozen works published in a half dozen periodicals and professional journals
- Author of the book On Gunnery
- Wrote or co-wrote over a dozen doctrinal and technical publications
- Writer and columnist for the *North County Times* newspaper in San Diego, California

Education:

- Master of Business Administration from the University of Southern California (Expected)
- Master of Arts in Military Science from American Military University
- Bachelor of Science in Business Administration from the University of Colorado at Denver
- Marine Corps Command and Staff College, Amphibious Warfare School, and Basic School

Qualifications and Certifications:

- Joint Terminal Attack Controller Evaluator (JTAC-E)
- Top Secret with Sensitive Compartment Information (TS/SCI) security clearance
- United States Army Training and Doctrine Command Certified Instructor

Figure 1 (cont'd): Chronological Resume Example

Resume Style #2: The Functional Format

The Functional Format resume is best for people who are changing careers (like transitioning military folks), those with gaps in their employment history, or people who want to emphasize their skills for a particular job or specific company. The focus is on *what* your experience or skill set is, not *when* you gained it.

Pilots are a great example. It takes a lot of work for aviators to earn their wings, and during a typical pilot's career he or she will spend thousands of hours in the air. They will fly different airframes and receive qualifications that range from landing on an aircraft carrier to flying in the dark using night-vision goggles. Even though an aviator will leave the service with dozens of different qualifications in numerous aircraft and thousands of hours in the cockpit, all of those things are related to the single function of flying an airplane. When he or she earned those qualifications or flew the different aircraft really doesn't matter: what matters is that he or she has the skills that a pilot needs.

For men and women who are hanging up their uniforms the functional format is a very useful way of showing the talents and skills that they have developed and used during their time in the military. Even though many of the jobs that servicemen and women perform during their careers are not directly transferable to the corporate sector (think rifleman, tank gunner, artillery mechanic; you get the idea), the underlying skills and capabilities are relevant and desirable to employers. Things like leadership (that rifleman was probably a small unit leader too), teamwork (tank gunners work as members of small and very close-knit tank crews), and detail oriented task management (that artillery mechanic worked on intricate equipment, ordered parts, and managed supplies on a daily basis).

The functional format is best to show those skills and to articulate how they can be useful for a corporate employer. Remember, when you write it you need to recognize that your targeted audience is a person who likely has zero military experience. As with all resumes you really need to work hard to "de-militarize" it as much as possible; they don't know what a rifleman or squad leader is and certainly have no clue about the operations of the M1A1 Abrams Main Battle Tank's 120 millimeter gun system. Don't make it easy for the hiring manager to throw your resume in the shredder by making it too difficult to read with military jargon and whatnot. That said, more jargon is acceptable in the functional resume format because the target company is probably more familiar with the skill set you are presenting, and the reader will likely know some mil-speak. Just don't overdo it.

There are some great advantages to the functional format, and to maximize their impact it is best to target the resume specifically on the job or company you are interested in. That takes a little research on your part (hello, internet!) and the patience to make adjustments and tailor your resume for each company as you go. Focusing on the target in job hunting is just as important as focusing on the target on the rifle range, because if you don't have a clear vision of where you are aiming you won't hit the target or find a job.

If you do your homework you will find the functional format easier to write because you can direct the reader (in this case, the hiring manager) to what you want them to know about your abilities. By researching the requirements for a particular job or needs of the company, you can show how you fit the bill with the exact skills that the employer is looking for. You can also highlight all of those intangible things that you have been doing while in uniform, such as helping the community, training others, and developing leadership in those junior to you. It also allows you to cut out anything that you don't want in your resume, such as gaps in your job history or a lousy grade point average from high school or college.

Another advantage is that you can be much more succinct and direct with the functional format. Resume writing follows the rule *less is more*. The HR person who receives your resume has a stack of them to go through, and generally speaking you have only a few seconds to grab their attention before they move on to the next one. If they have no second page to turn to then you have a bit of an advantage because they all look at the first page, and if you can get yours down to a single sheet then they will see the whole thing and not have to decide whether to go flip to the next page.

The elements that I used in my functional resume are pretty standard. After the basic header information (name, email address, phone number) there are four sections, the same number as the chronological format except with slightly different content: A summary statement, Functional Experience, Professional Experience, and a bit about Honors, Education, and Publications. Here is what a one page functional format resume looks like:

Michael David Grice

123.123.1234
email@email.com
TS/SCI Security Clearance

Career Summary:

Combat proven Marine artillery officer who has led men and women in very diverse environments and in supremely challenging circumstances. Subject matter expert in aviation integration and command and control, close air support (CAS), surface and sea based fire support, Unmanned Aerial Systems (UAS) employment and integration, joint, coalition, and allied operations and planning, and leadership.

Functional Experience:

- **Aviation integration and Command and Control.** Successfully trained and led a joint Marine/Navy/Air Force Tactical Air Control Party in Ramadi, Iraq during highly kinetic operations. Developed procedures and techniques that resulted in the successful integration of Army Attack Aviation into Marine Corps battlespace. Qualified Joint Terminal Attack Controller (JTAC).
- **Close Air Support.** JTAC Evaluator and Instructor with over six years of experience, including three combat tours and over 200 terminal controls of Fixed- and Rotary-Wing Close Air Support aircraft. Developed and implemented a successful and widely emulated training, evaluation, and monitoring program for Joint Terminal Attack Controllers and Forward Air Controllers.
- **Fire Support.** Over 25 years of experience as an artilleryman. Experienced in light, medium, heavy, and rocket artillery systems, including decisively employing artillery in active combat operations. Expert in Naval Surface Fire Support including U.S. and Allied Naval Surface fires.
- **Unmanned Aerial Systems.** Successfully integrated and employed Unmanned Aerial Systems in active combat and training operations, including tactical, operational, and strategic level systems. Innovatively developed techniques and procedures to synchronize UAS with both CAS and artillery systems in combat.
- **Joint, Allied, and Coalition Operations.** In two assignments with 1st ANGLICO developed relationships in combat and in training with over 20 Joint, Allied, and Coalition organizations. Acknowledged as the most successful and highly trained fire support and liaison unit in the Marine Expeditionary Force. Successfully integrated Iraqi, Afghan, British, Danish, Canadian, Japanese, Special Operations, U. S. Army, U. S. Navy, and U. S. Air Force units into combat and training operations in CONUS and in the combat theater of operations.
- **Leadership.** Acclaimed leader and expert on all aspects of fire support. Led, mentored, and trained employed hundreds of fire support professionals in two wars. Personally cultivated and supervised over 25 fire support and terminal control teams from the platoon to the division level of employment, including reintroducing ANGLICO personnel to MEU operational deployments.

Professional Experience: *United States Marine Corps*

-**Commanding Officer**, 1st Air Naval Gunfire Liaison Company (Afghanistan 2010)
-**Fire Support Branch Chief/TACP Instructor**, Expeditionary Warfare Training Group
-**Special Operations Command Central Asian States Current Operations Planner** (Afghanistan 2008)
-**Executive Officer, 5th Battalion, 11th Marine Regiment** (155mm Towed Howitzers/HIMARS)
-**Brigade Platoon Commander**, 1st Air Naval Gunfire Liaison Company (Iraq 2005, 2006, 2007)

Education, Honors and Publications:

- EMBA candidate; University of Southern California's Marshall Business School
- Master of Arts in Military Science from American Military University
- Bachelor of Science in Business Administration from the University of Colorado at Denver
- Marine Corps Command and Staff College, Amphibious Warfare School, and Basic School
- The Leftwich Trophy for outstanding leadership; decorations for heroism and meritorious service
- Hogaboom Leadership, Chase Essay, and Geiger Aviation Writing Awards
- Over three dozen works published in a half dozen periodicals and professional journals
- Author of the book On Gunnery

Figure 2: Functional Resume Example

Figure 2 depicts the resume that I used when I was leaving active duty and had an opportunity to pursue a position with an organization that was conducting fire support and aviation integration training and operations. After researching the opportunity and talking to people who were familiar with the company and what they were looking for I highlighted those things that I had done in the past that were relevant to the job position and left out those things that weren't.

Based on my research, I wrote the summary statement to show how my experience was exactly in line with what the company was looking for. The intent is to keep the hiring manager's eyes on the page, and by grabbing his or her attention by showing that I had the skills that they were looking for up front it piques their interest.

The functional experience section is the meat of this format. I chose the six areas that I felt best met the needs of the company and correspondingly included my expertise and experience. Notice that there is no timeline associated with the areas, but instead a series of concrete examples of relevant and specific experience in each.

The next section covers professional experience. Again, there is no strict timeline associated with the bullets but I did include the years that I was deployed overseas to Iraq and Afghanistan. I chose to include those dates specifically because it showed that I had recent combat experience in fire support, which is important because the field is dynamic and the requirements and rules were constantly changing. Notice that only the jobs and deployments that are directly associated with fire support are included, though. My tours and assignments in other areas are irrelevant for this format and would have just resulted in a lot of wasted space and an unneeded second page.

Lastly there is the "Education, Honors, and Publications" section. This bit is where you can cherry-pick those things that you have done to highlight your skills and achievements during your career. In my case I was fortunate to receive some awards that are unusual and have been a published author. You should look through your awards, professional military education graduation certificates, and other certifications or qualifications and include those that will help break you out of the pack and highlight why you are the best candidate for the job. Don't be modest, either. If the Army, Navy, Air Force, Marines, or Coast Guard took the time to give you a medal for something, then you should use the award for more than just another trinket in your shadowbox.

Figure 2a shows my most recent and updated resume (as of 2015) that I keep ready for opportunities that may arise. It includes my post-Marine Corps experience and education (listed after my name). I personally prefer the functional format because it lends itself to more senior positions in which the ability to perform more complex and demanding jobs is more important than a recapitulation of experiences. It is also easy to update for specific opportunities with minor editing:

Michael David Grice, MBA/MA

123.456.7890
email@email.com

Professional Summary:

Diverse and accomplished leader, manager, and entrepreneur with successful P&L business experience. Expertly led and managed organizations of up to one thousand men and women in exceptionally challenging environments; also formed and ran a successful veteran focused nonprofit. Proven in the areas of leadership, business management and profitability, entrepreneurship, and veterans issues.

Key Skills:

- *Leadership.* Acclaimed leader of groups, teams, and large organizations in the government, nonprofit, and business sectors. Decorated for heroism and exceptional leadership in combat and recognized as the #1 Combat Arms leader in the United States Marine Corps with the Leftwich Trophy for outstanding leadership. Acknowledged as the top leader in his University of Southern California MBA Cohort with the Neil Armstrong Leadership Award.
- *Management.* Successfully managed budgets and accounts in excess of $100M; consistently met fiscal targets without exceeding allocated funds or wasting resources. Responsible for procurement, supply chain, maintenance, repair, deployment, and recovery of over 100,000 items ranging from consumables to complex multimillion dollar systems locally and overseas.
- *Entrepreneurship.* Successfully built an innovative and respected nationwide veterans service start-up nonprofit business that over tripled in size in less than 12 months, maintained positive cash flow, and coordinated the efforts of over 100 staff, supporters, and volunteers. Developed a successful program that brings veterans, mentors, and companies together to provide training, mentorship, and job opportunities for transitioning military personnel and veterans.
- *Public Speaking and Engagement.* Invited lecturer, speaker, and panelist for audiences ranging from small groups to over 1,000 in the areas of leadership, mentorship, business management, veterans issues, employment and affirmative action compliance, and military subjects.
- *Scholarship.* Taught as an adjunct professor for the National University School of Business and Management and for the Marine Corps University's Command and Staff College. Author of two books and over 40 articles published in a variety of periodicals, journals, and newspapers.

Professional Experience:

-	**Chief Operating Officer.** MedTech and BioTech Veterans Program (MVPVets)	2013-2015
-	**Founder and President.** The Decisive Leadership Group Consultancy	2012-2015
-	**Adjunct Professor.** National University and Marine Corps University	2008-2012
-	**Senior Analyst.** Power Ten Incorporated	2011-2012
-	**Commanding or Executive Officer/Director.** United States Marine Corps	2000-2011

Education, Honors, and Awards

- University of Southern California – Master of Business Administration
- American Military University – Master of Arts in Military Studies
- University of Colorado at Denver – Bachelor of Science in Business Administration
- Marine Corps Command and Staff College
- Hogaboom Leadership, Chase Essay, and Geiger Aviation Writing Awards
- United States Marine Corps Leftwich Trophy for Outstanding Leadership
- 15 Military Decorations for heroism, leadership, meritorious service, and efficiency
- USC MBA Cohort Neil Armstrong Leadership Award

Figure 2a: Updated functional Resume Example

Resume Style #3: The Combination Format

The most flexible but most difficult type of resume to compose is the combination format. As the name implies the combination format is actually a blend of the functional and chronological styles, which makes it more impactful in many industries. It is the preferred format in situations where you have a very good idea of the job you are seeking and can tailor your resume to show your skills (think functional style) and experience (think chronological).

The difficulty in writing the combination style is that even though you are bringing in the best of both worlds you still need to fit it into two pages or less without doing something cheesy like shrinking the font down to microscopic size or using bigger sheets of paper. Editing is everything, and you need to be as ruthless as possible.

What will greatly help you edit is researching the company and position where you are applying. This will help you refine both your skill set and experience so that you are showing only what is relevant to the job or firm; you don't have room for everything, so you can pick and choose what needs to be presented.

As with all things, there are some advantages and disadvantages to the combination format.

Advantages:

- If you have little experience in the work area that you are seeking you can offset it by showcasing your skill set
- Likewise, if you have a tremendous amount of experience you can use it to offset a limited number of entries on your chronological history
- If you are changing careers, you can emphasize both your skill set and your experience to show why they are relevant for a new career path

Disadvantages:

- If you have been job hopping the chronological section will still show the frequency of change in your employment history, as well as any significant gaps.
- If you have no experience and no skills in the area where you want to work this format will highlight both situations. You

may be hoping to change your life and go in a radically new direction, which is great, but since this resume style is tailored to demonstrate both your skill set and experience that may be problematic if you have neither.

In this format we also introduce a new element: The *Objective Statement*. This is where you, the applicant, clearly articulate the particular job or position that you are looking to fill. Interestingly, if you surf around and read some of the posts and articles about resumes you will see that the objective statement is a controversial subject. Many writers feel that it is unnecessary and wastes space, while others feel that it is an important component of a well written resume.

My take on it is that the objective statement is the best way to focus the reader (the hiring manager or your potential boss) on what it is that you can do for them. It makes their job a little easier. Think of it like the thesis for a term paper: you state your position up front and then support it throughout the rest of the document.

A large number of transitioning military folks seek work in the Civil Service or with a government contractor. The objective statement is particularly useful for those who are seeking those jobs because the requirements to fill those jobs are generally fully disclosed and readily available, which means that you can tailor your resume to fit the stated requirements. Showing the person who has to fill a position that you are the right person is the purpose of the objective statement, and a well written one that is supported throughout the resume has the advantage over someone whose resume is not focused.

Another aspect to the Objective Statement is that it is another opportunity to include key words that will be part of an applicant tracking system search for employers that use heuristic engines to match job posting key words with those listed in an applicant's resume. Make sure to include those key words!

The tight focus on the job you are seeking also allows for more latitude in the use of jargon and acronyms. If you are seeking a job with specific technical skills then the odds are that the reader of the resume will understand your area-specific terminology. Make sure to be judicious and use jargon sparingly unless you know for certain that the reader will understand what you are saying. My example resume contains a fair amount of jargon and acronyms, but in my research I found that using them in this case because the company was very familiar with the military lexicon of fire support. This is what it looks like (in two pages):

Michael David Grice

123.456.7890
mike.grice@email.com
Current TS/SCI Clearance

Objective:

To be a Senior Systems Analyst of command and control systems for the United States Marine Corps.

Career Summary:

Combat proven officer who has led men and women in very diverse environments and in supremely challenging circumstances. As a recognized leader I have been hand selected to command five different organizations including specially and highly trained units with hundreds of Marines and Sailors that conducted humanitarian operations as well as serving in two wars. Established and respected expert in leadership, training, education, fire support, planning, logistics, and command and control systems.

- Recent and Relevant Experience
- Broad Technical Knowledge
- Combat Systems Background

- Operations and Testing Expertise
- Multi-Disciplinary Understanding
- Accomplished Technical Writer

Accomplishments:

Recent and Relevant Experience	• Trained and led a Battalion level unit to combat in Afghanistan including establishing and utilizing applicable and current Command and Control systems • Trained and deployed teams with Navy and Marine Corps amphibious units • Integrated Joint and Coalition forces into Marine Corps Command and Control
Broad Technical Knowledge	• Familiar with C2PC, AFATDS, TBMCS, JADOCS, CPOF, MIMMS-AIS, and numerous other systems currently in use for training and combat operations • Personally employed C2PC, Blue Force Tracker, MiRC, ROVER, and EPLRS • Integrated all ground tactical radio systems including data in combat and training
Combat Systems Background	• Implemented the automation of Marine Corps Field Artillery with the Battery Computer System and Initial Fire Support Automated System • As a Joint Terminal Attack Controller I employed terminal and procedural C2 within the Marine Air Command and Control System in combat and in training • Trained 3d and 7th U. S. Navy Fleets and I and III Marine Expeditionary Forces on operational level fire support systems and functional integration
Operations and Testing Expertise	• Led the evaluation of the XM777 155mm Howitzer as the Test Director during MCOTEA's six week field and shipboard Operational Analysis • Wrote and presented the Test Director's Report, which included over 900 discrepancies requiring resolution prior to commencing the system's Low Rate Initial Production and fielding
Multi-Disciplinary Understanding	• Recognized for meritorious service by the United States Army, United States Air Force, United States Navy, and United States Marine Corps • Served on a component level Joint staff and in Army and Navy service schools • Represented the Marine Corps to the U. S. Air Force-led CAS community
Accomplished Technical Writer	• Completely revised, rewrote, presented, and implemented new and comprehensive artillery Cannon Gunnery Safety procedures • Author or co-author of over a dozen technical and procedural manuals • Published in six professional journals, magazines, and periodicals

Figure 3: Combination Resume Example

Michael David Grice

Professional Experience: *United States Marine Corps*

Commanding Officer, 1st Air Naval Gunfire Liaison Company   2009-2011
- Competitively selected to command and lead a unit of over 250 Marines and Sailors, including active combat operations in Afghanistan and contingency deployments with the U. S. Navy.
- Developed the operational design for Marine Corps integration with the Afghan Army that was adopted and implemented by the Commanding General of Marine Forces in Central Command
- Ensured the welfare of hundreds of people and managed over $45 million in equipment

Expeditionary Fire Support Branch Chief, Expeditionary Warfare Training Group   2008-2009
- Trained Marine and Navy staffs on the integration of fire support systems at the operational level
- Hand selected to represent Navy and Marine Corps positions for executive level briefings

Special Operations Command Central Asian States Current Operations Planner   2008
- Selected to deploy to Kabul, Afghanistan as an expert in security and planning operations
- Supervised the support and reporting requirements for over 150 special operations people from the SOCCENT Joint Operations Center in Doha, Qatar and Kabul, Afghanistan

Executive Officer, 5th Battalion, 11th Marine Regiment   2007-2008
- Supervised the acquisition of over $100 million in equipment and the training of over 600 people on new equipment and procedures as the organization transition from cannons to rocket artillery
- Successfully integrated new command, control, and communications equipment and procedures

Brigade Platoon Commander, 1st Air Naval Gunfire Liaison Company   2005-2007
- Led over 100 highly trained Marines and Sailors during two tough combat deployments to Iraq
- Innovatively developed procedures that integrated sister service attack helicopters into the Marine Air Command and Control System that were adopted as standard by the Army and Marine Corps
- Personally led a team of specially trained Marines on over 120 combat missions in Ramadi, Iraq
- Handpicked to represent the Marine Corps at executive level decision briefs and conferences
- Developed techniques to integrate Unmanned Aerial Systems into air and ground operations

Other Pertinent Experience   1984-2005
- Introduced the first automated technical and command and control system into Marine Artillery
- Test Director for MCOTEA's Operational Analysis of the XM777 LW 155mm Howitzer
- Recognized for exceptional performance as a Logistics and Maintenance Management Officer

Honors:

- Recipient of the Leftwich Trophy for outstanding leadership
- Military decorations for heroism and meritorious service
- Hogaboom Leadership, Chase Essay, and Geiger Aviation Writing Awards

Affiliations:

- Fellow, Marine Corps University's Lejeune Leadership Institute
- Adjunct Faculty and Seminar Leader, Marine Corps Command and Staff College
- United States Army Field Artillery Association

Education:

- Currently pursuing an MBA from the University of Southern California's Marshall Business School
- Master of Arts in Military Science from American Military University
- Bachelor of Science in Business Administration from the University of Colorado at Denver

3 August 2011

Figure 3 (cont'd): Combination Resume Example

As you can see it leads off with the "Objective" statement, which is followed by the "Summary Section". The summary section is a thumbnail sketch that backs up your objective statement and shows why you are the right person for the job. It also introduces the functional areas (as bullets) that showcase your skills that support your objective statement as well as your summary. And, of course, why you are undeniably the best person for the job.

Immediately following the summary section are the more detailed narratives for each of the functional areas that you identified in the Summary section. The title of this section of the resume is "Accomplishments", I and use it to show how my skills in each area make me the most qualified candidate for the position. It is important to remember that each skill *must* relate to the objective and summary; otherwise you are wasting space and confusing the reader. Remember: *Focus, focus, focus* on the job you are applying for! Anything that does not bolster your objective and summary is taking up valuable real estate on your resume that you do not have to spare.

The accomplishments section is the end of the functional component of the resume. The next section is a whittled down version of the chronological format, presented from the newest experience to the oldest.

This is where editing is really important. In a traditional chronological resume you have a couple of pages to work with, but now you are down to half of that space. What I recommend is to only go back in time as many years as are needed to directly support your objective and summary statements. For my resume I chose to go into detail on the jobs that I held for the previous six years because those jobs were directly related to the job I was pursuing. I then wrote a brief paragraph about other previous work experience that again supports the objective and summary statements.

The combination format ends with a recap of "Education", "Affiliations", and "Awards" that highlights those areas. Here is where it is OK to include some things that may not be directly related to the objective and summary. If you have received awards that are unique or show recognition for your great work or leadership, then by all means include them because they will show that you have distinguished yourself. Likewise, if you have completed education or training that shows a depth of experience beyond the scope of your target job that can help as well.

In a nutshell the combination format is the right one for most government and contracting jobs as well as others that are have clearly defined requirements for employment. The best part about this format is that it showcases both your skills and your experience, but to do so effectively requires a lot of research and ruthless editing.

*   *   *   *   *

Lessons Learned:

- ☐ Of the three basic resume types, the Chronological Style is the most common and most widely used.
- ☐ The Chronological format is best for those who have no interruptions in their job history and can show a logical progression in education, skills, and experience over time.
- ☐ The Chronological format is not the best resume for very specific skills or for those with little experience or education.
- ☐ The Functional resume format is best for people changing careers, with gaps in their employment history, or desire to emphasize specific skill sets for a particular job or specialty.
- ☐ Less is more. Shoot for one page. This Functional format is the easiest of the three resume types to get down to one page.
- ☐ The Functional format is the most tightly focused of the three styles. Look hard at your career and pick out those things that are directly related to the job you are seeking or the company where you want to work. Ruthlessly cut the irrelevant!
- ☐ Be selective in the military jargon that you include. For companies that you know will understand the military vernacular it is OK to use it. For example, if you are applying for a job at Bell Helicopter it is appropriate to talk about your zillions of hours and dozens of qualifications you earned while flying one of their attack helicopters, but don't go overboard. Even at Bell Helicopter there are people who likely won't understand everything that you may write about your specific experiences.
- ☐ The Combination Format is the most difficult to write because it contains elements of the other two styles. That does not mean cram two resumes into one; you must include the most important and relevant portions of the Chronological and Functional styles and cut out the rest. Whatever you do, don't play games with font size or margins in order to get more information on the page. Hiring managers like white space and standard margins. If you try to get clever your resume will end up in the trash, and that is no way to get a job.
- ☐ For all three formats remember to only include the things that matter; keep your hobbies personal items off of the resume.

- ☐ Proofread, proofread, and proofread. Then proofread again. Don't have your hard work discounted because of an error.
- ☐ Make it professional, and keep it short and succinct.
- ☐ You may have noticed some faint text in the lower right corner of my resumes. It is the date that the resume was written. I include it as a form of version control; I can tell which resume it is by the date, which keeps me from giving somebody an outdated one. It is in a very faint grey font so that I can see it but most readers will never even notice.

Part 2: Cover Letters

We have just spent about twenty pages on the thrilling subject of resumes. As a part of a job-seeker's correspondence toolkit, resumes are the heavy weapon that a hiring manager looks at to determine whether or not to call you in for an interview. Simply sending in a resume is not a good idea, however. It's not that easy.

Put yourself in the hiring manager's position. She has a pile of resumes on her desk and she has to work through them to find the best candidates for the position. A skilled manager will spend a few seconds on each resume, and in that time if you do not catch her eye your hard work will end up in the shredder.

The resume itself is not particularly eye catching because they all look pretty much the same. Without something to really grab the reader's attention your resume will never see the light of day. Fortunately, we have another bit of correspondence that can help with that: the *Cover Letter*.

Think of the cover letter as your introduction to the company. If you had thirty seconds to tell someone at the company why they should read your resume, what would you say? The cover letter is that thirty seconds, but instead of speaking directly to a person you need to be able to convince them to keep reading with the contents of the letter. If you don't, your resume won't make it into the "call for interview" pile.

A good rule of thumb is to expand on the objective statement from your combination style resume. The objective statement articulates what you, the potential employee, are seeking in terms of employment. It should match as exactly as possible the description of the job that the company is trying to fill, which you should be able to find out through your research on the company.

The second rule of thumb is to show, briefly, why you are the best candidate for the job. Highlight an aspect of your skill set or your experience that will intrigue the reader and get them to turn the page and read your resume. Here is an example of a cover letter that I used in conjunction with a resume which resulted in an interview and a job offer:

123 Anystreet
Anytown, California, 92000
Tel: 123.456.7890
email: name@email.com

Mr. John Smith   23 May 20XX
Big Corporation
987 Big Company Street
Anytown, California, 92000

Sir,

I am submitting my resume for your consideration. I am very interested in pursuing future employment opportunities and am eager to present my bona fides for your review.

I am currently a United States Marine Corps Lieutenant Colonel and will be transitioning from active service in the late summer of 2011. During my career I have served primarily as a gunner and terminal attack controller as my specialty, and have led units from the small team to battalion level command in both training and direct combat. As a staff officer I have served at the Battalion, Regiment, Division, and Sub-Unified Command level, and have served as an instructor and trainer for both officers and enlisted personnel alike.

My experience has been with both conventional and Special Operations Forces. As the commanding officer of 1st Air Naval Gunfire Liaison Company I was fortunate and honored to lead 1st ANGLICO in Helmand Province, Afghanistan, where we worked with Task Force Helmand extensively as well as with over 50 other Joint, Allied, Coalition, and Special Operations Forces units. My previous operational experience includes joint work with Special Operations Command Central, active combat operations in Iraq, and humanitarian assistance operations in East Timor. Additionally, I have a significant amount of experience in fires and fire support from the tactical to the strategic level as well as instructing in formal schools in both the TECOM and TRADOC environments.

As I leave active service I will be pursuing a Masters degree in Business Administration with the University of Southern California's Marshall Business School. I am eager to pursue employment that allows me to complete my education concurrently with interesting and meaningful work. The best way to contact me is via email, and I look forward to hearing from you soon. Thank you for your time and attention.

Yours Sincerely,

Michael Grice

Figure 4: Cover Letter Example

This particular letter was written for a job in the defense industry, where the job required experience in ground operations, fire support, and military training. Those focus areas were contained in the resume, but I highlighted them specifically in order to get the reader's attention – and it worked. Remember, the key is getting the hiring manager to keep reading! You really need to hone in on what the company is looking for and why you are the answer to their needs.

The format for a cover letter is pretty standard in the business world. It is similar to most other forms of correspondence, but to help you put one together here are the elements, from top to bottom:

1. Your address and contact information. Include street address, phone number, and email.

2. Company's Address. Include the hiring manager's name if you can find it.

3. Greeting. If you know it is a man, use "Sir", and if it is a woman, use "Ma'am". If you don't know, feel free to use "Sir or Ma'am", but stay away from anything that could be viewed as informal or unusual. Don't start off with *"Hey there!"* or *"Devil Dog"* because you will not look professional and they won't read past the greeting.

4. The body of the letter. Three or four paragraphs is about the right length, with the first paragraph telling the reader why you are writing them (i.e., "I am very interested in working at Big Corporation"). The second paragraph should emphasize your strengths and skills, and why you are the right person to hire to fill the need at the company. The third paragraph should be a positive reinforcement of the previous paragraphs as well as information on how you will follow up with them, and the fourth paragraph (if you have one) can be used to summarize the letter and politely bring it to a close.

5. Closing. Use something conservative and respectful, as you did with the greeting. "Sincerely" or "Respectfully" are fine, "Cheers" or "Semper Fi" or "Later" are not the best choices. Remember, the only impression the person has of you is what they read. Don't put something at the end of the letter that will make all of your work a waste of time.

6. Signature. Type your name at the bottom of the page with enough space to sign your name above it. I recommend writing your full name and avoiding nicknames or call signs. If you simply must go by "Smasher" you can introduce yourself more informally when you are there for an interview.

So, take a look at your resume and pick out the strengths that meet the requirements of the company that you would like to apply to for a job. Using the format in this chapter, emphasize the things that the company wants, and write as professionally possible. A solid cover letter, when accompanied by a professional and well written resume, is a huge step in the direction of landing an interview.

$$* \quad * \quad * \quad * \quad *$$

Lessons Learned:

☐ The cover letter is the gateway to the hiring manager who will read your resume. It is your first impression with the person or people who will make the decision to hire you, so you had better provide your best possible product. Make sure it is error free, professional, compelling, and well written or they will never turn the page and look at your resume.

☐ Emphasize the specific strengths or skills that the employer is seeking. Pick those from your resume and expand on them for your cover letter. Be certain that whatever you write in your cover letter is in your resume, though, otherwise the reader will wonder why there is a disconnect between the two.

☐ Keep it to one page! Brevity is crucial, and if you write more than one page then you are probably just rehashing your resume. Also, there should be a lot of white space in the cover letter; it should look less dense than the resume it is attached to. Remember, the cover letter is the attention gainer and the resume is the meat of your offering to the company. Don't cram too much in the cover letter.

☐ Tailor the cover letter to the company you are applying to. The resumes may be the same for multiple opportunities, but each cover letter should be individually focused on the company to which you are sending it.

Part 3: The Curriculum Vitae, or CV

We have talked a lot about resumes, but there are jobs out there that resumes are not really appropriate for. These are usually professional positions in areas such as education, medicine, research, or other disciplines where your pedigree is considered more important than a list of where you worked and what you did there.

There is no set format for a CV, but instead it should be tailored to tell the story of why you are the best candidate for a particular opportunity. If you want to go into education, then the CV should focus on your educational background, you experience as an educator or as an instructor/trainer, and the certifications that you may have that support your educational aspirations.

In my case, one of the jobs that I performed after transitioning was to teach at National University's Graduate School of Business and Management. To apply for the position required me to write a CV and not a resume, because the CV is the expected format for applications in education.

So what are the differences between the CV and the various resume formats? The principle difference is that you are not limited to one or two pages, but instead need to use the space necessary to establish your *bona fides* for the position (although a good rule of thumb is five pages or less). In my case, I was applying for an adjunct professorship, so the information I presented started with the experiences and credentials that pertained to training and education up front with the less relevant information either omitted or presented in a more limited way than I would have used in a traditional resume. I broke my experiences down into eight areas:

- Academic Credentials
- Teaching Experience
- Academic Appointments
- Conference Presentations and Invited Lectures
- Publications
- Professional Experience
- Associations and Affiliations
- Awards and Honors

My CV for the adjunct teaching position at National University was four pages long. There was not as much description of the various positions I had held or the jobs that I had done, but instead I presented a comprehensive account of my education, publications, experience, and other items that showed why I was qualified to be a professor. Figure 5 shows the CV that got me the job at the university:

Michael D. Grice MBA/MA
123.456.7890   email@email.com

ACADEMIC CREDENTIALS

Master of Business Administration   2013
    University of Southern California

Master of Arts in Military Science   2003
    American Military University, with Honors

Marine Corps University Professional Military Education
    Marine Corps Command and Staff College   2002
    Amphibious Warfare School, with Honors   1999
    Marine Corps Officer Basic Course, with Honors, Distinguished Leadership Graduate   1993

Bachelor of Science in Business Administration   1992
    University of Colorado at Denver

Associate of Arts in Pre-Business   1990
    Front Range Community College, member of Phi Theta Kappa

TEACHING EXPERIENCE

Adjunct Professor
    National University School of Business and Management   2013
    Marine Corps Command and Staff College (COTS), Marine Corps University   2008 – 2011

Fires Training Branch Chief   2008 – 2009
    Expeditionary Warfare Training Group Pacific, Coronado California

Director, Marine Corps Drill Instructor School   2004 – 2005
    Marine Corps Recruit Depot, San Diego California

Tactics Instructor   1999
    Marine Corps Officer Candidate School, Quantico Virginia

Gunnery Instructor   1996 – 1998
    United States Field Artillery School, Fort Sill Oklahoma

ACADEMIC APPOINTMENTS

Student Director, University of California Leadership Institute Case Study Program
Fellow, Lejeune Leadership Institute, Marine Corps University, Quantico Virginia

Figure 5: Curriculum Vitae (CV)

Michael D. Grice MBA/MA
123.456.7890   email@email.com

CONFERENCE PRESENTATIONS & INVITED LECTURES

Warrior Wives Conference   2013

University of Southern California   2012-2013
  MBA program; guest lecturer

Military, Veteran and Transitioning Military seminars and conferences   2011-2013
  Various (includes over three dozen engagements in numerous venues)

The Boyd and Beyond Conference
  The OODA loop in Fire Support Decisionmaking   2012
  The Boyd Cycle in Counterinsurgency   2010

United States Marine Corps Fire Support Conferences
  The effect of points of intervention on the kinetic decisionmaking cycle   2011
  United States Marine Corps Air Naval Gunfire Liaison Company Operations   2010
  Joint Terminal Attack Controller Training and Operations   2008

The Lejeune Leadership Institute Russell Leadership Conference
  Coaching, counseling, and mentoring   2009

Central Command Fire Support Conferences
  Integration of joint fire support agencies in Al Anbar Province   2006
  Combined Tactical Air Control Party Operations in Ramadi, Iraq   2005

Army Research and Development Command
  Army Research and Development Command Aeroballistics Training Conference   1996

PUBLICATIONS

Books:
Orders to Nowhere. Createspace, 2013
On Gunnery. Booksurge Publishing, 2009

Periodicals, Journals, and Newspapers:

20/20 Vision: Identifying the Signs of Stress. Naval Center COSC *Mindlines.* Winter 2013
Various columns. The North County Times Newspaper, March – October 2012
Leading with PTSD. The Marine Corps Gazette, August 2012
Why I Write. The Marine Corps Gazette, July 2012
What Color are Your Socks? The Marine Corps Gazette, February 2012
The Discussion Continues. The Marine Corps Gazette, January 2012

Figure 5: Curriculum Vitae (CV) (Cont'd)

Michael D. Grice MBA/MA

123.456.7890   email@email.com

For a Bit of Colored Ribbon. The Marine Corps Gazette, October 2011
What Happened to the Marine Corps Planning Process? The Marine Corps Gazette, November 2010
Leading Through Change. The Marine Corps Gazette, January 2010
The Human Terrain in Afghanistan. The Marine Corps Gazette, December 2009
Where is our Kilcullen? The Marine Corps Gazette, December 2009
Air Power's Limits. Armed Forces Journal, September 2009
Force Protection and the Death of Common Sense. The Marine Corps Gazette, August 2009
A Lieutenant and his Platoon's Journey. The Marine Corps Gazette, June 2009
ANGLICO: The Great Enabler. Field Artillery Journal, May-June 2009
In Defense of Kinetics. Armed Forces Journal, March 2009
A Walk Worth the Read. The Marine Corps Gazette, February 2009
Resuscitating the King. The Marine Corps Gazette, October 2008
Distributed Operations. The Marine Corps Gazette, March 2008
The Command Element for the Long War. The Marine Corps Gazette, August 2007
Fear of Flying. The Marine Corps Gazette, June 2007
The End of the Day. The Marine Corps Gazette, May 2007
AH-64 Attack Helicopters. The Marine Corps Gazette, March 2007
A Matter of Trust. The Marine Corps Gazette, October 2006
Marine Corps Joint Terminal Attack Controllers: a View from the Back of the Bus. Marine Corps
Gazette, July 2006
Winning on All Fronts. The Marine Corps Gazette, June 2005
Marriage in the Marine Corps. The Marine Corps Gazette, November 2004
An Observation on Leadership from the Peanut Gallery. The Marine Corps Gazette, September 2003
Lies, Damned Lies, and Fitness Report Statistics. The Marine Corps Gazette, May 2003
Train Like We Fight? The Marine Corps Gazette, April 2001
Surface to Surface Fire Support, May it Rest in Peace. The Marine Corps Gazette, July 1999
Arsenal of Freedom: The Springfield Armory 1890-1948. The Gun Report, 2004
The Development of Indirect Fire Techniques for Machine Guns. The Gun Report, 2004
Field Artillery – Rain of Freedom. The Field Artillery Journal, 2003
Updated Artillery Safety Computational Procedures. Eagle, Globe, and Blockhouse, Spring 1998

PROFESSIONAL EXPERIENCE

The Decisive Leadership Group   2012 – Present
    Founder and President

United States Marine   1984 – 2012
    Enlisted rank from Private to Staff Sergeant (1984 – 1992 Reserve),
    Officer Rank from Second Lieutenant to Lieutenant Colonel (1992 – 2012 Active Duty)
    Deployed to Japan, the South Pacific, East Timor, Kuwait, Qatar, Bahrain, Iraq, and Afghanistan

North County Times Newspaper   2012
    Military Columnist

Figure 5: Curriculum Vitae (CV) (Cont'd)

Michael D. Grice MBA/MA
123.456.7890   email@email.com

Power Ten, Inc.   2011 – 2012
    Senior Analyst and Writer

ASSOCIATIONS AND AFFILIATIONS

Boy Scouts of America
Marine Executive Association
Marine Corps Association
MCRD Museum Historical Society
Unites States Army Field Artillery Association

AWARDS AND HONORS

The Neil Armstrong Leadership Award, USC MBA Class	2013
The Chase Boldness and Daring Essay Award, Marine Corps Association˙	2011
The Hogaboom Leadership Writing Award, Marine Corps Association	2011
The Geiger Aviation Essay Award, Marine Corps Heritage Foundation	2008
The Hogaboom Leadership Writing Award, Marine Corps Association	2003
The Leftwich Trophy for Outstanding Leadership, United States Marine Corps,	2001
Distinguished Leadership Award, Officer Basic Course, Quantico Virginia	1993

Military Decorations: Bronze Star Medal x2, Meritorious Service Medal x2, Joint Service Commendation Medal, Navy and Marine Corps Commendation Medal with Valor device (for heroism in combat) x2, Army Commendation Medal x2, Navy and Marine Corps Achievement Medal x3, Army Achievement Medal x2, Air Force Achievement Medal, Combat Action Ribbon

Other Awards: The U.S. Field Artillery Association's Order of Saint Barbara and the Ancient Order of Saint Barbara, the U. S. Cavalry Association's Order of the Gold Spur for Combat

Figure 5: Curriculum Vitae (CV) (Cont'd)

As you can see, the order of information is very different from a resume.   There is no objective statement or professional summary (although you can use one if you would like), and it is more of a list of credentials, appointments, job history, and presentation of my body of written work.   Like a resume, the CV presents your story to a potential employer.   Unlike a resume, however, the CV tells more than your story – it shows why you are a professional that is qualified and capable of performing within a profession, not just doing a job.

*　　*　　*　　*　　*

<u>Lessons Learned:</u>

☐ A Curriculum Vitae, or CV, is a type of resume that is used within certain professions. Examples include educators, litigators, medical providers, psychologists, etc.

☐ If you are pursuing a job that requires a CV (for example, teaching as a professor) then make sure that it reflects your body of work and not just a list of jobs you have held. It is critically important to present the credentials necessary for a particular job.

☐ The format varies depending on the job you are pursuing. For example, if you are looking to teach, then your relevant training and educational experience should lead.

☐ Keep it to five pages or less.

Chapter 21: Getting a job, part 3: Interviewing

Interviewing for a job in the civilian world is very different than applying for a job in the military. When you signed up with your recruiter he was eager to bring you on board. He had a quota to meet, and you were an eager young man or woman who made his life easier by signing on the dotted line. He did everything he could to convince you that putting on a uniform and serving your country was the best possible thing that you could ever do, and as a result of his hard work you signed up, shipped off to bootcamp or Officer Candidate School, and served your country.

That is exactly what finding a job in the civilian world is *not* like. In fact, it is quite the opposite. In the corporate sector you are the one who has to get out there and find a place to work. You have to go through the nutroll of networking with people who can help you in your job hunt, researching a company, writing a resume, and going through the interview process. While there are professional headhunting and recruiting firms that can help you find a job, you need to remember that they are in the business of linking you, the candidate, up with a company that needs someone like you. They don't hire you; their clients do. You still have to do the hard work of writing a resume and interviewing.

We have already explored the wonderful world of resumes, and now it is time to dive into the job interview process. You've written a dynamite resume and married it with the perfect cover letter, and soon after sending it off to the company where you want to work the telephone rings. The firm would like to invite you to an interview!

It is a thrilling feeling when the phone rings and the hiring manager is on the other end of the line – kind of like having someone you like say "yes" when you ask them out on the first date. It is also slightly terrifying – also kind of like having someone you like say "yes" when you ask them out on the first date. Seemingly thousands of thoughts race through your head: What to wear? When should I arrive? What does the company expect from me? What will the interview be like?

It can be overwhelming, but in the following pages we will take deeper look at the various types of interviews that companies employ to find the right employees. Some are very traditional, such as meeting the hiring manager in his or her office, and some are very eclectic, with the interview including such hoops to jump through as impromptu essay writing, math quizzes, and team building exercises.

The long and the short of it is that all of the work that you have done to this point – researching the company, writing a resume, crafting a cover letter, and sending it in – is wasted unless you can close the deal in the actual interview.

Before we get into the actual interviews and how best to prepare for them, we first need to go over some basics.

Remember always that the purpose of the interview is for *the company to fill a need in their organization.* It is *never* about what a great person you are. If you fit the needs of the company then you might be hired. That's right, you are *only likely* to be hired.

Why is that? Why only likely?

I'm glad you asked. Your skills and talents are what got you the interview in the first place. In the eyes of the company, they are bringing you in and expending resources, such as the time of the hiring manager and any travel expenses that may be incurred, because you look good enough paper to be worthy of a closer look. Your resume opened the door, but it is up to you to go through it and secure a job offer.

Simply put, the interview is more about how you will fit in with the company's culture and the way things are done there than your skills. They want to see how you articulate yourself, how you dress, what your manners and mannerisms are like. They want to see if you trim your fingernails or pick your nose or scratch yourself in awkward places, or if you project the image that the company wants. That is what the interview is really all about.

So in this chapter we will look at how to prepare for specific types of interviews. Before that, though, let's look at things that pertain to all interviews.

First off is personal hygiene. Ask someone of the opposite sex that you know and respect how you look. Don't ask your mom or dad (because they still think of you as a kid in the third grade) but instead someone who will give you an objective opinion. Ask them to look at you in terms of a hiring manager. How does your hair look? If it is a super-motivated flat-top then you may want to consider growing it out a little bit. Your posture? If you slouch in your chair it will project an image of slovenliness. How do you speak? If every third word is the "F"-bomb or you use acronyms in every sentence then you need to change your vocabulary. Do you have any mannerisms that you are not consciously aware of? Things like drumming your fingers, wiggling your toes, or biting your fingernails? If so, recognize that you do and make a conscious effort to stop.

Make sure not to take anything that your friend says personally because they are really trying to help you out, and besides you asked them to do it! An unintended benefit is that you may actually pick up on some things that will improve your appearance and help you find a date for next Saturday night, but that is an entirely different subject.

Look at how you dress. As a transitioning military person you likely have a closet full of uniforms. You also probably have a single navy blue blazer and a rumpled pair of khaki trousers. That was fine for your time in the military, but it is completely underwhelming in the corporate sector. Time to do some shopping.

As we discussed earlier, I personally like shopping at *Nordstrom* or *Joseph A. Bank.* They both carry a quality line of professional clothing, and more importantly the staff members in those stores are there to help you build a complete, updated, and professional wardrobe. This is a bit more challenging than you may realize, but years and years of wearing exactly the same thing to work has a tendency to dull your fashion sense. Nobody wants to hire an employee who wears a suit fresh from two or three decades ago, and just as importantly the sweet threads you wear to a nightclub are definitely not going to make a good impression at your interview.

Talk to the salespeople. They will show you the current trends in professional attire as well as instruct you on how to coordinate your wardrobe. Believe it or not, there are color choices outside the green, brown, and khaki palette, and if you choose poorly you will end up looking either comical or color blind. Swallow your pride and listen to the experts. You will be better looking for it!

*　　*　　*　　*　　*

Lessons Learned:

- There is a lot more to interviewing than just showing up at the hiring manager's office. Before you show up, you need prepare, and a significant part of preparation centers on how you will come across in the interview.
- Have a trusted friend give you an honest evaluation of your appearance, habits, and hygiene. Then work on your deficiencies and shortfalls.
- Get a new set of clothes that is consistent with the company that you are interviewing with. Talk to the pros at a place like Joseph A. Bank or Nordstrom, and listen to what they say. You will look a lot more professional, and that will go a long way in

presenting a solid impression at your interview. They also have some wickedly good sales on suits and whatnot, so take advantage of them when you can.

Interviews, part 1: Oh, the places you'll go...

As you depart the military and hang up your uniform you are going to be placed in a new and unusual position. Throughout your time in the military your career path was largely determined by someone who worked in the manpower section or branch of your service headquarters. This individual was charged with filling open positions with qualified individuals who had the right rank, skills, and experience level. After reviewing the population of "movers" (those folks who had been in one place for three years or so) and comparing it to the list of openings (holes in the spreadsheet created as "movers" leave), the assignments specialist would pick someone and issue them a set of orders to their new job.

Sure, there was a lot of politics involved, particularly for jobs requiring higher rank and expertise. Sure, there was favoritism as bosses influenced the process to get "their people" into their units. Sure, some jobs required interviews of candidates such as serving as an *aide-de-camp* for a general or admiral. What there was not, however, was a free and open competition for jobs. The assignments branch made the decisions, and even if you did not like the assignment you were still in the military and the paychecks continued show up twice a month. If you don't get the job you want in the civilian world, you are unemployed.

Big difference, that.

As a transitioning service member you no longer have somebody in a distant headquarters telling you where to go or what to do when you get there. Now it is up to you to do that for yourself. We have already looked at the decisions needed to end up where you want to live as well as what industry or job you would like to pursue, so now we are going to drill down into how to actually get that job.

The last step in the job-seeking process is to go through the interviewing process with the company in hopes of securing an offer of employment. That is what we will be talking about in the rest of this chapter.

Interviews come in many forms and styles depending on the type of employment you are seeking. There are traditional types of interviews in which you show up at the firm at the appointed time, go into the hiring manager's office, and sit across the desk from the person who will determine your fate with the company.

In the modern age, however, you may not actually have to go to the office. You may have a telephone interview or videoconference in cases where the company is too far away for a face-to-face without incurring a lot of travel costs.

You may be interviewed over lunch. Or dinner. Or maybe even breakfast, so that the interviewer can learn about your manners and mannerisms while asking you questions. Maybe at a bar to see if you get loaded in the afternoon.

More senior positions often require much more in-depth interviews. Perhaps you will be interrogated by a panel of Vice Presidents, or maybe spend an entire day at the firm in order to meet a variety of people. Perhaps you will be flown into the company's headquarters, where you will be evaluated by everyone from the bus driver who picks you up at the airport to the people that you meet in the elevator on the way up to the interviewer's office.

For job opportunities that require certain technical skills there may be a test of some sort, and for other disciplines (such as management consulting) there may be a case example for you to study and provide your best solution to. The more exacting and specific the job requirements are the more likely that you will need to demonstrate your proficiency during the interview process in order to secure a job.

You may go through a series of interviews of different types. For example, you may have a phone interview that leads to a Skype meeting with the hiring manager which results in a plane flight to the company headquarters where you are grilled by a panel of executives to see if you are someone they want in the company.

It can be quite bewildering! How can you be sure you are ready to do your best? You have already done the prerequisites by submitting a quality resume and cover letter that opened the door to the interview, updated your wardrobe, and refining your manners and hygiene. What's next?

Quite simply, you need to do your due diligence and conduct some serious research on the company.

Get on the internet and search for sites or blogs that discuss the steps others took while interviewing for a particular firm. Use search terms like "interview preparation for company X" or "interview tips for firm Y". Read through them to determine trends. Make sure to focus on the level of employment you are seeking. Don't prepare for a mailroom interview if you are looking to be an executive, or vice versa. Spend an afternoon surfing the net and taking notes.

Also ask around. Use your network of friends and family to see if anyone has interviewed at the company or knows someone who has. Pick their brain to see what they learned.

You can also perform some interviews of your own by seeking out people at the company or industry and simply asking them. It takes a little *chutzpah* on your part, but it may pay off in the long run. It can be a win-win for you if it is done properly, or a guarantee that you won't be hired if you do it wrong. An informational interview is one in which you ask someone about the company in order to learn more about it, and the hiring process is certainly germane to the discussion. Just calling out of the blue to ask about getting hired, though, is a non-starter!

*   *   *   *   *

Lessons Learned:
- ☐ Interviews are different depending on the company, position, and level of responsibility. They are not all the same.
- ☐ Research what type of interview is normal for the job you are seeking. Use the internet, your personal network, and the informational interview to learn more about the company and their interview process.
- ☐ Prepare, prepare, prepare! Depending on the type of interview you will need to polish different skills. If it is a lunchtime interview, do yourself a favor and review your table manners. If it is a traditional interview, make sure to take your suit to the cleaners the week before.

Interview, part 2: The "traditional" job interview

So the big day has arrived: your job interview! It is pretty exciting, scary, daunting, and exhilarating all at once. The time you spent networking, writing a resume, crafting a cover letter, and getting it in front of human resources at a company where you would like to work has paid off. You have a date with hiring manager.

Just like all dates, though, there is a lot at stake. Instead of just a peck on the cheek after a movie, however, you are looking for another date in the form of follow on interview or maybe a long term relationship in terms of a job. Also, just like hoping for a peck on the cheek, you must make sure that you do everything right because if you don't you will find yourself back on square one with nothing to show for your efforts.

In order to make the best impression it is important to show up for the interview as prepared as possible, including everything from how you present yourself to how you speak to how well you think on your feet. To make it a little easier, we've broken down the traditional interview into four segments: research, preparation for the interview, the interview itself, and following up.

First off is continuing your research. You have already submitted your resume and it has resulted in a call for an interview. Good job! Now you need to refine your research into how to successfully complete the interview. You can search the net for general interviewing tips, but you will be better served to go to a site that provides real insight into company-specific interviews. My own favorite is glassdoor.com because interviewees post their interview experiences, including the types of interviews, questions, and how things went. It is well worth a few minutes of surfing to see what you are up against.

You should also ask around. Use your network to see if there is anyone who has interviewed with the company you are looking to join or who has interviewed at a similar company or for a similar job. They can provide a lot of insight into the process, particularly if their interview landed them a job.

Next you need to prepare, prepare, prepare and then prepare some more. You will learn some valuable information about the interview process through your research, but now you have to *use it!* What kind of questions do they ask? How do they ask them? You must prepare for questions ahead of time, even if you do not know what the specific questions will be. Nothing ensures a life of continued unemployment like giving the stunned mullet look to the interviewer because you didn't bother to prepare and don't know what to say.

Practice answering questions. The questions can come from your research or from items on your resume. After all, the company called you in because they found your resume compelling. You should review your resume and think about what an interviewer may hone in on, and then be sure to thoroughly prepare for questions along those lines. Transitioning military folks always have "leadership" in their resume, so you had best be ready to talk about it. Whom did you lead? What techniques or skills did you employ to get people to do what needed to be done? How will your leadership experiences apply in the company where you are interviewing?

Ask a friend or family member to go through a mock interview with you. Give them your resume and a printout of your research findings, and ask if they will be gracious enough to spend some time helping you practice. The best possible rehearsal for an interview is to have someone actually sit down with you and ask questions, followed by some candid feedback. If that is not possible an alternative is to practice in front of a mirror.

If you have the time, I would recommend that you do a full blown dress rehearsal that includes wearing your interviewing clothes and sitting on opposite sides of a desk. Rehearse the whole process, from arriving at the company to saying goodbye and leaving the building. If you practice once or twice it will reduce your anxiety and you will be more focused during the interview. Remember, the interviewer is taking everything in from your appearance to your habits to your level of anxiety, and if you are too uptight or nervous it will not bode well.

Now you are ready for your interview. Before you go, however, there are some basic things that you should do to ensure that you make an impactful first impression. That is incredibly important as an interviewee! If you make a poor first impression you likely won't have an opportunity to make another attempt.

In the military, you prepared for inspections in a disciplined and results-oriented manner. When you had a uniform inspection coming up you spent a lot of time making sure that your uniform was correct. You carefully measured where the ribbons and badges would be placed, cut off any spare threads (*Irish Pennants* for you old-schoolers), and pressed the creases in your shirt and trousers so sharply that you could shave with them. Shoes were shined and the edges of the soles were dressed to remove any scuffs. You got a haircut the day before the inspection to make sure that it was within the required standards, and then you ever so carefully got dressed and presented yourself to the inspector.

You should approach your job interview with just as much attention to detail. Get a haircut the day before. Critically look at your clothes. They should be either fresh from the cleaners or at least have all of the wrinkles pressed out. Your shirt or blouse should fit and your necktie, jewelry, or other fashion accessories should be professional looking, clean, and conservative. Shine your shoes! Even though society has largely moved away from shoe shining as a daily task, I know of one executive who was promoted over three more qualified peers because he took the time to shine his shoes (and the boss took notice). It shows dedication to your appearance and discipline to do the little things, both of which are a big plus in any line of work.

Leave for your interview early. Make sure that you allot enough time to show up at least ten to fifteen minutes before it is scheduled to begin. I recommend going at least an hour early and stopping by a coffee shop near the company's office. That way you will have plenty of time to spare in case of traffic snarls and to take care of things you may have forgotten. When you get to the coffee shop you can review your notes, have something to drink, and get your mind right for the interview. (Remember to have a mint after drinking your coffee to keep your breath fresh!)

After you finish collecting your thoughts at the coffee shop it is time to head across the street to the hiring manager's office. The first thing that you need to remember is that the evaluation begins at the moment your hand touches the company's doorknob, not when you meet the hiring manager. Maybe even before then, depending on the circumstances of your interview. Here is a real example of how one company evaluates its candidates:

The firm pays to fly candidates out to their headquarters for personal interviews. It is a thoughtful company that sends a van with a driver to meet the candidate at the airport and bring her right up to the company's front door. The driver brings the candidate in and directs her to a receptionist, who in turn points her to the floor and room where the interview will be conducted. After a quick trip up the elevator, the candidate meets another receptionist who confirms that she is in the right place and then notifies the hiring manager that the candidate has arrived for the interview. After a few minutes (and right on time) the hiring manger steps out and meets the interviewee.

If you are not paying attention, you would offhandedly think that your interview started when the interviewee shook the hiring manager's hand. If that is what you think then you would be wrong. Dead wrong. A part of the company's hiring process is to see what kind of person you are, including how you interact with "unimportant" people like van drivers and receptionists. The hiring manager will certainly go through the interview process with you, but your performance across the desk from the interviewer is only part of the hiring procedure.

The van driver and the receptionists are brought into the process. The interviewer will ask them what kind of person you are. Are you rude to people you consider beneath your level? Were you polite? Did you shake hands? Were you talking on your mobile phone in the van, and if so, was anything you said indicative of a reason not to hire you? Did you treat the receptionist professionally? Were you nice or dismissive? Would they want *you* to be somebody that they would work with?

This company is not only assessing employment candidates on their skills and experience. Corporate culture and a person's manners are important. Remember that! This is particularly important for senior military officers and enlisted folks who are transitioning. As a colonel or a sergeant major you are in a position of elevated prestige and responsibility that can lead you to forget that those at the bottom of the ladder are people too. This is not an indictment of senior military folks (after all, I used to be one) but it is the way the martial game is played. As a senior leader it is easy to focus on your peers and immediate seniors and juniors because that is how you do your job and accomplish your mission. Senior leaders are often so focused that they don't really see the people far below them because they are so intent on the things that are going on at *their* rarified level.

If you treat people at the company like junior subordinates on your way to the job interview it won't go well. That way of thinking is archaic in the corporate sector, and you had best be conscious of it or it will severely limit your ability to find a job. In the civilian world there is no rank, and if you give off the impression that you are still wearing yours it will certainly be held against you.

Anyhow, back to the interviewing process. You first walk through the door and meet the receptionist. Be professional, polite, and shake his or her hand. This is your chance to make a positive first impression. You don't need to be artificial or insincere, but just be polite. A genuine smile goes a long way, too.

From there you are off to meet the hiring manager. This is where you get a chance to make a *second* first impression, but this time with the hiring manager instead of the receptionist. Go in, take the seat that they offer, and get ready to prove why you are the right guy or gal for the job.

Here are a few pointers for those first critical moments of the job interview:

1. Have a firm, but not crushing, handshake.

2. Look the interviewer in the eye, and thank them immediately for the opportunity to meet with him or her. *Practice this!!* In your rehearsal make sure to go over what you are going to say when you meet the interviewer so that you don't get tongue tied. Something as simple as: "Hi. I'm Mike, and I want to thank you for the opportunity to meet with you today."

3. Don't come in carrying a bunch of stuff, and *turn your mobile phone completely off!* You should have your right hand free to shake the interviewer's hand, and your left hand should be carrying either a briefcase (which is overkill unless you were asked to bring something along that requires a briefcase) or a nice looking notebook (not a high school spiral notebook or pad of sticky notes, but a folio or pad and paper set that is professional, conservative, and not tattered). Make sure to have a nice pen, too. Something that looks professional and does not have "US GOVERNMENT PROPERTY" stamped on the side.

4. Focus your attention on the interviewer. Don't look around the office like a visitor in a museum. You are there to get a job, not admire the books on the shelf.

5. Sit down on the front half of the chair, fold your hands into your lap, and smile. Don't kick back, cross your legs, and drape your arms over the chair. As the interview unfolds you can relax a bit, but if your mannerisms indicate you are a slacker then it does not matter how well you dress because you will then be regarded as a well-dressed and unhired slacker.

So now the first few moments are over. The interviewer is evaluating you on everything you do and say, so keep that in mind. Don't bite your fingernails, pick your nose, or check your phone. Sit upright, look at the interviewer, and answer his or her questions.

Think of the interview questions as opportunities for you to show why you are qualified and how well you can express yourself, but don't turn an answer into a monologue by rambling on for five or ten minutes. In your rehearsal you should focus on answering each question in a period of thirty seconds to two minutes. Any longer than that and you will likely start to bore the interviewer. Besides, you probably can't say anything in ten minutes that you can't succinctly articulate in two.

Don't try to answer them exactly as you did in your rehearsal, but instead listen closely to the question, take a breath, and then answer it as straightforwardly and honestly as you can. You don't want your answers to sound canned or rehearsed. They should be conversational. Also, leave your military jargon and barracks language at home! Nobody, and I mean nobody, in the corporate sector is impressed by the liberal use of the "F"-bomb in an interview.

An interview is not an interrogation, so it is ok for you to ask a few questions as well. You just make sure that they aren't stupid (like "how much will I make?" or "what happens when I call in sick?") because, unlike elementary school, there *are* stupid questions. Don't be a knucklehead and ask one!

Make sure to answer the questions that the interviewer asks. Don't try to steer the conversation in a different direction, but instead provide the answers that interviewer is looking for. No BS, either. If you don't know an answer or are unsure of what the interviewer is actually asking, be honest and say you don't know or that you need the question to be rephrased. The hiring manager has interviewed countless people before you, and your probability of fooling them with a BS response is about zero. Plus it will show that you are not the type of person that they want to hire because you are either dishonest or incompetent.

During the interview you may be asked if you would like something to drink. Always ask for water. That way you won't have any hot coffee to spill on yourself or carbonation from a soda making you want to burp at exactly the wrong moment.

Be prepared for signals that the interview is wrapping up. The interviewer may be up front and say that your time is up, or may begin saying things like "Do you have any last questions?" When the interview is over, it is over. Don't try to push the issue with stupid questions like "what are my chances to be hired?" or "how soon will you let me know your decision?" as they put the interviewer on the spot. He or she will let you know how you will be contacted. Let him or her take the lead with that information. Don't be needy and try to wheedle it out of them ahead of time. It will make you look bad.

When it is time to go, stand up, pick up your notebook, and shake the interviewer's hand. Thank them again for the opportunity to meet with them, and follow their lead from there. They may escort you to the reception desk or all the way to the exit. Feel free to make some small talk on the way out, but do not forget that the interview is not over until you are sitting in your car! Many jobs have been lost because the interviewee blows it on the way out of the building by doing something stupid (like being rude to a receptionist, throwing the "F"-bomb around, or picking their nose in the hallway).

The last step in the interview is to write and send a thank you note to the interviewer. No kidding. An old fashioned thank you note, just like the ones you used to send to Santa Claus when you were a kid. This will show your sincerity as well as cement your desire to work at the company. Many hiring managers will not hire a person who neglects to follow up with a note. It is an expectation and an essential element of business correspondence. If you don't have any thank you notes at home, stop by a stationery store and pick some up. Or even better, have personalized notecards made. It is a nice touch.

*   *   *   *   *

Lessons Learned:

- ☐ The interview is the result of all of your hard work up to that point, so don't wreck it with a poor performance. Follow these four steps: Research, Prepare, Attend the interview, and Follow up.
- ☐ Treat the interview like an inspection: get the little things right and the big things will take care of themselves. Look at your clothing as you would your uniform and square it away as you would for your commanding officer.
- ☐ Shine your shoes!!!
- ☐ Rehearse with a friend ahead of time by using questions garnered through your research and from your resume. Be ready to answer questions by practicing ahead of time.
- ☐ Head to the interview early, and use the extra time before you go through the company's front door to prepare, reduce your anxiety, and make sure you are ready.
- ☐ The interview is your opportunity to present yourself in the best light possible: dress well, be well groomed, be polite, and use professional language. Not doing any one of the above will likely result in you not getting a job.
- ☐ Be respectful and polite to every person you meet. You should assume that they are part of the hiring team at the company, and if you are rude to the receptionist the word will get out.

- ☐ The first moments of an interview are critical, so don't blow a shot at making a great first impression. Be on time, well dressed, polite, and turn off your phone!
- ☐ Answer the questions you are asked. Don't try to BS the interviewer. Also, answer in a period of thirty seconds to two minutes. No monologues.
- ☐ If a drink is offered, make it water. Coffee, tea, or soda may be tastier, but you are not there to get refreshments. You are there to get a job and the possibility of disaster through a spilled cup of coffee or an errant soda-caused burp is not worth it.

Interviews, part 3: Not so traditional job interviews: The Phone (or Skype) Interview

So you have sent in your resume and heard back from the hiring manager.

That's great!

She would like to interview you as soon as possible.

That's even better!

Over the phone.

Um, ok, you think. That sounds good. Interviewing over the phone should be easy.

Au contraire, my friend. Job interviews over the phone are not simple and you can certainly screw them up. They are not easy to get right and take just as much preparation as a face to face meeting, at least they should if you want to succeed and get the job.

There are countless reasons why a company may want to interview an applicant over the phone, or perhaps even over Skype or another video or audio interface system. The company may be on the other side of the country or even the other side of the planet, and a phone call is infinitely cheaper than a plane ticket and a hotel room. The hiring manager may be travelling. You may be travelling. A common reason may be that the company's hiring process begins with a phone interview to determine whether or not you are worth bringing to the office for a second look.

Regardless of the reason, a phone or Skype interview is still a job interview and just because you are not going to the company headquarters is no reason not to adequately prepare. You should do your research, review your resume, and rehearse with someone using a phone or Skype. After all, you want the job, don't you?

The heart of the interview is the interaction between you and the hiring manager of the firm. Having a telephone or laptop screen between you and the person on the other side changes the venue, but the content is pretty much the same.

The telephone interview

What a phone interview is not, however, is easier. Here are a few reasons why:

First off, you don't get the sense of the company or the interviewer that you would normally pick up by walking through the lobby, meeting a few people, and shaking hands with the hiring manager. Instead, you are going from zero to sixty in the few milliseconds between "Hello?" and "Let's get started."

Secondly, it can seem deceptively informal and easy. So easy, in fact, that you may not take preparation as seriously as you would for a "real" interview. It is over the phone, so why not do it in your pajamas? Or over Skype, so all you need to do is put on a nice shirt and maybe a tie, right? Again, *au contraire*.

The worst things that you can do in any interview situation are to be unprepared or fail to take it seriously. Sure, you can do the interview in your underwear if you want and the hiring manager will never know. Sure, you can watch Sports Center with the sound turned down and the hiring manager will never know. *You* will know, however, and it will affect the interview. And not in a good way. You need to get your mind right, steer clear of distractions, and *focus*.

Here are some recommendations that will help you have a successful phone or Skype interview:

First and most importantly you must prepare for the interview in exactly the same manner as you would for a traditional interview. If you are a man, get a haircut (they can still see you on Skype, after all, and getting a haircut is never a bad thing), and if you are a woman make sure to apply your makeup. Wear your interview suit and tie or blouse and slacks, research the company, and review your resume. Be ready fifteen minutes before it starts, and clear your mind in order to focus on the interviewer and the questions that you will be asked.

Prepare a location for the interview. The interviewer is likely in their office, but you can be pretty much anywhere that you have good reception on your cell phone. That said, driving down the freeway or sitting at your child's soccer game are remarkably bad ideas for obvious and noisy reasons. The hiring manager is devoting their time exclusively to you in order to determine if you would fit in their company, so the least you can do is reciprocate.

In my case, I was once interviewed by company president for a position with his firm over the phone. The timing was such that the only time we could talk was while I was driving down the interstate. It was very difficult to focus and concentrate on the call while driving at 70 miles an hour, and there was no way that I could refer to my resume or notes. I also could not write down any notes either, as my hands were on the wheel. The reception cut in and out a few times as I drove, and all things considered it was a poor interview. Even though he was gracious about it, I was embarrassed by the experience and swore to myself never to do it again.

Instead of your car you should find a place that is quiet, has good lighting, and is as office-like as possible. Sit at the kitchen table instead the couch, for example. We are all creatures of habit, and if you are sprawled out on a barcalounger instead of sitting at a desk you may well act or sound as though you are sprawled out on a barcalounger instead of sitting a desk.

Use your land telephone line if at all possible, too. You don't want to drop the call or endure a poor connection because that will reflect negatively. Have a copy of your resume laid out in front of you, take a deep breath, and call the hiring manager exactly on time. Not early. Not late. On time. Clear everything away except a copy of your resume, a notepad, and a bottle or glass of water. No distractions!

Skype (or other real-time video interviews)

For a Skype interview you need to go a step or two farther. What does the background look like? It should be bland or uninteresting, if possible. Is the light coming from behind you? From the front? From the side? Remember, the interviewer is going to see you and your surroundings, and if the light makes you look like Bela Legosi in a 1940s vampire movie it won't help. Your Twisted Sister poster collection is probably not the best background, either.

Back to the interview. Make sure that the quiet place you have found stays quiet: turn off your mobile phone, the dishwasher, television, radio, and everything else that makes noise. Put a post-it note over your doorbell advising visitors not to ring and to come back later.

Close all apps and programs that are running on your computer before you begin the virtual interview. You don't want to be distracted by any emails or instant messages that may pop up on the screen because the interviewer will instantly recognize that you are ignoring them and paying attention to something else. That is a guaranteed job-offer killer.

Start off by introducing yourself and follow interviewer's lead from there. Once the introductions are complete, ask the person on the other side of the Skype feed if they can see and hear you well enough and make adjustments that may be needed. From that point on the interview is similar to the traditional interpersonal style. Except that, like a phone interview, it is difficult to effectively gauge the interviewer's mood, expressions, or mannerisms. Skype offers a little better insight because you can see the interviewer's face, but that's about it.

Remember to keep your answers short (in the thirty second to two minute range) and to speak slowly. Being interviewed is anxious business, and you may unintentionally speak faster than normal. That can result in the interviewer not understanding what you are saying. To help with this, try taking a breath after hearing each question, restate the question to yourself in your mind, and then start talking. It will make you appear thoughtful (which is good) and articulate (which is also good). Keep in mind that the hiring manager has done countless interviews, and you want to make a solid impression by not sounding like a knucklehead.

Remember that you are on camera during the interview. Sit up straight, look at the interviewer on the computer screen when he or she is talking and look into the camera when you are answering. Also, be conscious of what you are doing with your hands. A famous actor once said that one of the hardest things about acting is knowing what to do with your hands, and that applies to interviews as well. Put them in your lap or sit on them if you need to, because if you fidget or pick at your nails all the interviewer will see on the screen is you fidgeting or picking your nails. You don't want to distract the interviewer.

As it draws to a close make sure to thank the interviewer for his or her time and make sure that you finish the interview professionally. We are all prisoners of our past experiences, and if you habitually say goodbye by saying pithy things like *"Later!"* or *"Out here..."* then the last impression the hiring manager will have of you is not particularly professional. A simple *"Thank you for your time today. Goodbye!"* will go a long way.

As with all interviews make sure to follow up with a thank you note. It is fine to send an email immediately, but go that extra classy mile and send a note in the mail too. It is important, expected, and if you don't you will be viewed as less desirable than those who do send in thank you notes.

*   *   *   *   *

Lessons Learned.

☐ A phone or Skype interview is just as important as a traditional interview. It is imperative that you treat it as such. Make sure to thoroughly prepare, get dressed in your interviewing clothes, and be on time.

☐ Tips for preparing the interview setting: sit at a desk or table, sit up straight, use your land line, have some water and your resume at hand, and for a Skype interview be sure to check out your background and how the lighting affects your on-screen appearance.

☐ Take a breath, restate the question, and then provide answers in the thirty second to two minute range. Try not to talk too fast!

☐ Make sure that there are no distractions, and turn off apps, televisions, mobile phones, or anything else that could interrupt your interview.

Interviews, part 4: Not so traditional job interviews: Lunch, Dinner, and Cocktails

There are many kinds of interviews, and we have covered several of them thus far. Next we are going to take a trip to your hiring manager's favorite restaurant or bar and learn about just how similar interviewing for a job is with a drink or a cheeseburger in your hand is to a traditional interview.

Just how similar is it, you ask?

It is a little similar. And it is completely, totally, and utterly different at the same time.

It is similar to all interviews in that the goal of the interview never changes: the company wants to fill a staffing need and you want to find a job. That's about where the similarity ends. The devil is in the details, and there are a lot of details to an interview in a bar or a restaurant. Trust me.

Why would a company want to conduct an interview outside the office? There are a lot of reasons, but we'll drill down into four significant ones:

- First, you may not be able to get your schedules to align during working hours, and the hiring manager may simply find it easier to interview you outside the normal workday.
- Second, it may be a small company. Small companies often don't have hiring managers, or may not even have managers at all. Small business owners may be busy running their businesses during normal hours and the only way they can squeeze interviews in is to meet with you for a meal or a drink.
- Third, the company may still be feeling you out. The interviewing process is often a lengthy one that may begin with a phone call that is followed by a lunch meeting and then, if things go well, a more formal interview at the firm.
- Fourth, the company may be seeing what kind of person you are outside the formal interviewing arena. They want to observe your manners, your social awareness, etiquette, etc. This is particularly the case for positions that place the employee in the public's view, because the firm doesn't want to hire a caveman to represent them in the business world. It is also an opportunity for the company to evaluate how well you will fit into their culture by observing you in a social environment.

Regardless of the circumstance under which you find yourself in this type of interview, the most important thing to remember is that you are being observed, evaluated, and judged from the second you meet to the second that you leave. Don't forget it!

Again, the best way to proceed with an interview at a restaurant is to treat it like a date. You don't want to look like an idiot in front of a prospective significant other, and you certainly don't want to look like an idiot in front of a potential employer. This type of interview is one where you can really make a knockout impression or have the opposite effect of making the person across the table run screaming out the door.

The choice is yours.

The basics in dating apply to lunch or dinner with a hiring manager. Dress nicely, just as you would for an interview, show up a few minutes early, and double check yourself in your car's rearview mirror before you get out of the car. It is always embarrassing to find out after it is all over that your necktie was crooked or that your was hair was sticking up like Don King's after a title fight.

You should also do a little homework about the restaurant before you go. Look at their menu online, and decide what you would like ahead of time. The hiring manager probably uses the restaurant routinely and knows exactly what to order; it will be awkward if you are stumped by what to order when the waiter shows up. I recommend that you order a salad because it is easy to eat with a knife and fork (not a burger that you eat using your hands, which can get ketchup on them and result in an uncomfortable handshake at the end of the interview) and a simple salad will not put you in the awkward position of trying to eat the world's greasiest cheeseburger without making a mess out of yourself in front of your interviewer.

That brings me to a significant point about military people, food, and table manners. Most military folks view consuming food as a method of calorie loading: we need to feed the machine to keep the machine going. We eat too fast, talk while we eat, and generally just shovel it in by starting at one end of the plate and stopping when we run out of food on the other side. Not only is this not a way to impress a date, it is certainly not a way to impress an interviewer.

Remember your manners! Be polite to everyone (including your server), use the proper utensils (don't eat everything with your spoon because of your years and years of experience eating rations using only the issued plastic spoon), and SLOW DOWN! A good rule of thumb is to take a bite, chew it at least ten times, swallow, and then take another bite. Take small bites and pace how quickly you eat your meal with the interviewer. You will be talking through the meal, and it is quite embarrassing to try to answer a question right after you shove half of a steak into your gaping maw. To help with this, try paying attention to yourself the next time you eat alone. I'll bet you will be surprised at how much the military lifestyle has affected your table manners as you mow down french fries like a belt of bullets feeding into a machine gun.

Treat your interviewer with the same deference and respect as you would a date. Allow them to be seated first, and follow their lead in ordering. Avoid alcohol and drink only water or iced tea. Remember, you are being evaluated through the entire process, and if they sense that you are a three martini lunch kind of person then you will likely find yourself pursuing an interview with another company.

Place your napkin in your lap and keep your elbows off the table. As with a date, it is a good idea to have some topics of conversation ready. Lunch and dinner interviews tend to be less formal and more social. The hiring manager will be feeling you out to see if you are a cultural match with the company in addition to asking about your skills and expertise.

Remember the rules of the military mess: do not discuss politics, religion, or sex. Any one of those topics will be a guaranteed job-offer killer. Even if the interviewer initiates a conversation in one of those areas you should do your absolute best to steer the discussion back to the company and your interest in working there. One thing that may help is reading a newspaper or listening to the news on the radio before the interview in order to have something to chat about when you need to fill some time.

Here are a couple of other do's and don'ts to keep in mind: don't complain about the food (do you want to look like a whiner?), don't get a to-go box for your uneaten food (you will look cheap), don't order dessert unless the interviewer does, and lastly do be both appreciative and gracious when he or she picks up the tab. It is assumed that the company is paying the bill, but it is good form to be thankful for the free lunch or dinner that you just enjoyed.

So there are some tips for an interview over a meal, but what about an interview in a bar or lounge? That is again similar, but also very different.

Think of being interviewed in a bar as the same as running through a minefield in your underwear: it can be both embarrassing *and* lethal for your career. You can do just fine, however, if you remember that it is an interview the entire time you are in the cocktail lounge. My recommendation is to order one drink and nurse it all night. One of the best drinks to have is a gin and tonic because you can just keep topping it off with tonic water throughout the evening and nobody will be the wiser. Keep the conversation clean and on topic, and even if the interviewer gets hammered don't give into temptation to join him down the boozy trail.

You may be interviewed in a bar for the same reasons as you would be for a meal, but now you have the added factor of involving alcohol. This is a big deal because we all act differently after a few shots of loudmouth juice:

A prospective employee spends an afternoon interviewing with a company. He meets people at varying levels of the company and impresses them all with his savvy demeanor and job skills. So much so, he thinks, that they invite him out for drinks after work.

While having a few cocktails he shifts out of "jobseeker" mode and back into "military" mode, complete with a liberal sprinkling of the "F" bomb and barracks humor. He had a great time, but was very surprised when he was informed that he would not be working at the company.

The trip to the bar was part of the interview. They wanted to see what the interviewee was like outside the office, and they learned enough to know that he was not someone that they wanted in their firm. He blew his shot because he was not savvy enough to see that rule number one of interviewing is that the interview is not over until you start working at the company or they tell you to go away.

Now *that* is a lesson worth learning.

* * * * *

Lessons Learned:
- You are being evaluated the entire time that you are being interviewed, from the moment you walk in until the moment you leave. There are many more things to get wrong in this environment, so limit your possible mistakes by preparing before you go. Check the restaurant location and menu online before you leave home.
- Be ready for some chitchat, but stay away from politics, religion, sex, or anything that is controversial.
- Be polite to everyone. The interviewer will notice if you are a jerk, and you will NOT get a job offer. I guarantee it.
- Eat a salad. Avoid the Monster Burger.
- Manners, manners, manners! Slow down. Bite, chew, swallow, repeat. Don't shovel food into your mouth like a hungry recruit.
- Be gracious and don't forget to mention how much you enjoyed lunch or dinner in your thank-you note.
- If alcohol is involved, order one drink and nurse it. Keep the barracks language and humor at the barracks. It has no place in the business world.

Interviews, part 5: Curveballs and questionable questions

The purpose of a job interview is to determine whether or not you are suitable to join a company's team. How the interviewer figures that out, however, can be unusual, uncomfortable, and sometimes downright odd. It can also be illegal. You need to be prepared for when the interview goes in an unexpected direction.

You expect to be asked about your experience, skills, education, and training during a job interview. You may not be expecting some of the tools that firms use in their hiring process to find the best candidates for the job, though. Some companies will ask you to take a personality test (to see what you are *really* like), submit a handwriting sample (to be analyzed by handwriting experts), have your picture taken (so that others who are involved in the hiring process can see what you look like), or something equally unexpected. These questions and tests are perfectly legal, even if they seem a bit unusual.

What about questions that are not legal?

There are some questions that are not permitted, by law, to be asked of an applicant. Although they vary from state to state, they generally fall somewhere in the following list:

- Age
- Gender, sex, or sexual preference
- Race, ethnicity, or heritage
- Disability
- Faith or religious beliefs
- Marital status
- Pregnancy or children

There are a few more for serving military veterans:

- Classification of discharge
- Military related disability status (particularly PTSD)
- Post-military benefits status (healthcare, pension, etc.)
- Whether you are in the National Guard and Reserves

Professional interviewers are well aware of which questions are permitted and which are not. Not all interviews are conducted by professional hiring managers, though. Many are conducted by small business owners, retail store managers, restaurant chefs, and others who may not be fully trained in the various aspects of human resources and employment law. These interviewers may ask a question that they shouldn't without realizing it, but even though they don't know the law they are still required to follow it.

There is another possibility, too. The person conducting the interview may be asking you questions that they know are illegal but they go ahead and ask them anyway.

Regardless of the circumstance, when one of these questions is laid on the table it is up to you to figure out what to do about it. You have about a millisecond to decide whether you will answer it or not. How much do you want the job? That is what it all boils down to in the end. If you stonewall, refuse to answer, or debate the legality of the question with the interviewer the probability of you landing the job will rapidly approach zero. However, if you feel that the interviewer is crossing the line intentionally then perhaps the company is not really a place where you would like to work anyway.

You have to ask yourself the simple question: "Is answering that question worth getting a job with this company?" If you answer yes, then do as you are asked. If not, then don't. It is as simple as that. The downside is that you may be guaranteeing that you won't get the job. Do you have to answer an illegal question or fulfill an odd request?

Nope. You can say no. And probably not get the job. It is up for you to decide.

That said, if you believe you have been discriminated against by an employer when applying for a job or while on the job because of your race, color, sex, religion, national origin, age, disability, or military discharge status, you can file a charge of discrimination with the U.S. Equal Employment Opportunity Commission (EEOC). The law, after all, is the law.

*   *   *   *   *

Lessons Learned:
- ☐ Not everyone conducting an interview is a professional. They may ask questions that they shouldn't out of ignorance.
- ☐ There are illegal questions, unusual questions, and uncomfortable questions. Regardless of where those questions lie on the spectrum, it is up to you as to whether or not to answer them.
- ☐ There are some questions that pertain specifically to serving military and veterans. Your military and VA benefits are personal in nature, as is any pension of disability payment that you receive. Disclosure of that information is up to you, should any such questions come up.

☐ It all boils down to how much you want to work at the company. Questions may be asked innocuously, and making a big deal out of it will likely cost you a job offer.

Interviews, part 6: Military-specific considerations

As you interview for your dream job there are a few considerations that you need to keep in the back of your mind. Unlike civilians who are free to pursue any and all employment opportunities, you may actually be precluded from taking advantage of some of the prospects out there because of your status as a member of the military. Ignorance of the law is no excuse, either. You need to take the possible ramifications of taking a job while still in uniform very seriously.

There are several issues that can seriously affect your future career and, if you are not careful, cost you thousands of dollars or land you in jail. This is not an exhaustive or all-inclusive list or discussion on the subject. It is, however, a look at three aspects of post-military employment that can get you into trouble.

First is the most obvious one: your security clearance. When you leave active duty your clearance becomes inactive. If you join a company during terminal leave or accept employment with a firm that requires a clearance before you get out, the company can keep your status active by adding you as an employee and sponsoring your clearance.

If, however, you are unemployed (even for one day) after you get out then your clearance will need to be reactivated. In that case, you have up to 24 months to reactivate it before it fully lapses. Different clearance levels have different characteristics; Top Secret clearances, for example, have a five year shelf life. If you get out at year four of the Top Secret clearance window then it is only good for another year even if it is reactivated immediately after you are hired. Be sure to list an accurate clearance status (e.g., "Top Secret Clearance active until 2016" or "inactive Secret Clearance"). You don't want to misrepresent yourself as having a clearance that has lapsed or expired.

Second is the concept of *Conflict of Interest*. In a nutshell, this is a situation in which your work while in uniform places you in a unique position to either profit from your position or have undue influence over the matter at hand. An example of this is a contracting officer who can influence the spending of government dollars on a particular contract; he may be enticed to choose one bid over another if his future job depended on it. The same goes if he influences his military connections after he gets out to bias a contract decision. Not all instances of conflict of interest are as obvious, however. If you are seeking a job in your specialty area (which is perfectly logical and normal) it is a good idea to get a copy of the job description and show it to a Staff Judge Advocate (military lawyer). They can give you an opinion as to whether it conflicts or not. This is a big deal because often the simple appearance of a conflict may create problems whether a true conflict exists or not. Better safe than sorry.

In my case I had gone through the entire resume, interview, and job offer process with a great company. I was still on active duty at the time, and they were going to hire me after I began my terminal leave. The job was perfectly in line with my skills and experience, and it would have been a very simple transition from wearing a uniform one day and a suit the next.

As a result of participating in the Ruehlin seminar, however, I became alarmed because it seemed that there may have been a conflict of interest. In my military duties I was responsible for writing requirements that were likely to result in creating contracted job positions that the very company that had presented me with a job offer would compete for! I made an appointment with a Staff Judge Advocate friend of mine and explained the situation to him. He advised me to not take the job until I had left active duty because the possibility that my accepting a job with the company would be in direct conflict with my duties while in uniform, and as a result both the hiring company and I could get into hot water. Even though I had no intention of violating the law, I turned down the offer and kept a clear conscience.

Lastly, and most interestingly, is the rule against foreign employment. The Emoluments Clause of the U. S. Constitution prohibits any person "holding any office of profit or trust" in the Federal Government from accepting any gift, emolument, office, or title of any kind from any foreign state without the consent of Congress, and that includes retirees. In order for you to work for a foreign government you must first receive permission from your service secretary, as in the Secretary of the Navy, Army, or Air Force. Needless to say, this is not a simple process! You will need to apply for a waiver from the Secretary *in advance* otherwise you are breaking the law and the government may come after you to recoup the monies that you received up to the amount of your retirement pay. Ouch!

*   *   *   *   *

Lessons Learned:

☐   Your security clearance is a big deal for many employers because obtaining one costs thousands of dollars, and if you have an active clearance (particularly a Top Secret one) it makes you a more desirable candidate. Misrepresenting the status of your clearance, however, makes you a knucklehead.

☐   Conflict of interest is a very murky and thorny problem. You can get yourself, your new company, and possibly other people in a lot of hot water (and potentially legal trouble) if you are not careful. Talk to your local Staff Judge Advocate if you have even inkling that there may be a conflict between your current job in uniform and the one you are pursuing.

☐   Even if you are retired you are still considered to be an office holder in the U. S. Government, and as such you must ask for permission to work for a foreign government. This can even apply to you if you are not directly employed by a foreign government; for example, if you are in a law firm and receive a share of the profits that are received from a foreign government it is considered to be in violation of the law. Make sure that you are not going to get into trouble by researching who your prospective employer's customers are.

Interviews, part 7: After the interview: What's next?

You have just finished interviewing with the company of your dreams. As you walk out the door you need to remember, though, that the even though the meeting part of the interview is over the whole process is not yet done. To have the best shot at landing a job offer you still have some work to do to finish it up.

Or, if you don't want the job that badly, you can just get in your car, drive home, and have a cold one to celebrate the time that you wasted on the interview and the job opportunity you missed out on because your competition is going to go the extra mile and finish _their_ interview properly. The choice is up to you.

The smart thing to do is to continue to treat the job interview like a date. Just as you want your relationship with the right pretty girl or handsome guy to get more serious the same can be said about your interest in the company. You are certainly curious as to how things went during the interview because you to want to step things up a notch and get into a meaningful relationship with the company. Just like you want your date to call you back the day after dinner and a movie you desperately want the hiring manager to give you a ring with good news.

Even though you have left the building there are still several things you can, and should, do to increase your chances to land a job. If you don't do them the worst that will happen is you won't receive an offer. If you do the following things, though, you still may not get a job but you will come away from the experience with a stronger reputation and a better understanding of how to become a stronger candidate for employment. Here, in my humble opinion (and in the opinions of many hiring managers) are the things that you should perform after the interview:

1. *Make some notes about the interview.* What questions were you prepared for? What questions were you unprepared for? What was the interviewer's name and title? You should have exchanged cards during the interview, and the back of the card is a good place to jot down the interviewer's preferred form of address ("Mr. Smith" or "Bob", for example). You should take notes while the interview is fresh in your mind because otherwise you will forget those brain-hiccups that you had, and if you forget them then you are likely to repeat them again in future interviews. A better idea than writing on the back of a business card is to obtain a small notebook that you dedicate to the interviewing process, and using it as a logbook or journal to record your post-interview notes.

2. *Send a follow-up note to thank the interviewer for their time and attention.* In the note make sure to use their preferred form of address (that you remembered to write down on the back of their business card as soon as you left the interview) and be sincere in your message. You should be professional and courteous, but not overly familiar. After all, you are still making an impression, and a poorly written note will do more harm than good. Here is an example of a short and acceptable thank-you note:

Dear Bob,
Thank you for the opportunity to meet with you on Tuesday. I am very excited about the opportunity to join XYZ Company, and I learned a great deal about the firm during the interview. Our discussion about the corporate culture and dynamic work environment reinforced my strong desire to join the company, and I

think that my skills and experience are a great fit for the _____ position. I feel that I can be a strong contributor to the firm.

If you need to contact me for any follow up questions or additional information I can best be reached at xxx-xxx-xxxx or via email at mike@anymail.com. I look forward to hearing from you soon.

> *Sincerely,*
> *Mike Smith*

3. *As you close out the interview ask the hiring manager for the best way to contact them in the future.* This is important because it gives the interviewer an opportunity to establish expectations for future communications. He or she may be open to a call or email or may prefer that you wait to hear from the company before you contact them. Make sure to pay attention! You can shoot down your chances at a job if you call them after being asked to wait. Just follow their lead.

4. *Think hard about your experience at the interview.* Are you going to be a good fit at the company? Did you learn anything that was unexpected or that is not in line with your goals? If you did, then do some serious soul-searching in order to decide whether or not to continue pursuing a job there. Don't just take the first job that comes along if it is not a good fit.

5. *Prepare yourself for the company's call.* It may be a letter, an email, or a telephone call, but regardless of how the firm reaches out to you the news will be either good or bad. This is where character really counts; if the news is good then it means that you have a follow on interview in your future or a job offer letter on the way. If the news is bad then it means that you will need to look elsewhere for a job. If the news is good then you need to be humble, respectful, and thankful for the opportunity to work for the company. If the news is bad, then you need to be humble, respectful, and thankful for the opportunity to interview with the company. Even though you did not land a job with that particular company it doesn't mean that you can be a jerk about it; remember, you are building a reputation along with your resume. If you are obnoxious because you didn't get the job the word will get out. If you are respectful, the word will get out too. The hiring manager who did not hire you may know of a company that is looking for someone with your skill set, and if you make a strong positive impression it may help network you into a new opportunity. A truly classy touch is to send another thank you note to the hiring manager who *did not* hire you, thanking them for their time and attention. You should also contact the

interviewer who did not hire you and ask them for their candid evaluation of how you did on the interview. Any feedback that helps you improve your interviewing skills is helpful.

Remember that the hiring process does not end with the interview. It ends with either a job offer, an invitation for a follow on interview, or a rejection. You can improve your chances for a job offer by following up on the interview.

*   *   *   *   *

Lessons Learned:

- ☐ Write down your impressions of the interview as soon as possible so that you can learn from it. You want to make your strengths even stronger and eliminate your weaknesses, and the only way to effectively do that is to learn from your experience.
- ☐ The interview is not over when you walk out the door. Hiring managers are people too, and sending a thank you note for their time is a nice touch that will be noticed. It is a normal part of the hiring process, and if you don't send a note then you fall behind others who do. Send the thank you note immediately after the interview. If you had to travel to the interview, then write the note and drop it in a local mailbox to ensure that it arrives quickly. *Strike while the iron is hot!*
- ☐ Reflect on the interview. Did it reinforce your desire to work there or uncover some negative aspects about the job or the company that make you have second thoughts?
- ☐ Be gracious when you finally get the results of the interview. This may take a while because the hiring process at most companies takes time, so be ready to wait. When you get the news, be respectful and courteous regardless whether it is good or not. Remember, your reputation is always growing, and if the word gets out that you are a jerk it will hurt your chances elsewhere.

Chapter 22: _Getting a job, part 4: Learning a new skill_
called negotiation

In the military one learns a good many things: How to stand at attention and march smartly about. How to carry and shoot a rifle, eat out of a ration bag, and how to live out of a backpack for weeks on end. How to fix a tank or fly a jet. How to do lots and lots of things.

One thing that you don't learn, however, is something that everybody else in the business world learns with their first job: how to negotiate.

Negotiation is a very important element of the job acceptance process. When a candidate is offered a position with a company he or she begins the discussion of employment considerations with the hiring manager or human resources person responsible for bringing them into the company. Things like compensation, benefits, work hours, vacation time, career progression, retirement plans, insurance, and countless other perks that are part and parcel of employment are also part of the conversation. In the corporate world all of these items are negotiable, and both job providers and job seekers know it.

In the military the situation could not be more different. When a young man or woman joins the military they are provided a comprehensive pay and benefits package that is firmly set by law and regulation. There is no negotiation for a better salary or more flexible hours; in fact, there is no negotiation at all. Pay, allowances, and benefits for military folks are no secret, either. The pay scale, which is based on rank and time in service, can be viewed on the internet. So are all other monetary benefits, special pay conditions (such as jump and dive pay), and housing stipends. They are entitlements, not perquisites. In the military you get what you get, just like everybody else in uniform.

As a result of the defined pay and benefits in the military those in uniform never really engage in the process of employment negotiation, and that places them at a disadvantage when they hang up their uniforms. In the civilian world _everything_ is negotiable.

Everything from the salary you will earn to the amount of vacation you can take to where you can park your car is on the table. It is up to you, the job seeker, to get the best compensation package that you can, and if you don't know to engage in the back and forth of negotiation then you risk leaving valuable things on the table. Although there are few guarantees in life, there is one guarantee in negotiation: you will never get things that you don't ask for.

Fortunately, you can arm yourself for an employment negotiation by doing a little research and preparing for it.

The research bit can make an enormous difference in the negotiation process because it provides you with valuable information about the company as well as what you can and cannot ask for. You can surf the internet (at sites like www.glassdoor.com or www.payscale.com) and ask your friends and contacts (especially those at the company or in the industry) about the salary for your desired position and the benefits package that the firm offers.

As the job seeker you have leverage in the negotiation up until the point that you accept the job offer and the terms that it contains. Once you say "yes" the negotiation is over, and you are highly unlikely to be able to change anything. At that point anything that was left on the negotiating table will vanish like a thief in the night.

So what are the types of things that you can ask for? Here is a quick list of twenty things that many companies will entertain and which may or may not be similar to military benefits:

1. *Performance bonuses. Can you make more money if your performance merits it?*

2. *Flexible hours. Maybe a four day work week with longer workdays?*

3. *Work location. Work from home?*

4. *Overtime pay. How much will you be compensated for working extra hours?*

5. *Retirement plans. What kind do they offer? How much will the company match in a 401K?*

6. *Vacation time. You received 30 days a year in the military and the base in the civilian world is two weeks unless you negotiate for more.*

7. *Travel expenses. Can you get a company car? Mileage compensation or a gas station credit card?*

8. *Non-monetary compensation. Can you earn stock options or shares of the company's stock?*

9. *Career flexibility. Can you create a path that starts in one area of the company and then move to another?*

10. *Time off. How about personal days? Sick days?*

11. *Health care. Is health insurance included? What are the plan's deductibles? Is there an on-site clinic?*

12. *Insurance. You had SGLI in the military at a steeply discounted rate. Does your employer offer life insurance?*

13. *Meals. Is there a company cafeteria? Are meals subsidized?*

14. *Child care. Can you bring your child to work? How about a nursing room for those who wish to nurse infants?*

15. *Tech equipment. How about a company smartphone or laptop?*

16. *Discounts. If the company produces goods, can you purchase them at a discount? Is there a company store?*

17. *Memberships. Will the company provide memberships to a health club or gym?*

18. *Travel. Will you be expected to travel in coach, business class, or even better when you travel? How about upgrades?*

19. *Education. Will the company pay for you to pursue an MBA or other educational opportunity?*

20. *Relocation expenses. Will the firm pay for you to move your family to the city where you will work?*

These are only the tip of the pay and benefits iceberg. If you don't do your homework and come to the bargaining table knowing what you can and should ask for you will get less than you could have. In the next few pages we will talk about how to prepare for a negotiation by rehearsing and doing a little self-examination to make sure that you do the best job possible at the bargaining table.

We have already looked at many of the differences between military and civilian employment benefits, so we won't go too deeply down that rabbit hole other than to point out that many of the benefits on the military side of the fence are not freely offered by civilian companies. Take, for example, the military subsistence (meal) and housing subsidies. You get them while in uniform, but they don't come freely in the corporate sector; civilians pay for food and housing out of their salaries. All of those special payments and allowances that fattened up your military paycheck helped mitigate the comparatively low pay that comes with wearing the uniform. An added benefit is that those payments are tax-free, which in the corporate sector is not the case.

As a military man or woman you are also free to shop in the commissary, gas station, and PX, all of which provide subsidized food and trade goods that are free of state and local sales taxes. While retirees can still take advantage of shopping on base, those who do not stay in for 20+ years or retirees who move to a locale without a military base nearby are out of luck. These subsidies, coupled with tax free shopping, are not offered by the corporate sector. Once you get out you get to pay full price for your groceries and consumer goods, and you get to pay sales tax, too.

My point is that many of the monetary and non-monetary benefits that you received while in uniform went a long way towards stretching your paycheck. When you get out your salary alone pays your bills, buys food, and fills your tank with gas. Since that is how the "real" world works, you need to make sure to get the best benefit package you can from your employer, and to get such a package you need to be able to negotiate.

Negotiation is a skill, just like any other. You can get better at it if you work at it, and the best way to improve is to practice and rehearse like you did for you job interviews.

Before you start rehearsing, though, you need use your research to craft a plan of action and prepare yourself just like you would for a mission in the military. Unlike military plans, though, yours does not have to be intricate or complicated. Instead, your plan should contain those elements of compensation that you feel are important to you. It should also contain those elements of compensation that are not important to you.

Why should the unimportant bits be included you ask?

Because they are all part of the plan. The art of negotiation is based on meeting mutual agreement, and getting to a point where both you and the human resources manager agree on your pay and benefits is based on the give and take that you both engage in during the negotiation process. If you only have those things that are important to you on the list then you are at a disadvantage because negotiation invariably requires you to give a little to get a little. You can give a little by sacrificing those things that are unimportant to you and, in turn, get a little something back that you truly want.

Here is an easy example.

You feel that flexible work hours are very important to you.

You also feel that employer-provided health insurance is not important to you because you are already covered medically by the VA and TRICARE.

In the world of civilian employment the cost of health insurance is high and by all accounts is only going to get higher in 2014 with the Affordable Care Act. The fact that you are willing to give up employer-provided healthcare is a significant savings to the employer. Even though you do not need to use the company's insurance you can offer to keep your current insurance plan (and save the company a lot of money by not using theirs) in exchange for a flexible work schedule.

If you don't have a plan to give up those things that you don't really want or need then you are giving up a significant amount of leverage. Be smart and plan your negotiation out!

Here are some basic planning considerations that I recommend you think about as you plan for your pay and benefits negotiation:

1. What do you want from the company? Sure, you want a job, but what do you want in return for your time and dedication?

2. What does the company want from you? Sure, they want an employee but generally want to pay as little as possible for one; you will need to show the company that you are worth the cost of your employment.

3. What is the <u>absolute minimum</u> that you are willing to accept from the company? This is very important. The Human Resources person has a lot more experience negotiating than you do, and if you are not careful they may well negotiate you out of the things that you hold dear.

4. What is your alternative? In official negotiating terms this is known as the "BATNA", or *Best Alternative to a Negotiated Agreement.* In other words, what are you going to do if the company is unwilling to meet your absolute minimum? This is important because you want to leave the negotiation with a job, but if you cannot reach an agreement you should know when to walk away. The best BATNA is to leave the negotiation on good terms that can be leveraged into another negotiation with that or another company that will ultimately be agreeable to you both. Don't burn any bridges.

After you put together your plan you need to do a little rehearsing, just like you did for your job interviews. Find someone to conduct a mock negotiation with, and then listen to their feedback. It will pay huge dividends. I guarantee that you will be surprised at just how difficult negotiating can be! By rehearsing you will learn if you are too brusque or direct or overbearing, all of which are very common traits that come with military service. You want to be convivial and professional because it is what the company expects, and by rehearsing with another person you can fine tune your style of engagement.

Here are a few things that military people tend to do while they negotiate that end up working against them:

- Being too rigid and organized. Just because you have a plan doesn't mean that you need to unyieldingly stick to it. Do not treat your plan as a checklist and start at the top and work your way to the bottom. The negotiation is a conversation that will go in many directions before it is completed, and if you come across as too mechanical and inflexible it will hurt you.

- Being unwilling to engage in a dialog. Often, military folks are used to just accepting "no" a bit too easily because they are inexperienced in negotiating. Remember, the Human Resources manager wants to hire you as cheaply as possible, and if you just roll over every time he or she says no then you are making his or her job pretty easy.

- Being ignorant of what benefits are available for discussion. This goes back to the previous chapter about interview preparation: make sure to do your research. If you do not ask for something I guarantee you will not get it. At this stage of the game nobody is looking out for you except you.

- Being ignorant of how much money they really need to make. A good rule of thumb is that you need to nearly double your base military pay to obtain the same level of compensation in the civilian world. Taxes go up and tax-free benefits go away. In the civilian world you get to pay bills that you may not have thought about: for example, if you lived in the barracks or in base housing you did not have to pay for electricity, water, natural gas, or trash removal. Guess what: in the civilian world you get to pay for all of those things and more!

*　　*　　*　　*　　*

Lessons learned:
- ☐ Military benefits are set. Corporate benefits are not. To get the best salary and benefits possible you are going to have to negotiate for them.
- ☐ Not all companies offer all benefits. You need to do some research to see what the company offers, and then be prepared to ask for them.
- ☐ Salary is usually the biggest aspect of the negotiation, but it is not the only element. Unlike the military, many corporate benefit packages are tailored to the individual employee.
- ☐ Use your network of contacts and the internet to research what will likely be on the table during the negotiation. Don't look

foolish by asking for something the company does not offer, and don't forget to ask for something that they do.

☐ Do some research on your own finances and see just how much money that you are going to need in the civilian world. Remember that taxes take a big bite! If you were in the civilian world you could count on 30-40% of your BAH and Subsistence Allowance to go to the IRS because it would be counted as income. Find out how much money you *really* need.

☐ List out those benefits that are important to you and also those that are not. You will use both lists during your negotiation. Make sure that those benefits you want are offered by the company.

☐ Rehearse with someone; you need the practice. Remember, the Human Resources manager does this a lot more than you do.

☐ Find out what your BATNA is and stick to it. It is OK to walk away from the negotiation if the result would be below your absolute minimum level of acceptability.

Chapter 23: *From Marine to Veteran*

On January 1st of 2012 I officially made the big step out of my combat boots and into my flip flops. It was indeed a significantly emotional and personal event, but it also marked an enormous change in my status in the eyes of the federal government. You see, on that day I officially became an ex-member of the Department of Defense and the newest customer of the Department of Veterans Affairs. This jump is significant for a lot more reasons than I realized, and it can be confusing and overwhelming if you aren't ready for it. And I wasn't nearly as ready for it as I thought I was.

The day you become a civilian again marks the day you can no longer take advantage of many of the benefits you enjoyed in uniform. If you are moving on after an enlistment or two and are not joining the retired rolls, then pretty much all of the benefits disappear with your last short haircut. No more tax free shopping at the Post Exchange and no more subsidized groceries at the commissary; you are fully back in the civilian world and get to pay full price (tax included) for your next pair of cargo shorts.

If you are retiring, however, you are still entitled to some benefits. You can still shop at the PX and the commissary, which is nice. You can take advantage of many of the recreational facilities, too, such as the campgrounds, gymnasiums, and beach cottages. Your priority slips to one peg below those still on active duty, but that's ok. After all, you're retired now, so you have all the time in the world. Or not, but that's another story we'll talk about later.

Either way, whether you are retired or simply out of the service, you still have a governmental agency that is looking out for you.

Enter the VA.

So what exactly does the VA do for you? Well, let me fill you in. First, though, a little bit of VA history.

The Veterans Administration's lineage stretches back all the way to the Revolutionary War when the Continental Congress made provisions for pension payments to soldiers who were disabled as a result of their service. Over the next hundred years or so, the benefits and provisions grew with the nation's involvement is wars at home and abroad, with the most significant being the War Between the States. Recognizing the sacrifice of those in uniform and their families, none other than Abraham Lincoln said of the importance of the government's duty to the veteran during his final Inaugural Address:

"To care for him who shall have borne the battle and for his widow and his orphan..."

By the beginning of the 20th century there were many programs to help veterans and fulfill Lincoln's charter. There were veterans' retirement homes as well as hospitals and other facilities, with the responsibility for taking care of vets shared between several federal agencies and the individual states. The magnitude and the carnage of the First World War made it evident that a consolidated and coordinated federal system was needed to meet the demands of the many thousands of veterans (and their families) that were part of that titanic struggle.

In 1930 the Veterans Administration was created by act of Congress. It consolidated all of the federal programs and responsibilities under one cabinet level department and took the onus of care off the backs of the individual states. With the Second World War the department expanded dramatically and evolved into the VA as we know it today.

So what can the VA do for you? Here is a quick list of some of their major programs:

- Home loans
- Educational benefits
- Life insurance
- Special adaptive housing benefits for wounded service members
- Medical care
- Psychological care
- Burial honors

Within those major programs are dozens and dozens of smaller ones. Take, for example, the educational benefits. The GI Bill isn't just for college. Programs are available to teach you trades and skills completely free of charge, and depending on your status you may even be paid a housing allowance to go to school.

When you take off your uniform for the last time it is important not to that there is an entire government agency that still has you in mind, and there are a lot of programs that can help you as you explore what is next in your life. The educational benefits and home loan eligibility don't disappear on your last day of service, and depending on your disability evaluation or retirement status you may be entitled to free health care as well. Make sure to talk to someone at the VA during your transition journey. I guarantee you will be surprised at how much they can do for you.

*   *   *   *   *

Lessons Learned:

☐ Once you hit your EAS date you no longer fall under the DOD but instead become a "customer" of the VA. This is a big deal because you can't go back to the military for pretty much anything once you transition over. It is *very* important to get as much done as you possibly can before you officially get out. If you don't you will face some daunting hurdles on the path to civilianhood.

☐ The benefits are astounding in many cases, but it is up to you to seek them out. Nobody is going to come to your house and educate you on the various programs. Go to www.va.gov and surf around. You'll be pleasantly surprised at just what the Veterans Administration offers.

Chapter 24: The hazards of going it alone with your VA disability claim

I have a good friend with whom I was fortunate to serve two tough tours in Iraq. Like me, after a long career he decided one day that it was time to retire from the Marine Corps. Unlike me, however, he stuck it out until the bitter end and hung up his uniform after a full thirty years (the maximum) of active service.

He is a great guy who lived one of the hardest lives you can live in the Marine Corps; he started out as an infantryman and then became a reconnaissance Marine and ultimately a Special Operator, meaning that he began his career as a grunt who carried heavy loads long distances and lived in the dirt to a recon guy who carried heavier loads longer distances and lived in the mud.

During his career he did all of the high speed and sexy things that are the stuff of recruiting posters. He jumped out of airplanes, and not just enough times to earn his jump wings, but hundreds and hundreds of times from helicopters and airplanes both at very low and extremely high altitudes. He became an expert diver, marksman, and small unit leader.

He helped the Marine Corps blaze the trail into the Special Operations world. He helped build what is now called MARSOC (MARine Special Operations Command – another acronym!) and was a critical leader in a Marine Special Operations Battalion. He went overseas to Kuwait and Iraq and Afghanistan to fight, and during his distinguished career he deployed *thirteen* times.

It all came at a tremendous cost, however. He suffers from a long list of physical ailments that are related to doing all of those incredible things; his ears ring from being around gunfire for years on end, his joints and back are so painful that he sometimes can barely move, and he has many other conditions that resulted from three decades of hard service.

At the end of his impressive career he did what all separating servicemen do. He went through the VA evaluation process. He ensured that his physical problems were recorded in his medical record and was then examined by a VA physician.

With all of his maladies he was certain that he would be assigned a relatively high disability rating. After all, many people served for far less time and in far less strenuous and physically demanding environments were rated as significantly disabled. He wasn't looking for anything he didn't earn and deserve, mind you, but was just looking for what was fair.

He went to all of the required medical appointments and not long after retiring he received the Veterans Administration's letter that announced his disability rating.

For 10%.

For tinnitus. Ringing in the ears.

To say he was angry is an epic understatement, and upon taking his case to his state VA representative they agree and are challenging the ruling.

How did he end up with such a low rating when he has so many demonstrable maladies?

My friend attributes it to his physical evaluation. The doctor didn't really examine him, but instead simply asked him questions about his conditions. He did not order tests or even conduct a thorough examination, but instead had an amiable conversation with my friend and apparently wrote down some notes.

The point is that in order to receive the most accurate evaluation it is imperative that you take an active role in your VA physical evaluations. Demand that the doctor examine those things that you know are wrong. Don't just let the overworked doctor hurry through your exam.

Otherwise you may likely find yourself under-rated for your service connected disability, and to get it corrected will make an already disturbingly long process even tortuously longer.

So this is a cautionary tale. You may save yourself a lot of time and inconvenience by taking an active role in your VA evaluation, so I recommend going into the doctor's office with the intent of having each and every issue thoroughly examined, addressed, and recorded.

After all, if you don't do it, who will? Well, there is help out there, if you seek it out. My friend did, and with the help of an advocate he is appealing the results of his evaluation. An advocate can make all of the difference in the world, and that is what we will be looking into next. (His appeal was successful, and in late 2013 he was rated at 80%)

Finding an advocate

A significant part of the separations process is the medical evaluation that all veterans go through in order to determine whether or not they rate disability benefits. It can be a confusing and overwhelming process even if you are healthy and don't have any lagging medical problems, but as my friend discovered, it can get downright impenetrable if you have significant issues or service-related disabilities.

It is not because the VA is an uncaring monolithic government agency. They are really trying to help the millions of veterans who need their assistance. They are doing the best that they can, but despite the ongoing modernization of various systems within the VA and an increasing budget they are simply buried by the sheer volume of veterans who are either already in the system or are now joining it. It is likely to get worse in the near term, too, as the services begin the post-war drawdown.

That is all well and good for the VA, but what about the individual veteran? Is he or she on his or her own to try to navigate the bureaucracy? No. Fortunately there are some great organizations out there to help ensure that veterans receive the benefits they are entitled to. In addition, those organizations will act as an adviser and advocate for veterans as they wend their way through the benefits claims process.

Several chapters ago we examined the ins and outs of the pre-separation TAP process, and in that chapter I wrote about the helpful guy who reviewed my medical record. Although I didn't really understand the significance of meeting with him at the time, after months and months spent working my way through the disability claim process I finally got it. He represented the Disabled American Veterans (DAV), which is a nonprofit organization that exists solely to help out veterans. All veterans, not just those with disabilities. At the TAP course he explained all of this to me, but it was such a blizzard of information over those five days that I really didn't pay as close attention as I should have. Fortunately, I did listen to him when he asked me to sign up for the DAV as my advocate, because it allowed him to review and prescreen my medical record before I was evaluated by the VA.

So what is the DAV? It is a nonprofit Veterans Service Organization, or VSO, that exists to help any and all veterans. Here is a blurb from their website (www.dav.org):

The 1.2 million-member Disabled American Veterans (DAV) is a non-profit 501(c)(4) charity dedicated to building better lives for America's disabled veterans and their families.

The DAV was founded in 1920 by disabled veterans returning from World War I to represent their unique interests. In 1932, the DAV was congressionally chartered as the official voice of the nation's wartime disabled veterans.

In addition to assisting veterans with the many issues that they face after leaving the service they are an advocate for people like me who were being evaluated by the VA for possible medical disability benefits. This is a great help because they have a lot of people with a lot of experience with the process, and they will go to bat for you in case you run into snags or are given a disability rating that does not reflect your actual physical condition. They make the confusing process manageable and will help you through it, which is a great relief to those who have absolutely no idea what to do as they transition (like me).

At any rate, the DAV representative prescreened my record and in doing so set me up for a much smoother evaluation process several months later with the VA. He identified prior medical conditions, injuries, and issues that I had completely forgotten about. They were all relevant to the claims process because they would probably get worse later in life, and if they were not identified during the VA physical then I would be ineligible for VA medical coverage to deal with them.

They also help with all kinds of other things that are veteran related; things like job placement assistance, counseling, and representing veteran's interests to Congress. The DAV is there to help you, so when you go through your transition courses make sure to track the representative of the organization down. He or she will gladly help you navigate through the wickets, and you will be amazed at how much you will come to rely on them to clarify the confusing claims process.

*   *   *   *   *

<u>Lessons learned:</u>

☐ There are a lot of organizations out there that will help you with veteran's issues and the transition to civilian life. I am working with the DAV, but the Veterans of Foreign Wars (VFW) and American Legion are also great organizations that can help you out. There are literally dozens more. They all have slightly different charters so do some research and see which one works best for you. Even better, join as many as you can because they are not competing with each other and they all want to help.

☐ Even if you are certain that you will have no disability rating it is still important to affiliate with a veteran's advocacy group. There are a lot of benefits that are outside the medical realm that they can help with, and if nothing else they are a great bunch of people you can rely on if you need advice or just somebody to talk to.

Chapter 25: Final Physical Exam....or not.
Welcome to the VA!

The last chapter was about the Veterans Administration and Veterans Service Organizations, and not long before is a chapter about what I thought was my last and final set of physical examinations related to my military service. I soon found out that as usual I was wrong, and that both the VA and even *more* physical examinations were inextricably linked to the journey that is transition.

Just as peanut butter goes with chocolate and peas like carrots the Veterans Administration and physical examinations go together too. It turns out that I was right about my military final physical examination being the last one that I would go through in uniform, but what I didn't realize was that it would be immediately followed by my *first* physical examination out of uniform by the VA.

The VA, among a host of other things, is responsible for determining whether or not you are eligible for a disability rating and associated compensation for any injuries or conditions that you suffered as a result of your service. The military's final physical is just your last checkup on the way out the door; the VA physical is your first checkup on the way into civilian life. In addition to finding out if you are disabled in any way the VA makes sure that you don't have any conditions that require additional treatment once you take off the uniform.

There are plenty of examples of both disability related conditions and continuing treatment requirements: they range from losing a limb or an eye in combat to tinnitus caused by the roar and whine of aircraft engines to physical therapy to help recover from surgery. Regardless of circumstance, the VA is responsible for the care of the veteran's service connected injuries and conditions, and in order to determine what type of care a veteran requires they need to have their doctors take a look under the hood (or hospital gown, as it were).

As my active duty days drew to a close I finished up all of my required checkups and paperwork to head out to the civilian world. On my last day in uniform I received my official orders back to my civilian life, and with a handshake and a cheery "see ya later" I set out on terminal leave and started my life back on Civvy Street. One of my first stops after my terminal leave began (and after recovering from the farewell party hangover) was to the VA office, where I dropped off my DD-214 and began the process of becoming a "customer" of the VA.

(As we learned earlier, the DD-214 is the most important document a veteran can possess because it is the key to veterans benefits as well as official proof that you served in the military.)

Along with my DD-214 I handed over a copy of my medical record. You should make two copies of your medical record: one for yourself and the other to turn in to the VA. This is VERY important because you are required to turn the original in to the military administrative clerk during your final checkout, the VA needs a copy to determine disability ratings and other medical concerns, and it is only prudent to make sure to keep a copy for your own records.

The nice lady in the office asked me a few questions. She then took a quick look at my records and started making some calls. Within a few minutes she had set me up with three appointments at a contracted medical office that the VA uses to evaluate separating veterans. She said that I would be receiving some information in the mail, and that it was now on me to ensure that I did everything necessary to complete the evaluation process. She also said that it could take anywhere from four months (in the best of all possible worlds) to a year or longer (which is not unusual) for my case to be evaluated and any disability rating to be issued. If I didn't do what I was supposed to it could take literally forever, because although the VA is there to help veterans, they are not there to hold your hand and drag you through the process. That's up to you.

Anyhow, I left the VA office with a few appointments and the pleasant, though pointed, reminder that it was up to me now. In order to take advantage of all of the great medical benefits that I had earned and to see if I had a disability rating I would need to take the initiative to attend appointments without anybody besides myself reminding me. There would be no Drill Instructors to tell me what to do next. Welcome back to the real world.

*　　　*　　　*　　　*　　　*

Lessons Learned:

- ☐ Make at least one copy (two if you can) of your complete medical and dental records. Your separations office on base should let you use the copier to make copies, and if they don't, you can use the copier at the career counseling center. If you don't want to stand over a copier for hours fighting paper jams and toner outages, you can take it out in town to a Kinko's or other copier business. It will cost a few bucks, but time is money. Your original record will be surrendered in exchange for your orders home, and the VA needs another copy to evaluate. Remember this: the VA and the DOD are separate governmental agencies and if you think that they will coordinate your transition for you then you need to take another urinalysis test. They are as separate as North and South Korea.

☐ Make sure that you leave the VA office with physical evaluation appointments. Your claim for medical benefits will not start until the evaluations are complete, so if you blow off or forget an appointment your case will just languish on some desk somewhere until it crumbles into dust. If you want benefits, then you need to do the legwork to make sure the process moves along.

Part 2: The wonderful world of VA medical examinations

The VA has become a very busy governmental agency during the last few years. The wars in Iraq and Afghanistan have spurred the dynamic growth of all of the armed services, and now that combat in Iraq has ended and Afghanistan winds down there are many thousands and thousands of new veterans leaving the service. The burgeoning numbers are compounded by the government's budget deficit and military belt tightening as the growth that the Army, Navy, Air Force, Coast Guard, and Marines experienced in the latter part of the last decade retrenches and the population of the armed forces shrinks back to pre-war levels or lower. Add all of the "new" veterans to those from World War II, Korea, Vietnam, Desert Storm and the Cold War and soon you have a huge population of veterans for the VA to oversee.

The meteoric rise in the VA population has slowed some things down, and one of those things is the completion of the disability rating evaluation. The disability evaluation is performed by the VA to document and, if required, provide compensation to veterans for physical or mental conditions that were caused or aggravated by their military service. The process is a pretty fair one, but it requires the veteran to put some effort into ensuring that all of the documentation is in their record and that they attend all of the required appointments.

In my case, I initiated the process right after I checked out of the Marine Corps and started my terminal leave. On that day I turned in all of my required files (including my original medical and dental records) and received my orders back to civilian life. I also received two versions ("Member 1" and "Member 4") of my all-important separation document, the DD-214. With these important papers in my hot little hands I trotted down to the Veterans Affairs office on base and signed up for a walk-in appointment to see what to do next.

After waiting about a half hour to see a counselor, I went in and meekly laid myself at the mercy of the VA, professing my utter ignorance of what I needed to do. Fortunately, the woman who took my case had seen plenty of knuckleheads like me before. She perfunctorily but professionally ran me through the requirements.

"Do you have your DD-214?"

I handed it over. Well, actually I handed her a copy. As an aside, when you check out make sure to ask for a half dozen or so "Certified True Copies" of your form because some agencies will not accept an uncertified FAX or photocopy. The admin shop will make copies and stamp them as certified, which will come in handy later. Trust me.

"Do you have your medical record?"

I patted the thick folder on my lap.

"Have you been pre-screened?"

I explained that my record had been evaluated by the Disabled American Veterans counselors during my Transition Assistance Class, and I showed her the form that they filled out.

"When do you EAS?"

I told her that my last day was New Year's Eve, and she paused. In a speech that she had obviously given hundreds of times before she explained how the timeline for VA claims works. It is important to file at the right time, she said, because depending on when a vet files has a tremendous impact on how quickly the case will be evaluated. Based on your EAS if you file too early, your package gets sent off to a regional evaluation center and it may take up to a year to get evaluated. In my case, since I was three months from my EAS I fell into the "too early" category. If you file too late your package gets sent off to the same place and it will likely take a year. Too late is defined as after your EAS. She explained that if you submit your claim 60 days or less before your EAS then your case will be evaluated by the local VA office, and that the turnaround rate is about four months.

It was my choice.

She smiled at me across the desk and sweetly inquired if I would like to submit my claim today or if I would like to submit it in a month or so...

...and a month later I was sitting across the same desk from the same nice lady. Since I was now in the "sweet spot" of claim submission I presented her with all of my information and got started.

Here is what she needed to initiate my claim:

1. A complete photocopy of my medical and dental records (the records accompany the claim throughout the evaluation process and when it is completed they are returned).

2. A copy of the pre-screening checklist that was performed at the Transition Assistance Class by the Disabled American Veterans representative.

3. A copy of my DD-214. Not just any copy, mind you, but the "Member 4" copy. Why do I know this? I know because I submitted the wrong one, of course, and had to resubmit the correct one a month later when my error was identified by the VA. It behooves you to look at the bottom of the form and bring the correct copy!

With the thick packet in front of her she began making some phone calls. Although I had completed my military physicals I now had to have my VA evaluations completed. After ten minutes or so of coordinating dates and times, she handed me three appointment reminders for the three evaluations that I would need to complete in order for my case to be adjudicated.

These three appointments were totally on me. I was required not just to show up, but to complete the pre-appointment paperwork, which was basically a questionnaire that asked about each and every item that I had identified as a malady or injury that was incurred during my service. Such things as a dislocated shoulder (When did it happen? How?) to a broken ankle (what treatment did you receive? Any surgery?). Filling out the paperwork was a little tedious, but without it my claim would not see the light of day.

Within two months all three appointments were finished. They were efficiently and professionally done by a contractor, and by the time my EAS arrived my claim was wending itself through the VA office.

After about four months a letter arrived in the mail from the VA. Wow, I thought, she was right! Less than four months and I got my results. Sweet! Rather smugly I opened it up.

Not so smugly I read what it said. "Dear Michael," it read, "we are sorry to inform you that your case is still under review...." D'oh. I still had a month to go before hitting early side of the average settlement timeline, but that was OK. The good thing about being retired is that time was not necessarily one of my problems. I could wait.

I had no idea how long the wait would be.

*   *   *   *   *

Lessons Learned:

☐ Talk to a VA counselor as soon as you can. Make an appointment while you are still on active duty if you can, because even if they can't help you until you go on terminal leave they can explain the processes and procedures that you will need to follow to obtain evaluations and benefits. Forewarned is forearmed.

☐ Schedule a meeting immediately after going on terminal leave. You can officially start your evaluations and benefits requests when you have your DD-214 and final orders. It really behooves you to start as early as you can because the VA is overwhelmed with the huge number of veterans applying for benefits. If you wait all you do is compound the problem. It is a first in, first out system that is irrespective of military rank or position. Don't think that your uniformed high ranking muckety-muck status means anything to the VA because it doesn't.

☐ Get as many "certified true copies" of your DD-214 as possible. I have had to give out several so far, and it is easy to get them when you check out. Much less easy later, trust me. Having spare copies on hand will save you from wasting time running around, making copies, and getting them certified. Again, trust me.

☐ Make sure to provide the correct documentation to the VA. It cost me a month because I submitted a "Member 1" vice a "Member 4" DD-214 with my claim. What's the difference? As far as I can tell there is one additional block of information on the "Member 4" version. Apparently it is a pretty important block!

Part 3: Behind the curtain: The VA Disability Claims Process

The last section began the story of my experience with the Veterans Administration's physical exam process. It took a few months to get through the paperwork and to actually see a doctor or two, but soon enough I had completed all of the required evaluations.

Before I knew it a week had zipped by after my last appointment. The week stretched to two, then three, and then a month. Followed by another month. At the three month mark I began to get concerned.

Why was it taking so long? It turns out that the process was glacial because so many people like me were filing for disability evaluation, and the VA was struggling with the staggering load of cases. My case was in the hopper, and in good time it would move forward. The wait was for good reason, too, because the VA is responsible for thoroughly and accurately evaluating each and every veteran. That takes a lot of time.

The purpose of the VA medical evaluations and claims process is to document any injuries or physical issues that were caused or exacerbated by military service. The evaluation is important for two specific reasons; first, if a service member is injured while on active duty it is important for that injury to be documented in case it requires treatment after they get out of the military and second, in cases where the service member has incurred chronic conditions or disabling injuries they are eligible for financial compensation.

If a veteran broke her ankle while on active duty, for example, and gets out while she is still going through physical therapy she isn't just pitched out into the street. Her injury still requires treatment, so it is annotated during the physical exam and she will be able to use the VA medical system to get through the necessary physical therapy and get back on her feet. Once she is better she goes on her way and may never need the VA again. However, since the VA evaluated her ankle and documented the injury, in case she needs future treatment it is in the system and can still have that service-related injury treated by the VA medical system. Taking the example further, if the veteran with the broken ankle is left with a limp for the rest of her life she will likely be evaluated as having incurred a service connected disability. Depending on the rating that the disability is assigned (I will devote a lot of ink to disability assessment and ratings later on, don't worry) she may be eligible for a disability compensation check every month.

So being evaluated by the VA is important!

Back to my case.

I started my VA evaluation process as soon as I went on terminal leave, and before my EAS I had completed all required VA physicals. As I wrote earlier, however, I slowed down the evaluation and claims process because I submitted the incorrect DD-214, which was caught by the case manager and rectified after I sent in the correct copy. Although it seemed a bit random to me, there actually is a pretty well defined process that claims go through which shouldn't have been a surprise because after all the VA is a governmental agency that runs on thoroughly bureaucratic processes.

You can check the status of your claim by logging into the VA's ebenefits website (www.ebenefits.va.gov; it is password protected and you will be required to set your password early on in the evaluation process). Below is a breakdown of the claims process stages from the VA website, beginning with when my claim was initiated during my first meeting with the VA representative after going on terminal leave:

"Claim Received" - *Your claim has been received by the VA. If you applied online with VONAPP (Veterans on Line Application - the web based application for VA benefits) Direct Connect, you should see receipt in your list of Open Claims below within one hour. If you applied through the U.S. mail, please allow mailing time plus one week for us to process and record receipt of your claim.*

This is essentially an electronic receipt from the VA to show that they have received your packet and application. It provides proof that they have your information and it has been entered into the tracking system. If you do not see your status change within 30 days of submitting your package then you should contact the VA to find out if there is a problem.

"Under Review" - *Your claim has been assigned to a Veterans Service Representative and is being reviewed to determine if additional evidence is needed. If we do not need any additional information, your claim will move directly to the* **Preparation for Decision** *phase.*

It is during this phase that my errant paperwork was discovered. It took about a month, but the system works because the claims representative discovered that I had submitted the incorrect paperwork and notified me. It cost me a little time, but once I sent in the right documentation, my claim continued along to the next step.

"Gathering of Evidence" - *The Veterans Service Representative will request evidence from the required sources. Requests for evidence may be made of you, a medical professional, a government agency, or another authority. It is common for claims to return to this phase, should additional evidence be required.*

This phase is the one in which your case is assembled. Think of it like building a car; before it can be assembled the wheels and seats and motor all need to be on the factory floor. The VA is collecting the reports from your VA induction physical exams and examining your medical records. Once they have all of the source documentation they move on to the next phase.

"Review of Evidence" - *We have received all needed evidence. If, upon review, it is determined that more evidence is required, the claim will be sent back to the* **Gathering of Evidence** *phase.*

I was contacted during this phase to provide a more detailed description of how I incurred an injury while in Iraq. Again, the system works because the VA identified, through their due diligence, that I did not have enough documentation to support a portion of the claim. I filled out the form and described the situation in greater detail, and with receipt of the completed form my claim moved further along the path to completion. This is where having a solid medical record comes in because if they can easily find documentation of your conditions in your records as well as your examination then it makes their job easy. If they cannot find proof, their job gets harder because they must then request another physical examination or try to find substantiating records. That can add considerable time to the process.

"Preparing for Decision" - *The Veterans Service Representative has recommended a decision, and is preparing required documents detailing that decision. If more evidence is required, the claim will be sent back in the process for more information or evidence.*

This is where my case sat for over six months. I did receive monthly letters from the VA apologizing for the delays in processing, so I knew that my file isn't lost behind a filing cabinet or being used as a doorstop. I really did appreciate that they took the time to let me know that they were just behind schedule and that they were still working on my case.

"Pending Decision Approval" - *The recommended decision is reviewed, and a final award approval is made. If it is determined that more evidence or information is required, the claim will be sent back in the process for more information or evidence.*

You are getting close! The claim has been compiled, examined, reviewed, and recommendations have been made. As with all bureaucratic endeavors, though, there is a requirement for a review of the claim package prior to the final decision being made. Ensuring that everything is in order is the purpose of this step.

"Preparation for Notification" - *Your entire claim decision packet is prepared for mailing.*

Victory! Your claim is done, and now the VA is about to send you back your medical records along with the decision that they have made in your case.

"Complete" - *The VA has sent a decision packet to you by U.S. mail. The packet includes details of the decision or award. Please allow standard mailing time for your packet to arrive before contacting the call center.*

Look for a package from the VA on your doorstep. It will contain your medical record copy and a sheaf of papers that notify you of the result of your claim as well as the benefits that you are entitled to as a result. Happy day!

*   *   *   *   *

Lessons Learned:
- ☐ It takes time. A lot of time. It is important to meet with the VA as promptly as possible once you have your DD-214 in your possession because the process is so lengthy. You procrastinate at your own peril; if you can get your case initiated 60 days or less before your EAS you will likely have your case reviewed by the local VA office instead of having it sent to the main evaluation center. The anecdotal difference is about eight months. I was informed that it should take about four months after all of my information was provided for a local review as opposed to a year or so for a national level review. It pays to be prompt. (Although, in the long run it turned out not to matter in my case. It ended up taking about two years to fully adjudicate, for reasons covered in the following sections.)
- ☐ Get all of your ducks in a row before you initiate your claim. Missing or incorrect paperwork will stymie you progress, so avoid having the VA go through the nutroll of contacting you to update the package. In my case, I provided the incorrect DD-214 and had to provide greater detail about an injury, and both of those transactions took time. I recommend that when you fill out the pre-appointment paperwork that you go into

excruciating detail in regards to any injuries that you suffered. The few extra minutes that you take filling out the form may save you the loss of a month in processing time later.

Part 4: A travelogue of my VA disability claim adventure

I began my transition process about nine months before I got out, and as I went through the required and optional transition seminars I was educated about the benefits that all honorably discharged veterans are eligible to receive. As a retiring Marine I learned that I was eligible for more benefits than those who served one or two enlistments (such as pension and access to VA medical care for me and an entitlement to TRICARE for my family). Such benefits are great! They were earned through over a quarter century of service in uniform and no small amount of time getting shot at in combat zones.

In addition to the need for VA medical care I was evaluated to determine whether or not I was eligible for a disability rating as a result of the maladies, wear, and tear that I experienced while serving in uniform. It is perfectly reasonable to be evaluated for any such problems, but unfortunately the time it takes for the claims evaluation process to reach completion is far from speedy.

As I said, my adventure with the VA took a considerable amount of time. Over two years passed between the first meeting with the Camp Pendleton VA representative and the settlement of my claim. After the initial flurry of medical evaluations and appointments, weeks stretched into months without any apparent progress. At month eight I received a couple of notifications. The first was a letter that was identical to the letters that preceded it telling me that my claims process was still under review. Not surprising, really, because the average time to review and approve a case is well over a year.

The second occurred when I logged into the VA ebenefits website. Surprisingly, I saw that there was some progress. Hooray! My status had changed from "Preparation for Decision" to "Regulatory or Procedural Review". I wasn't exactly sure what that meant, but I grew cautiously optimistic that it was an indicator of progress.

I drilled into the website to see what the new status reflected. Here is what the website said:

Claim Received: *08/17/2012*
Claim Type: *Regulatory or Procedural Review*

Estimated Claim Completion Date: unavailable. We are currently unable to provide you with a projected completion date for this type of claim. Please await further claim status notification for this Regional Office.

Hmmm. That told me pretty much nothing at all. I read on:

Next Steps:

We will review all available evidence and make a decision on your claim upon receipt of all requested information as outlined in the headings, "What Do We Still Need from You?" and "What Have We Done?".

Several factors will determine the duration of the "Development" phase, including:

- *type of claim filed*
- *number of disabilities you claim*
- *complexity of your disability(ies), and*
- *availability of evidence needed to decide your claim.*

Now that sounded promising! My case was in the "development" phase. I still wasn't sure what exactly that meant, but I continued to hope that it indicated progress.

At any rate, my claim continued to wend its way through the claims wickets. Not that I was informed of the process. You shouldn't wait for the VA to tell you about your updated status via the postal service, because they probably won't. The form letters that I received from the VA monthly didn't tell me anything new. To keep your finger on the pulse of your case you should be checking the VA ebenefits website frequently to see if your status is moving forward. Otherwise things may be going on with your claim that you are unaware of.

Just a word to the wise: keep up on your claim! After all, if you don't, who will?

Part 5: News from the Veterans Administration

A month later…

There are a few events in life that take nine months to complete. Things like a school year, a sailing trip around the world, or having a baby.

None of those things happened to me. What did occur, however, was that my VA Disability Evaluation was completed. And it was completed only nine months after I submitted my paperwork. I did a little surfing around the internet and found that nine months was close to average for a claim to wend its way through the system.

So I had nothing to complain about, really. My claim was processed in the same amount of time as pretty much everyone else's. But hold on...

As with everything in life there is a catch.

A catch that I discovered when I opened the claim packet that arrived in the mail from the VA. One afternoon a thick envelope was waiting by my front door, and upon opening it up I found my medical records and a letter explaining, among other things, my ratings. It seemed pretty straightforward.

But, as with all things related to transition, it wasn't.

It turns out that the evaluation process was only partially complete. I had a couple of things that were "not included" in the evaluation because the VA required more information. Apparently I was to be contacted in the future for a follow up examination to address the remaining issues.

So, I had apparently received my evaluation results in the mail but I had to wait to be contacted to complete my evaluation? To say I was confused is an understatement. About half of my claim was settled, and the other half was not.

You see, as I departed active duty I was thoroughly examined by both military and Veterans Administration physicians as a part of the final physical process. The Navy doctors and corpsmen checked me out and documented everything that was relevant into my records, and the VA then followed up with an examination of their own to determine what conditions, if any, that I had developed during my service would be considered disabling. Having the conditions rated as disabling is important because the VA treats those conditions free of charge.

In my case, about half of the conditions that had been identified during my physicals were rated as disability-related conditions and would be addressed by the VA in the future. The other half were marked as "deferred" because they needed additional information. The letter went on to say that they had requested a medical examination, and that I would be "notified of the date, time, and place to report." It sounded reasonable, so all I had to do was be patient and wait.

One month went by.

Then two. Then three. Four. Finally at month five I decided that my phone wasn't going to ring any time soon and I needed to do something about it. But what?

Thinking back to my experience at the Transition Assistance Course I remembered that a representative from the Disabled American Veterans had talked me through the VA medical evaluation process as he evaluated my medical record. I had signed a limited power of attorney that appointed the DAV as the Veterans Service Organization that would represent me in my VA proceedings, and now it was time to give them a ring and ask for some help.

After rummaging through the rather tall pile of transition related documents that occupies a significant portion of my desk I found his business card. "Aha!" thought I. "A call and it will all be fixed!"

Wrong again.

I did call the number, only to find that I was calling the wrong number. It turns out that the gentleman that I had worked with during the TAP seminar was not the same gentleman that I would be working with in my dealings with the VA. The guy at TAP was fully engaged in meeting new veterans and helping get their claims processes started. Once the veterans were in the DAV system they (including me!) would be working with representatives at their regional office located in San Diego.

So I called *that* number. Unfortunately their offices were closed for the holidays, so I called back once the holidays were over. I *finally* linked up with a live person, a very nice lady, took down some basic information and instructed me to wait for a representative to call.

After a day or two of swapping voicemails because of missed calls the DAV representative and I finally linked up on the phone. I explained my dilemma to him, and he patiently explained what needed to happen next.

"What you have," he said, "is a partially completed claim. At this point there really isn't anything the DAV can do for you because our process begins when the initial VA claim is settled."

Sensing my frustration, he continued.

"What you need to do is to contact the VA and set up an appointment to get the ball rolling yourself. You need to do this quickly because if you don't follow up on the listed conditions they may be disallowed because you are not showing that they are still a problem." He then gave me the appropriate phone number for the closest VA office and we said our goodbyes.

Hmm...so I needed to get my sore knees and bad back looked at again? I had signed up for TRICARE Prime, so I could go to the doctor, but my decades of "sucking it up" had precluded me from making an appointment for something that did not involve broken bones or arterial bleeding.

So I called the VA the next day. After a similar game of telephone and voicemail tag I spoke with a very helpful gentleman who understood exactly what my dilemma was. He checked his calendar and squeezed me into an appointment the next week, when he promised to get my ship sailing in the right direction.

*　　*　　*　　*　　*

Lessons Learned:

- ☐ Contact your VSO immediately after you receive your VA claim settlement letter. I lost about five months as I waited for the VA to contact me before I finally got on the ball and started engaging the system.

- ☐ The VA is perpetually buried in claims and the best thing to do is to take charge of your own case. Waiting just means that others who are being proactive are jumping in line ahead of you.

- ☐ Your VSO can explain the intricacies of the settlement letter in a phone call, but you have to contact them to initiate the conversation.

- ☐ The next call you make after the VSO should be your local VA office in order to initiate the next steps in the evaluation process. If your claim is settled, then you need to contact them to be registered in their computer system so that you can access healthcare providers. If your claim is not fully settled, then you need to get registered and schedule appointments with the appropriate professionals in order to finish up your claim.

Part 6: Entering the system

The appointment on the following Wednesday was a real one, complete with a real live person as opposed to another endless and annoying game of telephone tag. The instructions were simple enough: I was directed to gather together my documentation and to show up at the local VA clinic by ten in the morning. Upon my arrival I would be meeting up with the Benefits and Enrollment specialist.

So arrive I did, and right on time. I walked into the lobby of the recently built and still sparkly building and sauntered up to the reception desk. Much to my chagrin there was no one at the desk, so I rather aimlessly just leaned on the counter until somebody arrived. I was hopefully that someone would arrive because there were two chairs behind the desk, and they looked recently abandoned.

After a few minutes of pointless leaning I decided to find someone who could help me. I wandered past the reception desk and into the halls beyond. After walking from one side of the building to the other in hopes of randomly finding the office I was looking for I gave in and asked an employee (who was readily identifiable by her hospital scrubs and prominently displayed VA Identification badge) for help.

"Go to the lobby and check in with the girls up front," said she.

After explaining the absence of said girls, the employee shrugged and pointed back the way I came. "Just go back to the lobby. Someone will call for you."

I was not particularly optimistic that said calling would occur, but I meekly headed back to the lobby anyway. Joining a few other patient souls in the chairs that ringed the perimeter of the room, I found a tattered copy of Time magazine to fill my time as I waited for the call that I was not certain would come.

After ten minutes of reading about Time Magazine's view of the world circa 2011, a door that had previously gone unnoticed burst open. An energetic gentleman with short graying hair and an startlingly positive outlook on life fairly leapt onto the scene and immediately started asking each of us in the lobby why we were there.

After a staccato interchange between the people sitting next to me, he turned in my direction and asked if he could help me. I explained that I was there to meet with the enrollment section. He smiled and said "That's ME!" and pointed me towards the still-open door and one of the vacant offices on the other side. "Take a seat, I'll be right there."

So in I went, clutching my sheaf of medical records and other documents, wary to see what would happen next.

John, as I learned his name to be, had obviously introduced a few people to the VA system before I showed up. Probably thousands of them. He had it down! He handed me a sixteen page long questionnaire to fill out and began firing questions at me faster than a belt fed machine gun.

"Retired?" "Yep."

"How long were you in?" "Twenty seven years."

"Social?" (As in *what was my social security number*, which is the key that opens my files in pretty much every government database). I gave him my precious nine digits.

"Marine?" "Yep."

"What did you do in the Marines?" "Where do you live?" "Do you have TRICARE?"

Each question was accompanied by his furious banging on the computer keyboard as he entered my information into the computer. I was vainly trying to complete the form as he talked, which he noticed.

"Don't worry about that paperwork right now. That is for the social worker, who I will introduce you to in a few minutes."

Social worker? Really? What was that all about?

"For now, let's just get you in the system..."and from there we were off on a journey of questions and answers that lasted ten or fifteen minutes. I won't subject you to the lengthy details, but here is a rundown of the pertinent ones for those of you who will be headed to the VA:

- The difference between TRICARE and the VA. He patiently explained that TRICARE is insurance, and the VA provides traditional medical care, just like your regular family physician. While that statement sounds obvious, the ramifications are significant. If you are injured in an accident or have an emergency away from your normal VA provider, TRICARE takes care of it because that is what insurance is for. The VA is not insurance, so you would be in trouble when the bills came due for emergency treatment because the VA does not pay for such events because the VA is not insurance.

- Online enrollment. I had previously enrolled into the VA healthcare system because several months ago they had thoughtfully sent me an email with instructions detailing how to sign up. The email, which suspiciously looked like spam (but wasn't) encouraged me to register via the VA website, which had a link to an automated form known as the 1010EZ. I logged in and filled out the form, and it reduced the amount of time I spent with the enrollment specialist by at least half.

- The Packet. The sixteen page packet that he handed me was the OIF/OEF/OND (Operation Iraqi Freedom, Operation Enduring Freedom, and Operation New Dawn) enrollment questionnaire. In a nutshell, it was a long questionnaire that asked a lot of questions about my mental health, combat experiences, and exposure to traumatic brain injury (TBI). The form would be used by my social worker. More on that later.

- Explanation of how the clinic works. This particular clinic is divided into three teams (Red, White, and Blue: pretty catchy!) and each team had a staff of its own. In my case I became a member of Team White, and with my assignment came my choice of primary healthcare providers. Since I did not know any of the doctors personally, I happily chose the one with the next available appointment time, which was only a month away.

- My first appointment with the doctor would be a "welcome aboard" type of physical examination, and I would be required to visit the hospital's lab the week prior to the appointment and surrender various bodily fluids. Joy.

- Appointments. In order to set up an appointment, I would not be allowed to call the doctor or the clinic directly. Instead, I would have to call *central appointments* (via a 1-800 number) in order to contact someone at the clinic. That is pretty much the same as life in uniform, so it wasn't a shock, but it certainly is annoying. If I want to ask the doctor about a medication, for example, I need to call central appointments and leave a message. Then, when the doctor gets the message and has the time, he or she is supposed to call me back. I hope I don't have any time critical severe allergic reactions!

- ID Card. Towards the end of the interview he announced that it was time for me to get my VA ID. I sat up straight and looked at the camera that was mounted above his computer screen, and when he said smile I did so. With a click of his mouse and a flash of bright white light, my crooked smile was forever etched into the VA database. About ten days later my ID card arrived, and fortunately my photo is not too terrible. No second chance for a new picture!

As soon as John was done with the interview he guided me to another office and introduced me to one of the clinic's social workers. She asked if I had completed my form, and as I had not she gestured for me to take a seat and fill it out.

I did so, and after ten minutes of scribbling I knocked on her door. She invited me in, and after taking the sheaf of papers from my clutches she began *her* interview.

Now, you should understand that this is probably the first time in my life that I have ever been in a room with a social worker. I have met people in that line of work in the past, but never have I actually been professionally engaged by one. Honestly, I had no idea what social workers actually did, but after spending a half hour with a professional I was pleasantly surprised to learn that they fit a niche that is needed in the VA: helping veterans who are having difficulty transitioning back to the civilian world deal with the often confusing processes that come with the title "veteran", not to mention little things like Post Traumatic Stress Disorder, Traumatic Brain Injury, and other psychological issues.

At any rate, she had the unenviable task of manually inputting the responses I scribbled on my questionnaire into the computer database. Obviously some parts of the VA could use a little modernization, but she explained that she actually got more out of re-inputting the data because she could interact with the client (me, in this case) and flesh out her perspective on the information. This is important because she was evaluating things with real impacts on veterans, such as combat stress problems and indicators of violence, self-harm, and suicide. She was there to make sure that we, the combat veteran population, were looked at objectively and offered the appropriate levels of care.

After an hour or so spent chatting with the social worker, she led me to the appointment desk at the combat stress clinic. The results of my survey indicated that meeting with them would be a good idea, and to be honest I believe it is a place that all combat veterans need to visit. The wars of the last decade have seen an unprecedented level of stress on the military forces, with many veterans deploying to war time and again, and then again, and again. The frantic deployment tempo means that many veterans bring issues and problems home, and the VA is there to help deal with them. Going to the clinic is the first step along the way to getting better, and whether you think you need it or not you should stop by.

*　　*　　*　　*　　*

<u>Lessons Learned:</u>
- ☐ After your claim is settled, either partially or in full, you should be receiving an email inviting you to enroll in the VA via their website. Initially I thought the email was spam, but after several attempts I finally paid attention and registered. Doing so greatly streamlined my in-person registration process. As an aside, they

used the email address that I provided months earlier as I was transitioning out, so it behooves you to make sure that you provide an address that you will utilize for a long time to come.

☐ The VA is just like every other government bureaucracy. Get ready to do some things twice, and if you are lucky, three times or more. It is just the way it is. Suck it up and march on.

☐ It will help for you to bring whatever documentation from the VA you have accumulated thus far. I recommend that you buy a pocket folder or folio specifically to keep all of your VA stuff in. Even better, get yourself a dedicated filing system for all of the stuff that you are amassing because if you don't you will end up with a disorganized pile of documents approaching the stature of the Eiffel tower. If you don't believe me, just come to my house and look at the pile on my desk.

Part 6: This is not the appointment you were looking for...

A week later I found myself reporting to the clinic for my first official appointment. It was interesting, but not really what I had expected. Or what I was hoping for. It was, however, insightful because it provided a glimpse into the road that lay before me as a "customer" of the VA healthcare system as well as an introduction to many of my fellow veterans who frequent the local clinic.

The appointment was with the VA Clinic's PTSD Services unit. As I wrote in earlier, I spent an hour or so with my designated social worker whose job it is (among other things) to assess whether or not I needed to be evaluated for the effects of combat stress. Her assessment was based on our meeting as well as the sixteen page questionnaire that I completed beforehand. Since the questions were all about combat, and having spent a whole lot of time in and around a significant amount of it in two different war zones, she determined that it was certainly appropriate for me to go in for a PTSD evaluation.

That brought me to my inaugural appointment, which was the *Post-Traumatic Stress Disorder Services Orientation*. I wandered into the clinic's Mental Health Services waiting room and, after checking in, was handed yet another set of forms to fill out. After ten minutes of answering questions about my propensity for self-harm, manic episodes, and depression, I was finished. Just in time, too, because as my government issued pen scratched out the last checkmark a young woman opened the waiting room door and asked those of us waiting for the PTSD orientation to follow her.

I joined a rather eclectic group as we accompanied her to a smallish room ringed with chairs padded with leather seats and backrests colored in the oddly disturbing green that is prevalent in hospitals and movies about psychiatric institutions. They must have got them on sale somewhere, because I don't think they would match anyone's home décor unless there was a time machine that could take us back to about 1968. To their credit, though, they were actually pretty comfortable.

Out of the twenty odd-colored seats ten or so were filled by my fellow attendees. There was an elderly veteran of the Second World War, Korea, and Vietnam (as his hat proudly proclaimed), a man in his sixties, a few gentlemen in their 50's, a young woman who never took off her sunglasses, a tattooed young man barely out of his teens, and me. It was not at all what I was expecting. I had figured that my meeting would be with young veterans from the recent decade of war, but to my surprise we veterans of Iraq and Afghanistan were in the minority. There were three of us, one veteran of Desert Storm, the aforementioned WWII vet, and the rest were from the Vietnam War.

I know this because the young woman who led the session (another clinical social worker) had us introduce ourselves before we began the session. In addition to asking where we served, she asked us to share why we were here. The recently discharged veterans were pretty obvious, but the others were a surprise. Each of them had been referred to the session by their primary care provider, which I found to be fascinating. After hearing their introductions and listening to their conversations it became evident to me that many of these veterans were just now entering the VA medical system. To me, that was a surprise because I had never really considered *not* entering the system.

That reveals a tremendous difference between the experiences that "new" veterans have in juxtaposition to the "old" ones. Our transition process from active duty included a mandatory introduction to the VA, along with an education in the basics that the VA provides. Many veterans of WWII, Korea, Vietnam, Desert Storm, and the Cold War received no such exposure. As a result, thousands and thousands of veterans who are eligible for help and care never bothered to pursue it until they really needed the services that the VA provides. Unfortunately, for many of them, the help that the VA offers ends up attempting to make up for years or decades of neglected conditions. That was the explanation for why so many of the people in the room with me were there for the first time despite having removed their uniforms before Disco Fever ruled the dance floor.

Anyhow, back to the session. After introductions, the social worker ran through a dozen or so power point slides that described the multitude of programs that the VA offered in the clinic. This particular clinic was focused on combat veterans who were at risk for PTSD, and the services that they provide were all focused on countering and healing the effects of combat stress. She started with textbook definition (according to the American Psychiatric Association, which apparently comes up with such things) of PTSD, which included things like experiencing traumatic events, re-experiencing previous trauma, hyper-vigilance and hyper-arousal, and avoidance of things that remind you of traumatic events. Considering that everyone in the room has served in combat, the probability that at least some of these symptoms would apply to us was about 100%.

After an explanation of what PTSD was all about she assured us that recovery from it was possible. The VA offered over a dozen different methods to assist with recovery including individual and group sessions on topics like anger management, coping, spiritually based recovery, couples and family therapy, anxiety disorders, and women's groups. The goal of each program is to help the veteran reach a positive outcome within three months, with a positive outcome being that the veteran being better able to cope with his or her condition.

Not surprisingly the clinic was overwhelmed with veterans who needed help. The wait time to join in the programs was eight weeks or more. The social worker explained the process for getting into one of the groups, and that is where I realized that this was actually not the appointment I was looking for. Actually it was not even really an appointment at all, but instead it was just an orientation.

Towards the end of the session she explained that for us to participate in any of the offerings we would have to set up another appointment in which we would actually meet with a healthcare provider who would then assign us to a group. An intake appointment, she called it. That was the first indicator that this was not the appointment I was looking for. The second indicator was her announcement that the clinic did not have anything to do with disability claims.

I was actually hoping to get my disability claim back on track. It had been five months since I had been notified that the claim had been partially settled and that I should wait to be contacted by the VA for further evaluation. After spending almost half a year listening to the sound of no telephones ringing I called the VA to get the ball rolling. I had wrongly assumed that once I was in the system that the claims process would proceed as a matter of course and that this appointment was a part of the plan.

Nope.

I would need to call another number for that, or I could stop by the Veterans Service Office (VSO) that happened to be just across the hall. They would be able to help those of us working on our claims, she said, but unfortunately not today because their office was closed.

D'oh.

She then reviewed all of the forms that we completed prior to the session, and then she called each of us out individually to set up appointments for the intake interview. I was a bit disgruntled, but resigned myself to just go with the flow and left the session with an appointment for an intake appointment some six weeks in the future and the phone number to the clinic's VSO office which would help me with my claim.

I also left reminding myself that the VA was a bureaucracy and that patience was a virtue. I was still disgruntled, though, and not feeling particularly virtuous. So it goes.

*   *   *   *   *

Lessons Learned:

- ☐ The medical side of the VA is different from the disability claims side of the VA. Make sure to stay engaged with your VSO to ensure that your claim is moving forward, and also be specific with the VA representatives when you are making your appointments. I was not specific enough because I made some errant assumptions, and as a result I have lost another month or two of forward progress on my claim.

- ☐ Be ready to devote a lot of time to the VA. There are great programs available, but it will take a long time and plenty of repetitive red tape, paperwork, and meetings to actually see a provider. Breathe deep, think happy thoughts, and go to your happy place. Time will pass and you will get the help you need. It will just take a lot more time than you would like.

- ☐ Ask questions up front. Had I asked whether or not this appointment would help with my disability claim I would have saved some valuable time. Assume nothing!

Part 7: It was the appointment I was looking for...sort of.

Every once in a while things make sense. Unfortunately, during our journey into the wonderful world of the Veterans Administration, that once in a while proved to be frustratingly elusive.

Earlier we learned about the two seemingly unrelated and paradoxical events centered on my VA disability claim. Within the span of a single week I received a telephone call to invite me to an appointment at the local Veterans Administration hospital, which I took as an augury that my claim was turgidly stumbling forward. Interestingly, I also found that my claim was marked "CLOSED" on the VA's ebenefits website.

One step forward and a huge leap back? To say I was confused would be a gross disservice to the concept of understatement.

At any rate, I showed up for the aforementioned appointment and learned a little more about how the various processes at the VA work, or at least how they are *supposed* to work.

Unbeknownst to me that day's appointment was based on the interview that the VA social worker had conducted on the day I officially became a consumer of VA health benefits. The survey identified some items in my history that required further evaluation, and the appointment that I attended a few days ago was one of those items (in this case, it was for a Traumatic Brain Injury evaluation that was warranted because of my close proximity to noisy exploding things while in Iraq).

I checked into the medical center, and after filling out yet another questionnaire about various things related to my mental state was called to see the doctor. After a brief introduction, I followed her through the physical therapy section of the hospital to a small office tucked away behind the treadmills and medicine balls.

I spent the next 45 minutes or so answering questions about the noisy things that exploded in my vicinity and the possible effects that they could have on me these many years later. She then performed a series of physical examinations. After getting whacked on the knee and following her finger with my eyes and a dozen or so other tests she announced that she felt I was unlikely to be suffering from any long term effects of getting my bell rung in combat. "Maybe a concussion," said she, "but you seem fine to me. Any questions?"

Ahhh. Finally. I did have a question or two.

I inquired as to the purpose of my visit. Was I here for a disability related evaluation? I explained my confusion, and she gave me the patient smile of someone who has explained this to people a time or two before.

"No. This exam is based on the social worker's evaluation from the VA clinic. It has nothing to do with the disability claim process."

She saw my blank and vacuous stare, and continued.

"We don't have anything to do with claims. The systems are completely separate. If they want, they can access the records of this appointment, but that is up to them. We are the medical side, not the disability claims side of the fence."

With that bit of insight the light bulb went on in my head. Suddenly I understood why the two events that had occurred a month previously had confused me: I mistakenly thought that I was dealing with one agency when in fact I was dealing with two. And neither of them talks to each other.

How governmentally bureaucratic!

The medical side had set the appointment, and it was proof positive that the system (or at least their half of it) worked.

The claims side, on the other hand, clearly had something wrong.

With that shocking bit of knowledge, I set out to find out just what was amiss with my disability claim. After finishing the appointment, I went home and called the toll-free number for the VA. Not once. Not twice. Not three times.

I won't bore you with how many times I pounded the keys on my phone trying to reach a VA counselor, but after many fruitless attempts I resorted to calling at 5:20 (Pacific Standard Time) in the morning in an effort to get through. It worked. After waiting on hold for nearly 30 minutes, I finally found myself at last in contact with a real live VA person.

I explained my dilemma to the gentleman on the other end of the line and he looked into it. Apparently the ebenefits website was depicting the results of the most recent review that my case file had received and was incorrectly showing my status as closed. What had occurred was that my file was being reconciled to determine what still remained to be done, and once that reconciliation was completed that review was posted as closed.

For whatever reason (which the VA rep could not explain) the ebenefits site "sometimes" picks up the wrong status. I was one of the lucky few to fall in the wonderful world of "sometimes". Fortunately, my case was still open. The status on the website was wrong. Unfortunately, there was also no indicator of progress in my case, so it really didn't matter what the website said. I was still going nowhere fast, but apparently I am making good time.

Sensing my consternation, the VA rep offered to initiate an inquiry. The inquiry, he explained, means that someone in the office that held my claim would have to call me within the next ten working days to explain what was going on.

Hooray! All I would have to do was wait for the phone to ring, and once it did I would be able to talk to someone who could explain just what was happening with my disability claim.

All I had to do was wait. Again.

*   *   *   *   *

Lessons Learned:

☐ The VA medical system and the VA disability claims system are two unrelated and unintegrated silos. They each are performing their own important mission, but they do so independent of each other. Make sure to find out on which side of the fence your appointments fall or you will end up confused like I did by assuming that a medical appointment was for my disability claim or vice versa.

☐ Calling the VA during working hours is pointless and annoying. There is supposedly a callback feature that you can use if you call after working hours, but I could never get it to work. I resorted to calling early in the morning, right about the time that the call center opens, which is listed as 7:00 am Eastern time. The number is 1-800-827-1000. Good luck!!

☐ Write everything down, including the inquiry tracking number and the name of the person that you talked to. It will be useful later on in case the inquiry gets lost or the information that you received turns out to be erroneous.

Part 8: The call I was waiting for from the VA. Really!

After a month (not ten days as advertised) it finally happened. The VA called and scheduled my final disability evaluation appointment. Well, they didn't actually call, but instead they contacted me the old fashioned way: through the good old U. S. Postal Service. I received a letter that explained that I needed to be seen by the VA's contract provider for a few things that were not completely documented by my initial visit, and with the letter came a questionnaire regarding the issues in question. I filled out the questionnaire, and within a day or two I received a call from the provider's office to schedule an appointment.

A few weeks later I went to the contract provider that takes care of the claims side of the VA house. It was the same provider that I had seen a year earlier, and to their credit they were very efficient and polite. I was in and out of their office in less than 45 minutes, which was a pleasant surprise as I had anticipated spending the afternoon in the waiting room. With that appointment I had, in theory, finished up my claims process. I fervently hope that it was finally done! According to the VA representative with which I had spoken earlier the only items remaining in my case were the completed evaluation from the contract provider and a few administrative corrections in my file.

With that appointment the evaluation phase was finished. Now all I had to do was to wait for the administrators to correct my file, forward it to the team that was evaluating my claim, and finalize the process.

I've heard that story before, though. The question is just how long the wait would be.

*   *   *   *   *

<u>**Lessons learned:**</u>

☐ The medical side of the VA is completely separate from the disability claims side of the VA. In my case, the clue to the difference was that all of the medical issues were addressed by my local clinic while all of my disability evaluations were performed by a contracted provider.

☐ Be proactive. Call the VA and determine your status. I think it helped, as my case was languishing for months until I made some inquiries.

☐ As always, be patient!

Part 9: Finally settled!

The virtue of patience finally paid off when one day I learned that my VA disability claim was finally settled. Suddenly, after nearly two years of jousting in vain, I found myself with one less windmill at which to tilt.

Although I could finally put down my lance and return my trusty steed back into the barn, I found the whole process to be pretty confusing. Particularly confusing was figuring out just what being identified as a disabled veteran meant in *real* terms, such as the impact a disability rating have on my bank account and future medical care.

It turns out that if you have incurred an injury while serving in uniform, and that injury is determined to be disabling, then you are entitled to compensation from the Veterans Administration. That compensation is paid directly to the veteran by the VA, which is nice. It is also tax free, which is nicer.

If you are a veteran who receives a disability rating which entitles you to a monthly benefit payment, you will receive a check in the mail (or an electronic deposit into your bank account) for the scheduled amount of money.

But, as usual, things are not always that simple. Particularly for retirees who receive a pension for their 20+ years of service to the nation. Retirees like me.

In that case, any remuneration that you receive from the VA is offset by an equal deduction from your pension, with the only really difference in your retirement check being the portion from the VA that is tax free. For example (and this example is in round numbers to keep things easy), if your pension is $1500 per month, you receive a check for $1500 minus any taxes (let's say 20%, which is $300), or $1200.

Now, let's say that you receive a disability rating which results in a payment from the VA of $100. That $100 is not added to your check for a total of $1600. Instead, $100 of the $1500 that was paid by the Defense Finance and Accounting Service (DFAS) is now paid by the VA, so the total pension amount stays the same. What changes is how the taxes are computed.

Now you have $1400 that is taxable, which results in a slightly lower tax bill. Here is the math:

$1400 x 20% = $280 in taxes.

$1400 (from DFAS) + $100 (from the VA) = $1500 (which is your pension amount).

$1500 (pension + VA Disability) - $280 (taxes) = $1220.

Sooooo.....as a retiree you get an extra twenty bucks in your monthly check. If you are not a retiree, however, you get the full $100.

That seems really odd. But wait, there's more!

The reduction of your pension by the disability payment changes at the 50% disability threshold. If you are rated as having a disability rating of 50% or more, then the bizarre math problem that we just performed goes away. In that case, you receive your entire pension as well as the complete VA disability amount.

Sounds bizarre, eh? I'm not making this stuff up! Really!

The program which makes the math problem go away is known as Concurrent Retirement Disability Pay (CRDP). (For a more in depth explanation of the math problems above, you can read all about how it works at the DFAS website: www.dfas.mil/retiredmilitary/disability/crdp.html)

Back to my disability claim. I know that it was settled because the VA sent me a very nice letter saying that it was, and along with my final disability rating came a brief paragraph that indicated that I would be receiving a settlement check from the Defense Finance and Accounting Service (DFAS) as well as the VA. Intriguing, thought I. What exactly did that mean, and more importantly for my bank account, how much money were we talking about?

I received no VA compensation until my case was partially adjudicated some ten months after the claim was filed. During that time I was receiving my full military pension.

On the tenth month of the life of my disability claim the VA made a partial determination in my case. They rated me at a low level for a few conditions, but they needed to conduct more examinations to determine if I was eligible for a higher rating. The bottom line was that now I was eligible to receive some compensation from the VA.

Great!

The devil is always in the details, however, and instead of receiving a check on top of my pension the military deducted the amount of my VA compensation from my pension. The VA then did send me a check, but for the same amount that was deducted from my pension.

In my case, I received the partial amount until my claim was settled a whole year later. I then became eligible for not only the full VA compensation amount, but also a check that amounts to all of the compensation that I would have been paid had my claim been settled the day I left active duty. In other words, the VA would write me a check for the full amount of compensation I was eligible for, minus the money that I had already received. Here is an example of how that works:

To keep things simple, I will use $100 as the partial claim compensation amount and $200 as the final compensation amount. My claim took 22 months to complete, with a partial settlement issued at month ten. The math looks like this:

Total amount of VA compensation that the veteran should receive in this case is computed by multiplying the number of months eligible times the final compensation amount, as follows: $200 x 22 = $4400.

The amount of VA compensation that the veteran has received to this point is computed by subtracting the number of months he or she did not receive compensation from the total months eligible, and then multiplying that number by the partial settlement compensation amount, as follows: 22 - 10 = 12 months: 12 x $100 = $1200.

Now that we know how much the total amount of compensation the veteran is eligible for ($4400) and the amount of compensation that he or she has already received ($1200), we can determine the settlement amount from the VA by subtracting the amount received from the total amount: $4400 - $1200 = $3200.

So the veteran will receive a tax free check for $3200. Sweet!

But wait, there's more.

For those veterans who are retired from the military, they are owed the same back pay as shown above, but in addition DFAS is required to pay back the taxes collected on the back pay. For every month that you should have received a payment from the VA but didn't, that amount was taxed. Since VA compensation is tax free, you are due the taxes that you paid. It is calculated as follows:

From the problem above, you are about to receive a check for $3200 from the VA. DFAS has already deducted the taxes for the first $1200, but has not done so for the remaining $3200. In effect, you have been paid that amount and been taxed on it, so DFAS needs to cut you a check for the taxes (assuming a 20% tax rate as used in the problem above): $3200 x 20% = $640. Unfortunately, if you are retired and not simply out of the service you don't get $3200 (unless your disability rating is 50% or greater). You get $640. Not as sweet, but still a nice chunk of change.

But wait, there is still more!

In cases where your VA disability compensation rating is 50% or more, you are eligible for Concurrent Receipt of VA Compensation and Retired Pay through a program known as CRDP (Concurrent Retirement and Disability Pay; to learn more about the nuts and bolts of how the program works go to www.dfas.mil/retiredmilitary/disability/crdp.html). Concurrent receipt means that you receive checks from both DFAS and the VA, and that you are entitled to the full amount of eligibility from both. Now the numbers are quite different when you calculate them using the numbers above:

Since you are eligible to receive both checks, you will receive your full settlement check from the VA as well as back pay for the pension amount that was deducted and replaced by the monthly VA claim amount, less taxes on that amount. Sounds complicated, but it really isn't. The math looks like this: *(Full VA settlement amount)* $3200 + *(Pension amount deducted and replaced by the VA)* $1200 - *(taxes on the pension amount deducted and replaced by the VA)* $640 = $3760.

If your brain hurts, that's ok. The bottom line is that the DFAS and the VA are sending you a check or two that will cover the cost of whole lot of aspirin.

Chapter 26: The GI Bill

A big part of my transition was the decision to continue my education by pursuing a master's degree. Getting a college education is expensive these days, but fortunately for me and for all honorably discharged veterans the VA is there to help out with the Post 9/11 GI Bill.

For those of you who are unfamiliar with the GI Bill, here is a quick rundown of how it came about and evolved into what it has become today:

The GI Bill was created towards the end of the Second World War. In 1944 the federal government passed the **Serviceman's Readjustment Act**. Apparently calling the new law by its formal name was a mouthful, so it quickly became named after the people it was designed to help; the GIs who were returning home from the war (GI was slang for anyone in uniform, coming from the term "Government Issue" or "Galvanized Iron", depending on which story you believe). Anyhow, the veterans coming home from Europe and the Pacific were able to take advantage of a wide array of benefits which included home, small business, and farm loans, unemployment compensation, and educational benefits. As a result of the program a staggering total of nearly 8,000,000 veterans (almost half of all those who served during the war) pursued higher education.

Over the following decades GIs went to war again and again, and as they did the GI Bill was there to help veterans when they returned from places like Korea and Vietnam. In the 1960s benefits were opened up to veterans who did not serve in time of war, but over time the GI Bill dwindled until it was a shadow of its former self. It provided a stipend to help defray the cost of school, but that was all.

That changed with the attacks on 9/11 and the subsequent wars in Iraq and Afghanistan. With hundreds and hundreds of thousands of Soldiers, Sailors, Airmen, and Marines serving tour after tour in harm's way the Congress passed the **Post-9/11 Veterans Educational Assistance Act of 2008**, which quickly became known as the "Post 9/11" or "new" GI Bill. It focuses primarily on educational benefits for veterans as shown below, which I adapted from the VA's Post 9/11 GI Bill website (as of December 2013):

- The GI Bill will pay an eligible veteran's full **tuition & fees** directly to the school for all public school in-state students.

For the 2013-2014 academic year, those attending private or foreign schools will find tuition & fees are capped at $17,500. For those attending a more expensive private school or a public school as a non-resident out-of-state student, a program exists which may help to reimburse the difference (the "Yellow Ribbon" program, which can be as much as $10,000 per year).

- For those attending classes at the greater than ½ time rate, a **monthly housing allowance (MHA)** based on the Basic Allowance for Housing for an E-5 with dependents at the location of the school. For those enrolled solely in distance learning the housing allowance payable is equal to ½ the national average BAH for an E-5 with dependents ($714.50 for the 2013-2014 academic year).
- An **annual books & supplies stipend of $1,000** paid proportionately based on enrollment.
- A one-time **rural benefit** payment of $500 those eligible.

As you can see, the new GI Bill is pretty generous. Not everyone is eligible, however. In order to take advantage of the benefits the veteran must meet the following criteria:

- You must have served at least 90 aggregate days on active duty after September 10, 2001, and you are still on active duty or were honorably discharged from the active duty; or
- released from active duty and placed on the retired list or temporary disability retired list; or
- released from active duty and transferred to the Fleet Reserve or Fleet Marine Corps Reserve; or
- released from the active duty for further service in a reserve component of the Armed Forces
- You may also be eligible if you were honorably discharged from active duty for a service-connected disability and you served 30 continuous days after September 10, 2001.

In my case, I originally became eligible for what was known as the **Montgomery GI Bill** while I was enlisted back in the 1980s. I used it to help pay for tuition and fees as I pursued my undergraduate degree, receiving payments of about $150 or so per month. Fast forward a few decades, and as a result of serving after the terrorist attacks on 9/11 I became eligible for the new GI Bill as well. But there was a catch.

There is always a catch. It turns out that veterans are only allowed to take advantage of GI Bill benefits for a total of 36 months. If you are in school for a full year, then you use 12 months of benefits. If you take summers off, you use up nine months. In my case, I used up approximately 34 months of my benefits while I was enlisted, and that didn't leave much for me to use after I got out.

Fortunately, the Post 9/11 GI Bill recognizes that there are a lot of us in that position. The VA authorizes an additional 12 months of benefits (more on that later) for vets like me who took advantage of their educational benefits before the new GI Bill came into existence. In my case the added year of benefits resulted in about 14 months of total eligibility. That worked out pretty well because my MBA program was 19 months long, so most of the tuition and fees were covered. Good thing that I had been saving money to prepare for my graduate education or I would have been out of luck. School is expensive!

I was indeed fortunate because I fell into the unusual case of being eligible for two different GI Bills. It allowed me to utilize a total of 48 months of educational benefits, which was instrumental for both my undergraduate and graduate studies. For those who are only entitled to the Post 9/11 version they are held to a total of 36 months of educational benefits. That number is set in stone.

The recipient cannot get those months back if he or she makes a poor decision and uses the GI Bill to pursue an education at a dubious college or university. Like the shot clock on a basketball court, once those benefits are used up they are irretrievably gone. The "educational" institution takes the money and the vet loses out. Since there are so many veterans and so much money devoted to the GI Bill, veterans have become a lucrative target for disreputable schools. Many vets have been victimized by unscrupulous opportunists, and unfortunately too many of those institutions are still in business despite legislation aimed at putting them out of business.

Take this as a cautionary tale: be very, very, careful when you utilize the GI Bill. There are no refunds if you exhaust your hard-earned benefits at a diploma mill or a questionable "educational" institution; you are simply out of luck and there is no way to get the money back. Do yourself a favor and do your homework. Only enroll in a school that will meet your real needs and is not out to just shake you down for the benefits that you have earned through your service.

The GI Bill is a tremendous opportunity for veterans who are eligible to take advantage of it. I highly encourage any separating or retiring service member to pursue higher education, and to do so soon. It is an expensive proposition for the government to pay for such a generous program, and it probably won't last forever.

*   *   *   *   *

<u>Lessons Learned:</u>
- ❑ As with any VA program you must register for benefits. Go to www.va.gov and complete the VONAPP (Veterans on Line Application) in order to get started. You can complete the paperwork at any time, so get started as soon as you can in order to draw benefits as soon as you start school.
- ❑ There are different rules for public and private schools. Basically, the VA will pay up to the highest state school rate for the state you attend college, but for private schools there is a cap on tuition and fees. Make sure to surf around the VA's GI Bill website to find out what pertains to your situation.
- ❑ Another great benefit is the housing allowance that you receive from the VA while attending school. It only pays while you are in class (no spring break or summer payments) and it is also not allowed it you are still on active duty. It may be to your advantage to start your education after you get off terminal leave if you want to receive the full benefits available.
- ❑ Once you use up your GI Bill benefits they are gone forever. Make sure that you are committed to the education or training program that you use your benefits for. There are no do-overs and there is no way to regain money lost in pursuit of a degree or certificate you did not really want or need.
- ❑ There are unscrupulous shysters out there who will fleece you out of every dime of your benefits and leave you with at best a worthless degree or at worst nothing at all. Do your homework and only attend reputable school or college. *Caveat Emptor!*

GI Bill part 2: Transferring benefits from the MGIB to the Post 9/11 GI Bill

The GI bill is a great benefit that really helps veterans obtain an education or get vocational training that will provide the tools needed to enter the civilian workforce. I used the Post 9/11 GI Bill to help defray the costs of the MBA program that I enrolled in as I departed active duty. Having served before the day of the attacks on the World Trade Center, however, made me eligible for two GI Bill programs: the Montgomery GI Bill (MGIB) and the Post 9/11 GI Bill. As with all things related to transition, the fact that I was eligible for two programs made things more complicated.

As we discussed earlier, I was eligible for two programs because my service crossed over the eligibility requirements for both. The MGIB was in force up until the Global War on Terror began, whereupon it was ultimately supplanted by the Post 9/11 GI Bill. Veterans who joined after the eligibility window for the Post 9/11 GI Bill were automatically granted access to those benefits while in uniform and after they got out. Veterans who got out before 9/11 were eligible only for the MGIB. The vast majority of those whose service bridged over that fateful day (like me) could choose which program they wanted to use. (For those who are only eligible for the Post 9/11 GI Bill the following information won't have an impact on your education, but you may find it to be an interesting read.)

There are advantages and disadvantages to both programs, and it is important to do your homework and fully understand the nuances of each. Here is a great comparison chart that lines up all of the various programs that veterans may be eligible for (adapted from the official VA website):

(See note 1 for program titles)	Post-9/11 GI Bill	MGIB-AD	MGIB-SR	REAP	VEAP	DEA
Minimum Length of Service	90 days active aggregate service (after 9/10/01) or 30 days continuous if discharged for disability	2 yr. continuous enlistment (minimum duty varies by service date, branch, etc.)	6 yr. commitment (after 6/30/85)	90 days active continuous service (after 9/10/01)	181 continuous days active service (between 12/31/76 and 7/1/85)	Not applicable
Maximum # of Months of Benefits [2]	36	36	36	36	36	45

(See note 1 for program titles)	Post-9/11 GI Bill	MGIB-AD	MGIB-SR	REAP	VEAP	DEA
How Payments Are Made	Tuition: Paid to school Housing stipend: Paid monthly to student Books & Supplies: Paid to student at the beginning of the term	Paid to student	Paid to student	Paid to student	Paid to student	Paid to student
Duration of Benefits	Generally 15 years from last day of active duty	Generally 10 years from last day of active duty	Ends the day you leave Selected Reserve	Generally 10 years from the day you leave the Selected Reserve or the day you leave the IRR [4]	10 yrs from last day of active duty	Spouse: 10 - 20 years [3] Child: Ages 18-26
Degree Training	Yes	Yes	Yes	Yes	Yes	Yes
Non College Degree Training	Yes	Yes	Yes	Yes	Yes	Yes
On-the-Job & Apprenticeship Training	Yes	Yes	Yes	Yes	Yes	Yes
Flight Training	Yes	Yes	Yes	Yes	Yes	Yes
Correspondence Courses	Yes	Yes	Yes	Yes	Yes	Yes
Licensing & Certification	Yes	Yes	Yes	Yes	Yes	Yes
National Testing Programs	Yes	Yes	Yes	Yes	Yes	Yes

(See note 1 for program titles)	Post-9/11 GI Bill	MGIB-AD	MGIB-SR	REAP	VEAP	DEA
Work-Study Program	Yes	Yes	Yes	Yes	Yes	Yes
Tutorial Assistance 5	Yes	Yes	Yes	No	Yes	Yes

Notes:
1. MGIB-AD: Montgomery GI Bill Active Duty
    MGIB-SR: Montgomery GI Bill Selected Reserve
    REAP: Reserve Education Assistance Program
    VEAP: Veterans Education Assistance Program
    DEA: Dependent Education Assistance
2. You may receive a maximum of 48 months of benefits combined if you are eligible for more than one VA education program.
3. Spouses are generally eligible to receive benefits for 10 years. However, spouses of individuals rated total and permanent within 3 years of discharge and spouses of individuals who die on active duty are granted a 20 year eligibility period.
4. The Individual Ready Reserve (IRR) is a category of the Ready Reserve of the Reserve Component of the Armed Forces.
5. The VA can pay the difference between the total cost of tuition and fees and the amount of Tuition Assistance paid by the military.

In my case, I transitioned from the MGIB to the new bill because it resulted in me being entitled to an additional 12 months of benefits that I otherwise would not have been entitled to. While it was a good idea for me, it may not be good idea for everyone. Here is why:

The MGIB has many provisions, but for the sake of simplicity I will only cover the two major parts of the bill: the Active Duty benefit (also known as the MGIB-AD or "Chapter 30") and the Selected Reserve benefit (also known as the MGIB-SR or "Chapter 1606"). As the titles indicate, there were different programs for active duty personnel and those in the reserves.

In my case I was in the Organized Marine Corps Reserve while I was working on my undergraduate studies. During that time I used all but about two months of benefits from the MGIB-SR, meaning that I received about 34 months of benefits and had about two months of eligibility left over. Since a vet can only use 36 months of benefits under that program I initially thought I was out of luck. Fortunately, there is a provision that allows for vets like me to transfer between programs and take advantage of an additional 12 months of benefits.

As the table above indicates, veterans are eligible for a total of 48 months of benefits if they participate in more than one program. Individual programs may offer shorter benefit periods than four years, and for both the MGIB and the Post 9/11 bill this is the case because they are each 36 month programs. A vet can get the additional 12 months only if he or she is eligible for the both the MGIB and the Post 9/11 bills because the only way to get the extra time is to convert from the MGIB to the Post 9/11. There is no bill for the Post 9/11 to convert to, so there are only 36 months of benefits available.

There are two scenarios for transferring from the MGIB to the Post 9/11, and they have enormously different ramifications, so **PAY ATTENTION TO THE NEXT TWO PARAGRAPHS IF YOU WANT TO TRANSFER OVER!!!**

First, let's start with the MGIB-SR (Chapter 1606) program. This was my particular situation because had I used up about 34 months of benefits as a reserve Marine in that program. The VA simply added my remaining balance of about two months to the 12 additional months of Post 9/11 eligibility and *presto!* I had fourteen months or so of eligibility under the new bill to use towards my education. All I had to do was complete the VONAPP on the VA website and indicate that I wanted to apply for the new GI Bill. Once my application was approved I received my updated entitlement.

For the MGIB-AD eligible veterans the situation is **VERY DIFFERENT!** In their case, their 36 months of benefits is really 36 months of benefits. If they have never used their MGIB-AD and they switch over, they will receive 36 months under the new bill. If they use 35 months under the MGIB-AD and apply for the new GI Bill they will receive *only one month* under the new GI bill. Here is the key: in order to get the additional 12 months you must *completely exhaust* your MGIB-AD benefits, and I mean completely; use up every day because if you have only one day of eligibility left and you apply for a transfer you will get one day of benefits under the new bill, and the decision is irrevocable! Once you have used up the MGIB-AD you can then re-apply for benefits under the Post 9/11 GI Bill using VONAPP and receive 12 months under the new bill. Make sure that you do it right, though, because once you apply and are accepted for a transfer there is no going back. Don't say I didn't warn you!

It is easy to see how much of your MGIB you have used. All you need to do is call the VA and ask the counselor which program you currently fall under and how much eligibility you have left. Once you have that information, you can decide if you want to transfer over or not.

Education is a good thing, and the GI Bill makes pursuing a degree or certificate a lot more affordable. Take advantage of it!

*   *   *   *   *

<u>Lessons Learned:</u>

- ☐ The old and new GI Bills are different, and there are a lot of ins and outs that you need to consider before you pull the trigger on a conversion. Make sure to do some research and find out what works best for your situation.
- ☐ Once you do pull the trigger on a conversion from the MGIB to the Post 9/11 GI Bill it is irrevocable and final. There are no "do-overs". Make sure you are committed to the decision that you make!
- ☐ If you are uncomfortable with completing an online application, you can go online and download the fillable .pdf document here: www.vba.va.gov/pubs/forms/vba-22-1990-are.pdf. All that you need to do is fill it out and mail it in to the address listed on the form.
- ☐ If you have *any* questions, call the VA. You will be on hold for a while, but they have a nice callback service which you can use to have the counselor call you back so you don't have to listen to cheesy '70s disco cover tunes while on hold. I recommend calling early in the morning as my wait times went from an hour when I called in the afternoon to a few minutes when I dialed in as soon as they opened the lines.

Here is the VA's GI Bill contact information:
Website: www.gibill.va.gov
Telephone number: 1-888-GIBILL-1 (1-888-442-4551).
Be advised this line only accepts calls from 7:00 AM - 7:00 PM CST Monday through Friday, and you may experience long hold times.

Epilogue: What have I learned from all of this?

Transition has been a long and winding trail between my decades of service in uniform and the rest of my life in a business suit. I learned many lessons along the way, and sharing them is the whole purpose of this book. Looking back on it all, however, a few things stick out as being the most important. They are the things that I wish I had known when it all started.

The first of these is the importance of *time*. Time has a lot of interesting qualities, and while you are in uniform the most salient property that time has is that it is rarely your own. There is always another deployment, another field exercise, another inspection, or another critical planning session that will take your focus off of transition and burn priceless days, weeks, and months that you will never get back. As my career drew to a close I tried to row two canoes at once by staying fully engaged in my military job and dabbling in transition. As a result I started the process way behind the power curve.

Not everyone is the master of their own schedule, and the lower down the rank totem pole you are the less control you have. Having had to scramble and bend rules and call in favors to get through the process I can say with certainty that transition is a full time job. In the real world, however, it is extremely unlikely that any unit in any branch of the armed forces is going to allow their transitioning folks to spend the final year of their career in full transition mode. That said, a little knowledge goes a long way, and as a commander I could have been a better steward of my Marines' time. I should have let the members of my unit that were going through transition more flexibility and more support to help them through it. Unfortunately, like everybody else in uniform I had no idea how confusing the process was until it was too late to help them. By then I was scrambling myself.

My recommendation is that once you make the decision to get out you need to start planning. I mean *that day*. Break out a piece of paper and start writing out some goals, and from there figure out how to meet them. There are things that you can do while still decisively engaged as a steely eyed killer who may not want everyone to know is getting out such as get your medical record up to date (corpsmen and medics can be your best friends!), get your administrative matters squared away (try actually paying attention during your annual administrative audit because it is a great opportunity to get all of those pesky ankle-biting administrative annoyances taken care of), and doing a little research (you can find a lot of really useful info on the internet).

Another recommendation is that if you are a leader and your subordinates are getting out, help them along the way. Give them the flexibility to attend transition courses earlier than later and to get their affairs in order. I have met literally hundreds of transitioners who are trying to get it all done at the last minute. As a leader it is your responsibility to return better citizens to the nation, and you can help them immeasurably by facilitating their transition.

The second big lesson I learned is that transition is remarkably complex, and the smallest details can derail the transition train very quickly. I did not realize that I needed to be proactive to ensure that all – and I mean *all* – of my administrative and medical requirements were done. I found myself constantly losing time and energy as I had to go back to the admin shop or the aid station to get something signed or to fetch some seemingly irrelevant piece of documentation that I had neglected to bring. I had been in uniform for nearly three decades and had become complacent with administration and medical requirements. Year after year I was spoon fed by the admin shop and by corpsmen to get stuff done, and as I transitioned the spoon disappeared.

I could have avoided a lot of stress, lost time, and aggravation if I had only done some networking with others in transition to learn what they experienced on the way out. I should have talked to a few people who had completed their final physical or had completed their admin checkout. If I had done that I would have been much more efficient and much less irked by the whole deal.

The third lesson was one of humility. I had a great career, and as long as I was in the mix and one of the trusted agents that was always in the middle of the action it was great. My reputation was solid, I held great positions, and the future was tremendously bright. With my decision and subsequent announcement that I was going to retire that all came crashing down. When I announced that I was leaving I was viewed as if I had quit, and many people treated me like a quitter.

I bear no one ill will because of it, but instead blame myself because before I made the decision to retire *I* acted the same way. When other Marines got out I wished them the best and quickly turned away in order to get back into the mix. I didn't follow up with them, call them to see how they were doing, or anything else. I was just as focused on work as my peers, and those who had departed the pattern were no longer part of the game. I was just like that, and now that I am on the other side I can honestly say that I should have been a better person. But, sadly, I wasn't.

I left the Marines immediately after commanding a unit that I had taken to war and safely brought home. We had trained together, fought together, laughed, cried, and collapsed in utter exhaustion together. Once I began to transition, though, I went from the captain of a championship football team to the losing team's water boy. I was the same as everyone else who was transitioning, and it took some serious introspection and self-evaluation to get my mind right about it. Once I did, though, it was all good. I recommend *really* thinking about how you will emotionally feel about stepping out of the fast lane and heading down transition road. I didn't, and it was tough to reconcile while I was busy with everything that comes with getting out.

The last and most important lesson that I learned was just how difficult my military career had been on my family. My wife has a tremendously demanding career of her own, and leaving her on her own for deployment after deployment was incredibly difficult for us both. I missed so much of my kids as they grew up that I thank God that they still tolerate me. The Marine Corps is a harsh mistress that throws you out the door when she is done with you, and the people who pick you up off the street are your family. I had overdrawn my account from the family bank for too long, and once I was transitioned it was time to pay it all back. With interest.

If I had not recognized the strain that four grinding combat deployments within five years placed on my family I would have become estranged from them, and it most likely would have ended in marital disaster. Find some way to pay back your debt to your family. Use your terminal leave to spend time with them and bring them into the decisions that will shape the rest of your lives. The military has called the shots for you and your family, and now it is their turn to vote.

Finally, I can say that transition has been quite the ride. I often think about what it would have been like had I stayed in the military, but I always keep coming back to the same conclusion. I was going to get out sooner or later, and I chose to get out on my own terms and before my family fell apart. Transitioning when I did just brought the inevitable into the present, but it was an inevitability that I could control.

Am I glad I got out? Yep. Do I regret any part of my career? Nope. It was just time to go. So I left, and this book is the story of my journey into the rest of my life. I sincerely hope it helps you with yours.

Epilogue

Mike Grice enlisted in the Marine Corps Reserve as a private at age 17 and retired from active duty as a Lieutenant Colonel over 27 years later. After four combat tours in Iraq and Afghanistan, humanitarian operations in East Timor, and five challenging command assignments he was quite surprised to find that the transition from life in uniform back to the civilian world would be one of the most challenging, frustrating, confusing, and enlightening aspects of his career.

In addition to serving his country, Mike is an award winning writer and widely recognized expert in leadership. While in uniform he was decorated for heroism, meritorious service, and leadership and was also the recipient of the Officer Basic School's Outstanding Leadership Award and the Marine Corps' most prestigious leadership award: the Leftwich Trophy.

After his retirement he earned his Master of Business Administration from the University of California's Marshall Business School and founded *The Decisive Leadership Group*, a leadership and management consulting company. He also devotes a considerable amount of time to veterans' issues and helping others make the jump from the service back to the other side.

He lives in Encinitas, California with his wife Cheri and their two boys, Max and Alexander.

Made in the USA
Las Vegas, NV
25 October 2021